Empowering Exporters

Michigan Studies in International Political Economy

SERIES EDITORS: Edward Mansfield and Lisa Martin

Michael J. Gilligan
Empowering Exporters: Reciprocity, Delegation, and Collective Action in American Trade Policy

Empowering Exporters

Reciprocity, Delegation, and
Collective Action
in American Trade Policy

Michael J. Gilligan

Ann Arbor

THE UNIVERSITY OF MICHIGAN PRESS

Copyright © by the University of Michigan 1997
All rights reserved
Published in the United States of America by
The University of Michigan Press
Manufactured in the United States of America
⊚ Printed on acid-free paper

2000   1999   1998   1997   4   3   2   1

A CIP catalog record for this book is available from the British Library.

Library of Congress Cataloging-in-Publication Data

Gilligan, Michael J., 1964–
    Empowering exporters : reciprocity, delegation, and collective
action in American trade policy / Michael J. Gilligan.
        p.   cm. — (Michigan studies in international political
economy)
    Includes bibliographical references and index.
    ISBN 0-472-10823-9 (cloth)
    1. United States—Commercial policy.   2. Free trade—United
States.   3. Reciprocity.   4. Delegation of authority.   5. Pressure
groups—United States.   I. Title.   II. Series.
HF 1455.G488   1998
382'.63'0973—dc21   97-14923
                                                              CIP

For my parents

Contents

Preface

This book began as a study of international cooperation in trade policy. By the time it was finished it was much more a book about how changes in the *domestic* institutions by which trade policy is made produced the dramatic reduction in American trade barriers. The analysis in this project came to rely most heavily on the insights of the positive political economy and the new institutionalist schools of American politics than any particular international relations literature. There are many really superb studies that explain the liberalization of American trade policy with the institutional changes that occurred in 1934. Unlike those studies the present volume argues that the institutional changes produced liberalization not only by changing legislative-executive relations, but also by changing interest groups'—particularly exporter groups'—incentives to take costly political action.

My curiosity about international cooperation in economic policy began during my final semester, spring 1989, at the Woodrow Wilson School of International Affairs at Princeton University in a very interesting course on international macroeconomic policy cooperation cotaught by William Branson and Paul Volcker. It was also during that semester that I first took an interest in international trade policy, thanks to a course on that subject taught by Gene Grossman, who is a superb teacher of economics. In a sense, then, the Woodrow Wilson School at Princeton was where this project began. The following autumn I came to Harvard to begin the Ph.D. program in the Department of Government, where these interests, under the guiding hand of many fine scholars, would eventually develop into a dissertation.

Unfortunately it is impossible to name all of the many people who helped me with this project, but a few deserve special mention. First, my dissertation committee was a group of helpful teachers and top-notch scholars. Alberto Alesina was indispensable in providing the rigor of a fine economist in his comments on drafts of the dissertation. I greatly appreciate not only his expertise but also his kindness, good humor, and support during my work on this project. Jim Alt was extremely supportive of this project and of several projects since. It was with his help that I received a fellowship with the Research Training Group in Positive Political Economy at Harvard and MIT. Since my graduation from Harvard Jim and I have worked on several projects on trade policy together. His insights and advice are always valuable, and he has been very generous with his time in offering them to me. Robert Keohane offered many helpful comments and suggestions. It was at his urging that I added the historical overview in chapter 4, which I believe makes the book a better final product. Bob was also essential in helping me gain an International Institutions Fellowship at the Center for International Affairs at Harvard. Gary King provided many helpful methodological points throughout the development of this project. He also deserves extra special thanks for taking me under his wing during my first year in graduate school at Harvard. His kindness and patience made the year much less frightening and more productive than it otherwise would have been.

Many people at New York University have offered me a great deal of help on this project and others. Steve Brams has been extraordinarily supportive of me at NYU, and his advice, both professional and avuncular, is greatly appreciated. Alexander Schuessler read several drafts of the manuscript very carefully and offered me many helpful comments on it. Much of the work on delegation in chapter 3 was aided appreciably by discussions we had as he participated in a positive political economy seminar I taught at NYU in the spring of 1996. I have had helpful discussions with several other scholars at NYU about this project, including Anna Harvey, Russell Hardin, Ben Hunt, Stathis Kalyvas, and Gabriella Montinola. This project simply would not have been possible without the help of several research assistants at NYU who entered data from nine economic censuses by hand into the computer. The vast bulk of the data entry was completed by three people: Amy Freedman, Dermot O'Brien, and Dolly Voorhees. Helen Wu was also notably helpful and diligent in a variety of tasks on this project.

Generous financial support for this project was provided by a variety of sources. The Institute for the Study of World Politics supported me during the summer of 1991. The Center for International Affairs (CFIA) International Institutions Program gave me support for the fall 1991 semester, and the Mellon Foundation supported me for the spring semester and summer of 1992 with added support from CFIA. My last semester at Harvard was supported by the Research Training Group in Positive Political Economy at Harvard and MIT.

The generous support from these sources enabled me to work full time on my thesis research and finish the Ph.D. in considerably less time than the average. New York University generously supported me in the summer of 1994 with a Research Challenge Fund grant.

Many friends and members of my family have provided me with emotional and, in some cases, financial support throughout my education—my grandparents Jim and Clara Harrison, Roland and Mary Gilligan, John Traas, my aunts and uncles Frank and Sophie Brandt, and Hank and Gelly Rommelfaenger, and my dear friend Reverend Peter John Cameron, O.P. My immediate family—my mother, father and sister—deserve the most thanks of all. Finally, I would like to thank my wife Geraldine for the help she has given me on this project including data entry and copyediting, and, most of all, for her love and support.

CHAPTER 1

Introduction

I. Introduction

From at least the Civil War until the New Deal, American trade policy could be fairly characterized as follows: import-competing interest groups asked for protection, legislators gave it to them, and it would have been individually more costly for consumers to form a collective protest than to simply put up with the tariffs. And yet in 1934 all of this changed. The six decades that followed have produced a remarkable liberalization in the United States and in developed countries generally—all this despite the fact that domestic politics, according to some of political economy's best developed theories, should have prevented it.

Figure 1.1 illustrates this dramatic reduction of American tariff rates. With the exception of the Underwood Act of 1913[1] and the period of World War I (which disrupted normal trade patterns and coincidentally lowered the average tariff rate) tariffs in the United States hovered around 45 to 50 percent from the Civil War until World War II, reaching a peak in 1933 as a result of the infamous Smoot-Hawley tariff. In 1934 Congress granted President Franklin Roosevelt broad powers to negotiate reciprocal trade treaties with other countries that would reduce barriers to trade. The launching of the reciprocal trade agreements program was followed by large decreases in the American tariff rate after 1934. Since 1947 reciprocal trade agreements have been negotiated in eight "rounds" as part of the General Agreement on Tariffs and Trade (GATT), culminating in the creation of the World Trade Organization (WTO) in the Uruguay Round agreement signed in 1993. Through these efforts American tar-

---

1. As I discuss in more detail in chapter 4 the anomaly of the Underwood Act is attributed to several factors: an exceptionally activist president (Woodrow Wilson) who made tariff reform a top priority and the unusual institutional circumstances under which the legislation was created and considered (the bill was essentially considered by the floor under a closed rule) (Link 1956).

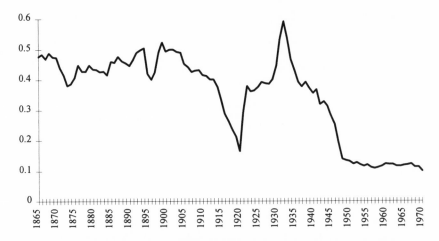

Fig. 1.1. Overall tariff rates, 1865–1970. Rates were caculated by dividing total tariff receipts by total dutiable imports. (Data from U.S. Department of Commerce, Bureau of the Census 1975.)

iff rates have been progressively reduced so that now they are roughly less than one-tenth what they were in 1933. Given the staunchly protectionist trade policy that existed with few interruptions from the Civil War until 1934, this reduction in trade barriers is the trade policy equivalent of the fall of the Berlin Wall.

Such profound reversals in policy are interesting in their own right, but there are practical reasons to search for an explanation for this dramatic liberalization. An answer may give us insights into the current American political economy with its strange coexistence between cooperation and liberalization (NAFTA, the Uruguay Round) and discord (exemplified by the periodic brinkmanship between the United States and Japan or the European Union over market access to American products). A compelling explanation for America's ability to conquer its protectionist habit may also give clues on how to break out of similar quandaries (like chronic federal budget deficits) that continue to plague the American political economy. Finally, many developing countries continue to struggle with their own liberalization programs, and an explanation of the American liberalization may provide clues to help them proceed with liberalization of their markets more smoothly.

The explanation for the puzzle provided here is that liberalization has succeeded because it has been *reciprocal* with liberalization in other countries. That is, countries' trade barriers have been reduced as explicit quid pro quos for trade barrier reductions in other countries. Reciprocity concentrates the benefits of liberalization on export interests that receive foreign trade concessions, and, therefore it helps those exporters overcome their collective action problems.

This enables them to lobby for liberalization to a greater extent than they would if the legislation was unilateral—that is, if there were no explicit foreign trade concessions. The greater lobbying by exporters, in turn, encourages legislators to accept greater liberalization than they would have been willing to accept without the greater export lobbying. The greater lobbying by exporters actually changes politicians' preferences on trade policy in favor of more liberalization.

This explanation relies crucially on three important concepts: reciprocity, delegation, and collective action problems. Each has been used in some form as an explanation of American trade policy by other scholars. However, as I will show in this and subsequent chapters, using one of these as an explanation of American trade policy in isolation from the others only generates other puzzles. Each of these concepts—reciprocity delegation and collective action problems—provides a piece of the puzzle of the American liberalization that interlocks with the other two. All three are required to provide the full picture of American liberalization.

In sections II through IV I will explain in greater detail what I mean by each of these concepts. Section V will then put the pieces of the puzzle together in an explanation of the American liberalization. I will address a few other factors that aided in the liberalization of American trade policy in section VI. Section VII will conclude and offer an outline of the rest of the book.

II. The First Piece of the Puzzle:
Collective Action Problems

Any worthwhile theory of American liberalization must include *collective action problems*, because political economists have recognized for decades that these problems are a central feature of trade politics. The term *collective action problems* refers to a class of maladies associated with political action by groups. For instance, larger groups may have higher organizational costs, and members of larger groups have smaller personal stakes in an issue, giving them less incentive to take costly political action. This latter point has been recognized for quite a while as a problem in trade policy. Pareto (1927) in his *Manual of Political Economy* wrote:

> In order to understand how those who champion protection make themselves heard so easily it is necessary to add the consideration which applies to social movements generally. . . . If a certain measure A is the case of a loss of one franc to each of a thousand persons, and of a one thousand franc gain to one individual, the latter will expend a great deal of energy, whereas the former will resist weakly; and it is likely that, in the end, the person who is attempting to secure the thousand francs via A will be successful.

A protectionist measure provides large benefits to a small number of people, and causes a very great number of consumers a slight loss. This circumstance makes it easier to put a protection measure in practice. (379)

And, in his classic study of the Smoot-Hawley Act, Schattschneider (1935) summarized the source of the problem succinctly: "Benefits are concentrated while costs are dispersed" (127–28).

The main interest in collective action problems, though, is with the public goods nature of political action. Mancur Olson (1965) pointed out that it is often difficult for political pressure groups to form because there is an incentive for their members to "free-ride" or let others pay for political action in the hopes of reaping its benefits for free. In the end less of the public good (political action) is supplied than is optimal. Olson also argued that groups that can use "selective incentives"–private, excludable benefits that accrue to members and not nonmembers–will have an advantage in collective action over those groups that cannot supply such incentives. In later work Olson (1982) himself recognized the obvious implications of his argument for trade policy: since import competing industries form a much smaller group than consumers do they have much less stringent collective action problems and can more readily take political action. Furthermore, producer groups can sometimes provide selective incentives such as closed shops or professional licensing requirements that consumer groups cannot. As such there is a bias in the political system in favor of protectionism. More recently scholars in the endogenous tariff literature (Magee, Brock, and Young 1989 and Mayer 1984 are exemplary) have also used collective action problems to explain the presence of protectionism.

Collective action problems make our puzzle all the more difficult, though, since we must not only explain liberalization but we must do so in a political economy that has a bias toward protectionism. As much as we might like to, though, we cannot simply ignore collective action problems–the decades of work by Pareto, Schattschneider, and Olson and more recently in the endogenous tariff literature are simply too convincing. Collective action problems and their bias toward protectionism are a fact of American trade politics with which any worthwhile explanation must deal. I will take up the issue of collective action problems more extensively in chapter 2.

III. The Second Piece of the Puzzle: Delegation

Several scholars of the American political economy have claimed that *delegation* of trade policy authority by Congress to the executive has facilitated the liberalization of American trade policy. There are actually several different versions of this argument, which I will review more fully in chapter 3 when I take up the issue of delegation in more detail. Common to all of them, though, is the idea that the president has more liberal preferences on trade policy than members of Congress do because his constituency is national rather than parochial. Therefore, after Congress delegated, the president was willing to liberalize when Congress was not able to do so because of constituency pressures. Destler (1986) argues that delegation facilitated liberalization because it insulated Congress, which is unable to resist constituency pressures, from those pressures. O'Halloran (1994) and Lohmann and O'Halloran (1994) argue that prior to delegation Congress set trade policy by means of a "universalistic logroll" in which each legislator was granted protection for his district in return for voting for protection for all other districts. This arrangement made all legislators worse off since the costs of protection to every other district outweighed the benefits of protection to one's own district. They argue that delegation allowed Congress to escape this logroll, making legislators better off. Schnietz (1993) argues that Congress delegated to the president in 1934 in order to commit future (possibly Republican controlled) Congresses from raising trade barriers.

These studies provide rigorous and convincing explanations for the liberalization of American trade policy. However, they also produce several puzzles of their own. For instance, if Congress was unable to resist constituency pressures in order to liberalize trade policy itself, why was it able to resist them to make an institutional change that led to liberalization? It is also hard to see how delegation could in any way insulate Congress from constituency pressures. Congress was still faced with periodic renewals of the president's delegated authority (ample opportunity for protectionist interests to pressure Congress). Besides, the "congressional dominance" literature (Weingast and Moran 1983 is seminal, but see chapter 3 for a fuller review) teaches us that even when Congress delegates to the president it still maintains a great deal of control over policy outcomes because the president must keep a majority in Congress happy or it will reclaim his delegated authority. As such, protectionist interests have every incentive to keep the pressure on Congress knowing that by doing so they can still affect the trade policy set by the president through their impact on legislative preferences. Second, if a universalistic logroll was the source of the problem why did Congress choose delegation rather than one of several other institutional innovations that also would have cured it? Third, one has to wonder if delegation alone was sufficient to bring about a liberalization as dramatic as America's. If the congressional dominance literature is right and the president is constrained by congressional preferences some shift in those preferences toward more liberal trade must have been necessary for legislators to submit to trade barrier reduction as deep as those in the United States over the last sixty years. Furthermore, since these studies are mainly concerned with the institutional characteristics of legislative-executive relations they do not really address interest groups' lobbying behavior and collective action problems[2] or take into account the foreign policy aspects of Congress's delegation to the executive— after all Congress did not delegate to the president the power to set *any* trade policy, only to reduce trade barriers *reciprocally* with other countries. This brings us to the third piece of the puzzle.

IV. The Third Piece of the Puzzle: Reciprocity

The final piece of the puzzle comes to us from separate literatures in international political economy and international economics. Scholars have recognized that countries' policies often produce externalities—actions taken in one country affect the welfare of other countries. These scholars have shown that if countries take into account these externalities they can be better off.[3] This is obviously the case in trade policy where trade barriers in one country harm the export industries in other countries. Agreements to reduce trade barriers in one country in return for trade barrier reductions in another country or countries can make all the countries better off.

In this volume I call this latter phenomenon *reciprocity*. Reciprocity perhaps more than the other concepts I have discussed so far means different things to different people. Keohane (1986) discusses the wide variety of uses to which the term *reciprocity* has been put. His own definition is "*exchanges of roughly equivalent values in which the actions of each party are contingent on the prior actions of the others in such a way that good is returned for good and bad for bad*" (8, italics in original). The cornerstones of this definition are *contingency* and *rough equivalence*. In trade policy, for example, contingency requires that each country reduce its trade barriers only as an explicit quid pro quo for foreign trade barrier reduction. If one country reneges on this arrangement, the other (or others) do as well. Rough equivalence is *not* a requirement that

---

2. Lohmann and O'Halloran 1994, O'Halloran 1994, and Schnietz 1993 do not include lobbying behavior in their models.

3. In the field of international political economy the articles in Oye's 1984 edited volume are emblematic. In international economics a few examples from a very large literature include Hamada 1976; Oudiz and Sachs 1984; Canzoneri and Gray 1985; Currie and Levine 1985; Rogoff 1985; Currie, Levine, and Vidalis 1987; Kenen 1988 for monetary policy; and McMillan 1986 for trade policy.

countries receive the same dollar increases in exports from each other's concessions or that trade will be balanced but merely a requirement that, to be reciprocal, exchanges must be essentially voluntary and not the result of dominance or exploitation.

Reciprocity as I use the term is consistent with Keohane's definition. Reciprocity simply signifies a voluntary *transaction* between countries to reduce specific trade barriers on each other's exports.[4] It is defined more formally in chapter 2 as a reduction in one country's trade barriers in return for a reduction in another country's (or countries') trade barriers. Rough equivalence according to my definition does not require that countries think they received a "good deal" in any sense other than that the deal was sufficiently welfare enhancing for the parties to the agreement to sign on to it voluntarily.[5] As I will show more formally in chapter 3 this is a requirement that all parties necessary for approval of the agreement are better off with the agreement than without it.

Reciprocity clearly can help explain the American liberalization—the United States liberalized because it received something in return—greater access for its exports overseas.[6] But this explanation is not of and by itself sufficient because it does not take into account the domestic economic and political factors, such as collective action problems and delegation, which other literatures have shown are important. By assuming particular preferences for *states*, it can explain liberalization, but it cannot explain why particular *people* within the government with their own personal interests would want to do so. This problem is particularly acute in trade policy with its domestic political bias in favor of protectionism due to collective action problems and with dozens of studies that have shown that domestic economic and political factors are very important in determining trade policy outcomes.

---

4. In earlier drafts of this manuscript I called this phenomenon "cooperation," but several scholars in the international political economy field objected to that name because it implied that U.S. trade policy was cooperative for half of the 1930s, a period generally agreed among international political economists to be noncooperative. Robert Keohane suggested the name "reciprocal conditional liberalization," which perhaps captures the essence of my argument better but is somewhat unwieldy. I settled for "reciprocity" despite its connotation to some of "fairness," but I want to be clear that I am really simply talking about trade agreements.

5. I recognize that this definition is at odds with the way the term *reciprocity* is used by some scholars. For instance, Rhodes (1993) also uses Keohane's definition but seems to apply it only to bilateral relationships (particularly between the United States and Japan). She also seems to interpret "rough equivalence" to mean that reciprocity is a *result* that is perceived as "fair" by both parties, changing Keohane's "rough equivalence" to "perceived equivalence," meaning that both parties to an agreement have to *perceive* that they gain as much from reciprocity as does the other.

6. "New liberal institutionalist" theory can augment this explanation. International institutions made these types of transactions less costly and thereby facilitated more of them (Keohane 1984).

V. Fitting the Pieces Together

A compelling explanation of the American liberalization, then, must contain the elements reciprocity, delegation, and collective action problems. The argument in this book synthesizes these elements as follows: after Congress delegated to the president the president negotiated reciprocal trade treaties with other countries in which American trade barriers were reduced in return for greater access by American exporters overseas. As usual protected interests lobbied Congress heavily to maintain their protection and end the reciprocal trade agreements program. However, now exporters had a stronger incentive to lobby in favor of the program than they would have had to lobby for unilateral liberalization. The reciprocal trade agreements mitigated the collective action problems of proliberalization groups that are inherent in the political economy of trade policy by concentrating the benefits of liberalization on particular exporters. As a result the amount of lobbying for liberalization increased.

Figure 1.2 is a graphic representation of the various steps in this argument, showing an attempt at liberalization both unilaterally and with a reciprocal trade agreement. In the first step Congress decides whether or not to delegate to the president. On the left side of the chart Congress does not delegate, and on the right side Congress delegates. If Congress does not delegate the House Ways and Means Committee proposes the legislation. In step 3, the costs of reducing protection are concentrated on protected interests while the benefits of reducing that protection are dispersed through the rest of the economy. These familiar collective action problems produce a strong lobby by the protected interests against liberalization but only a weak lobbying effort by the beneficiaries of the liberalization (consumers) in step 4. In step 5 the legislative vote is taken with liberalization having a lower chance of passage, ceteris paribus, because of the one-sided lobbying by protected interests.

In the right side of figure 1.2 Congress delegates to the president the power to negotiate foreign trade agreements. In step 2 the president negotiates a trade agreement with another country that reduces foreign trade barriers on American exports in return for reductions in protection of American products. Therefore in step 3 costs of the liberalization are concentrated on the protected interests, as they were in unilateral trade policy, but the benefits are also concentrated on those particular exporters who would now gain greater access to foreign markets. As a result in step 4 there is a strong export as well as import-competing lobby. This more balanced lobbying effort by interest groups on both sides of the trade issue actually changes legislators' preferences to favor more liberal trade policy, and Congress can more easily decide to continue delegating to the

Unilateral Trade Policy	Reciprocal Trade Policy
Congress does not delegate to the president	Congress delegates to the president
↓	↓
House Ways and Means Committee proposes liberalization	President negotiates a reciprocal trade agreement with a foreign country
↓	↓
Costs are concentrated on protected interests while benefits are dispersed throughout the rest of the economy	Costs are concentrated on protected interests and some benefits are concentrated on export interests
↓	↓
Strong import-competing lobby and weak consumer lobby	Strong import-competing and strong exporter lobbying
↓	↓
Liberalizing bill has little chance of passage (ceteris paribus)	Legislators prefer more reciprocal trade agreements

Fig. 1.2.   Graphic summary of the argument: liberalization with unilateral and reciprocal trade policy

president the power to negotiate further trade agreements with other countries.[7]

In short, the reciprocal trade treaties that the president negotiates concentrate the benefits of liberalization on particular export industries so that they have more incentive to lobby for reciprocal than for unilateral liberalization. Reciprocity can "empower" export interests to lobby for liberalization for which they otherwise would not have an incentive to lobby. This is what I mean by the statement that reciprocity increases the demand for liberalization—there is a

---

7. There is one complication in the sequence I described for the right side of figure 1.2. Since 1974 Congress has required the president to submit all trade agreements that he negotiates to Congress for an up or down vote—the so-called fast track procedure. Therefore, there would be an extra step in the right side of figure 1.2 for trade agreements negotiated after 1974 to take into account congressional approval of the agreements. This extra step is a very important tool by which Congress controlled the agreements negotiated by the president, as I will discuss in chapter 3, but obviously it does not change my main point in figure 1.2, which is that reciprocal trade agreements encourage more lobbying from exporters by concentrating the benefits of liberalization on them, change legislators' preferences, and thereby make liberalization more likely than unilateral liberalization does.

stronger lobby in favor of liberalization than would have existed without the international agreement.[8]

In this way my argument melds the collective action and reciprocity approaches to the American liberalization. It also augments the delegation approaches. My argument explains how Congress was able to resist constituency pressures in changing trade policy-making institutions (i.e., delegating to the president) when it could not resist them in making trade policy itself. Specifically, delegation did *not* insulate Congress from constituency pressures—instead it *transformed* those pressures to include a voice for liberalization from exporters. It also explains why Congress chose delegation rather than some other remedy to the universalistic logroll—only by delegating to the president to negotiate reciprocal trade agreements could Congress reduce foreign as well as American trade barriers and motivate exporters to take political action. Finally, the increase in exporter lobbying that is at the heart of my argument explains the progressive shift in congressional preferences toward freer trade, and congressional willingness to allow such deep reductions of American trade barriers. In this way my argument synthesizes these three key elements of any explanation of liberalization: reciprocity, delegation, and collective action.

VI. Other Factors

There are several other factors that undoubtedly contributed to the liberalization of American trade policy that I will not address in any detail in this book other than to control for them in the empirical analysis in chapters 5 and 6. Exogenous changes in the American economy comprise one set of factors. Milner (1988) argued that the increased interdependence of the international economy of the 1970s compared with the 1920s meant that there were more economic actors with a large stake in a stable world economy and that for this reason there was less lobbying for protection in the troubled 1970s than there was in the comparable 1920s. Revisionist historians have argued that the need to dispose of the

---

8. Kenneth Oye (1992) has also discussed the role of reciprocity in activating an exporter lobby, but he does not develop it beyond simple intuition nor does he test it in any rigorous fashion. Nor does Oye discuss the role of congressional delegation in American trade policy as I do in chapter 3. Furthermore Oye's main purpose seems to be making the claim that bilateral discriminatory reciprocity is better at concentrating benefits on exporters than is multilateral rule-based reciprocity of the type associated with the GATT (now WTO). I could not discern any justification for this claim from his discussion. In the model I develop in the next chapter the benefit that encourages exporters to take political action is an increase in the world price of their product. I see no reason why bilateral discriminatory reciprocity should be better at accomplishing this than global rule-based reciprocity is as long as the industry in question is a legitimate export industry with comparative advantage.

excess production of manufactured goods during economic downturns caused the American expansion into the world in the late 1800s (Lefeber 1963; McCormick 1967; Williams 1962). To these scholars the United States' search for markets has been the unifying theme of American foreign policy from before the Spanish-American War to the present. David Lake (1988) has argued that the growth of labor productivity and export dependence of manufacturing in the United States explains the move from protectionism to liberalization during this period.

Yet these analyses leave a few unanswered questions. First, they do not address the fact that, throughout American history, *some* sector of the economy has always been heavily reliant on exports—whether it was cotton growers in the South and grain producers in the Great Plains during the nineteenth century, or manufacturers in the twentieth century. By concentrating on the growth of manufacturing exports, these scholars cannot explain why the export-dependent interests of agriculture did not lead to a liberal, internationalist, foreign economic policy a century earlier. Relatedly these explanations do not take into account the presence of collective action problems.[9]

The theory presented in the following chapters will help answer these questions, by explicitly taking into account the collective action problems of the various economic interests. Throughout the late nineteenth and early twentieth centuries, factors inherent in industrial production put industry in a much better position to overcome collective action problems and lobby the government than agriculture enjoyed. Industry was geographically concentrated in a few states in the Northeast and the eastern Great Lakes region of the country. Agriculture was spread over hundreds of thousands of square miles throughout the country often in areas of great isolation where communication was very difficult. Industry was also economically concentrated relative to agriculture. The specific factors for various forms of industrial production were concentrated in a very few hands. The specific factors of agricultural production, however, were

---

9. The revisionist histories often suffer from a third shortcoming. Their accounts seem to suggest that American foreign economic policy should have become more liberal throughout the first part of the twentieth century—the time of the transformation from import-competing to export-oriented production of manufactures for the United States. However, American foreign economic policy was very much of a mixed bag during the early twentieth century. The United States attempted to expand its exports and took up a more internationalist foreign policy generally—adopting limited reciprocity treaties; expanding ties to South America, the Caribbean and the Pacific; and of course fighting the Spanish-American War and World War I. But the United States did not unambiguously liberalize its own market. American trade policy through most of the first thirty years of the twentieth century was highly protectionist—protectionism that did not reach its apex until the Smoot-Hawley tariff of 1930—well beyond the point in time at which the United States had become a substantial exporter of manufactured goods.

spread thinly over millions of people so that agriculture's already smaller real income changes from protectionism were even smaller. This further exacerbated the problems of concentration of benefits and dispersion of costs of protection described in chapter 2.

The inherent inability of agriculture to overcome collective action problems can explain its failure to effectively lobby its government for export promotion.[10] As I will describe subsequently, the farmers' collective action problems manifested themselves not only in an inability to lobby for export promotion, as industry was able to do, but also in an inability to lighten the heavy burden of the tariff system of this period, from which farmers did not benefit. The relatively less stringent collective action problems of industry enabled it to lobby more effectively for export promotion once it felt it could compete overseas, and reciprocity became a political issue. This may be why the United States adopted a more activist export promotion strategy as manufacturing became more export oriented, as the scholars previously mentioned have observed, and why we did not see an earlier use of reciprocity by politicians interested in liberalization.

Finally there is a class of explanations that attribute the American liberalization to its changed strategic position in the world or its Cold War rivalry with the Soviet Union. These arguments suggest that the United States was more willing to liberalize in order to stabilize the world economy like a good hegemon should (Kindleberger, 1986), or to shore up its alliances against communism. This point is fairly obvious—politicians often justified trade policies in this way—and no doubt it was operating to some degree. However, it does explain why the United States began liberalizing in 1934, at least a dozen years before the start of the Cold War and well before most scholars would date the beginning of U.S. hegemony. More important, these explanations, like those that rely solely on reciprocity, neglect the importance of domestic political factors like interest groups' collective action problems, and delegation. Having said this, these changes in the U.S. economy and strategic position undoubtedly had some effect on the willingness of important trade policymakers to liberalize, so I will control for these factors in the empirical analysis in chapters 5 and 6.

---

10. This is not to say that agriculture did not have *any* voice. Movements like the Grange in the 1870s and the Populist movement in the 1890s were able to sufficiently frighten politicians to throw agricultural interests a bone or two. However, these periodic instances of revolt did not have the impact on policy of daily lobbying of congressmen in Washington by large, wealthy, industrial interests. Agriculture had no such lobby. As a result agriculture found it difficult to lobby effectively until the mid-1920s when the National Farm Bureau Federation was formed and it and the other farm lobbies moved their offices to Washington (J. Hansen 1987, 193–228). As Olson has argued the National Farm Bureau Federation was very successful at offering selective incentives to overcome farmers' collective action problems, which contributed to some of its success in organizing for political purposes (Olson 1965, 153–59).

VII. Conclusion

Trade liberalization among developed countries has been a hallmark of the post–World War II era. The international relations literature has explained this only by not addressing the presence of domestic political conditions that should militate against liberalization. The existing endogenous tariff literature with its emphasis on collective action problems and the new institutionalist literature with its emphasis on delegation explain the domestic political economy well but ignore the international elements of trade policy. The theory presented here attempts to accommodate all three of these arguments. It will do this by using a model of the domestic political economy taken from the endogenous tariff literature and placing it in an international political economy in which each country's trade policy has an effect on other countries' exports. In the model that follows, reciprocal reduction of trade barriers concentrates benefits in the hands of the particular export interests that receive the foreign trade concessions and thereby helps alleviate the collective action problems of proliberalization groups so that they could lobby for liberalization.

The subsequent chapters are organized in three parts. Part 1 is theoretical, composed of chapters 2 and 3. Chapter 2 lays out somewhat formally a model of the domestic political economy that describes the bias against liberalization because its costs are concentrated and its benefits are dispersed. I then place this model in an international system in which countries' trade barriers reduce exports from other countries. I show that an agreement between countries to lower trade barriers on each other's exports concentrates benefits on particular export interests. Chapter 2 further shows how these increased benefits from liberalization encourage exporters to lobby for liberalization in a way that they would not for unilateral liberalization. Chapter 3 discusses congressional delegation to the president. It shows that the increased lobbying by exporters modeled in chapter 2 actually shifted legislators' preferences to favor more liberalization. As such, the president was able to make deep reductions in American trade barriers as part of reciprocal trade agreements and Congress was still willing to renew his delegated authority to lower them further as part of more agreements in the future.

Part 2, which consists of chapter 4, provides a historical overview of American trade policy from roughly the Civil War to the present and offers some preliminary qualitative evidence on the plausibility of the argument presented in part 1. The chapter reviews the highly protectionist period of American trade policy from the Civil War to the Great Depression. It shows that any proliberalization lobbying during the period was completely outclassed by protectionist lobbying. Chapter 4 then turns to the liberalizing period since 1934. It shows that, indeed, exporters did become more involved in the political process of trade policy making after the introduction of reciprocal liberalization, and, more importantly, that they did not lobby for unilateral but only for reciprocal liberalization.

Part 3 offers more rigorous quantitative empirical evidence of an increase in demand for liberalization as a result of reciprocity from legislative voting on twelve major twentieth-century trade bills. Chapter 5 provides the main evidence covering eight trade bills from 1890 through 1934. It shows that the demand for liberalization did increase substantially in the Reciprocal Trade Agreements Act (RTAA) of 1934 and its first renewal in 1937, as reflected in legislative voting. Chapter 6 extends the analysis up to the present, showing that the demand for liberalization remains high as expected from the theory. Finally, chapter 7 offers some conclusions and implications of the analysis and a few ideas for future research in the area.

Part I
Theory

CHAPTER 2

Reciprocal Trade Agreements and the Demand for Liberalization

I. Introduction

In chapter 1, I informally introduced the main argument of this book: the United States was able to mitigate the protectionist bias inherent in its political economy through reciprocal trade agreements that concentrated the benefits of liberalization on particular exporters, giving them an incentive to lobby that they otherwise would not have had due to collective action problems. Legislators then faced more balanced pressure from both sides of the issue and came to prefer more liberal trade, allowing the president to negotiate deeper reductions without endangering renewal of his delegated authority. The argument requires two things to happen. First, reciprocity must concentrate the benefits of liberalization on particular exporters. Second, exporters must respond to this concentration of benefits by taking costly political action that they would not have taken in the absence of reciprocity. In the following section, I will show the first of these steps with a standard Ricardo-Viner model of the effects of tariff changes on real incomes. I review Mayer's (1984) main result that the costs of a small reduction in a particular industry's tariff rate are concentrated on that industry while the benefits are dispersed throughout the rest of the economy. That is, tariff reductions comprise a substantial decrease in the protected interest's real income but a negligible increase in the gainers' real incomes. I will then show that reciprocal liberalization can assuage this effect by concentrating benefits on a particular export industry. The derivations of the results in section II are presented in appendix A. Appendix B provides some comparative statics of the results with some numerical examples to help illustrate the effects of the various parameters of the model. Section III proceeds to the next step in the argument by showing the conditions under which the concentration of benefits of reciprocal liberalization on exporters encourages those exporters to take costly political action that they otherwise would not have taken. Section IV offers some conclusions of this chapter.

II. The Effects of Unilateral and Reciprocal Liberalization on Real Incomes

The country modeled in this chapter is assumed to be large enough to affect the world prices of the goods that it imports. There are assumed to be n commodities, where $n > 2$, in the domestic economy. Furthermore, only unskilled labor is perfectly mobile between each of the n industries. The other factors of production are specific to the particular industries in which they are employed and cannot be used in other industries. There are n specific factors—one for each industry. Each constituent in this domestic political economy is assumed to have homothetic preferences, which can be expressed in an indirect utility function specified by equation (2.1):

$$U^i = U(p_1, 1, p_3, \ldots p_n, y^i) \tag{2.1}$$

where p_j is the price of the jth commodity relative to the second commodity, and y^i is individual i's personal income.[1] This personal income, y^i, can also be expressed as a share of the country's aggregate income, Y. That is, $y^i = \phi^i Y$, where, ϕ^i is constituent i's share of aggregate country income. Each individual's income share can also be expressed as his or her factor income as a share of the total factor income in the economy or:

$$\phi^i_j = \frac{R_N + R_j V^i_j}{R_N V_N + \displaystyle\sum_{j=1}^{n} R_j V_j} \tag{2.2}$$

where R_N is the wage rate of labor (the mobile factor), V_N is the total amount of labor in the economy, R_j is the return on the specific factor employed in the

---

1. Following Mayer 1984 I have used the indirect utility function, which expresses the highest utility individual i can achieve with a given income y^i and prices p_j, rather than the direct utility function, which expresses individual i's utility as a function of the quantities of goods he or she consumes. Although the direct utility function may be more familiar to readers, the indirect utility function is the natural choice and eases exposition of the model because trade policy effects utility directly through consumers' incomes and the prices of the goods they consume.

*j*th industry (i.e., the salary, wage rate, or rental rate, depending on the kind of specific factor), and V_j is the total amount of the *j*th industry's specific factor in the whole domestic political economy and is assumed to be fixed. V_j^i is the amount of the *j*th specific factor owned by individual *i*, and is also assumed to be fixed. Notice two implicit simplifying assumptions in equation 2.2. First, each individual owns one unit of the mobile factor (i.e., $V_N^i = 1$ for all *i*). Second, each individual owns only one type of specific factor. Therefore, each individual's income share, ϕ^i, is also indexed by the industry in which he or she owns a specific factor, *j*.

I will make the simplifying assumption that only one commodity, the *g*th, has a positive tariff and that the tariffs of the remaining $n - 1$ commodities are zero. This simplifies the analysis without changing any of the qualitative conclusions. The aggregate income (i.e., GNP) of the home economy can be expressed as follows:

$$Y = \sum_{j=1}^{n} p_j X_j + t_g \pi_g M_g \tag{2.3}$$

where X_j is the home country production of good *i*, t_g is the home country's tariff rate on imports of commodity *g*, π_g is the world relative price of good *g* for good 2, and M_g is the amount of good *g* imported by the country. Notice the implicit simplifying assumption in equation 2.3 that there are no export taxes. I will further assume that commodity *g* is unbiased with respect to the mobile factor labor—that is, a change in good *g*'s price leads to a change in the mobile factor's wage rate that is on average the same as the change in the factor rewards of all the other factors in the economy.

I will examine the effects of a small change in the tariff rate on good *g* from its "optimal" level. (Throughout this book "optimal," in quotes, refers to the tariff that maximizes national income and therefore is called optimal in the international trade literature. It is not necessarily optimal from the point of view of politicians or constituents within the domestic political economy.)

Under these conditions the effect of a small change in the tariff rate on good *g* will produce the following real income effects. First, on those who own the specific factor used in the *g*th industry:

$$B_{gg}^i = \frac{\partial U_g^i / \partial t_g}{\partial U_g^i / \partial y_g^i} \, dt_g = Y(1 - \beta_g) \beta_g \lambda_g^i \hat{p}_g \tag{2.4}$$

and on those who own the specific factors used in any other unprotected industry h where $h = 1, \ldots, n$ and $h \neq g$.

$$B^i_{hg} = \frac{\partial U^i_h / \partial t_g}{\partial U^i_h / \partial y^i_h} \ dt_g = -Y\beta_h\beta_g\lambda^i_h\hat{p}_g \tag{2.5}$$

where B^i_{jg} is the effect of a small change in t_g on the real income of the ith person who owns the specific factor used in the jth industry, dt_g is meant to symbolize the magnitude of the small change in t_g, $\hat{p}_g$ is the percentage change in the price of good g, and $\lambda^i_j = V^i_j / V_j$ or person i's ownership share of the jth specific factor. Appendix A includes the derivations of equations 2.4 and 2.5. The parameters β_j are defined more formally in appendix A, but for our purposes here it is sufficient to know that when commodity g is unbiased with respect to labor (as I have assumed) β_g is the share of the gth industry in the economy as a whole, or $\beta_g = p_g X_g / Y$, and that

$$\sum_{h=1, \ h \neq g}^{n} \beta_h = 1 - \beta_g$$

always (whether β_g is unbiased with respect to labor or not).

Since $(1 - \beta_g) > \beta_h$, if there are more than two industries, it is clear from equations 2.4 and 2.5 that $|B^i_{gg}| > |B^i_{hg}|$ among individuals with similar ownership shares of their respective factors. In other words, the costs of a tariff reduction are concentrated on owners of the gth specific factor while the gains from that reduction are dispersed across the owners of all $n - 1$ other specific factors. Each specific factor owner in the many unprotected industries gains much less from tariff reduction than the gth specific factor owner loses. In short, it shows Schattschneider's point, reversed in the case of a tariff reduction—"costs are concentrated while benefits are distributed."

Now let us look at the situation if t_g were to be reduced reciprocally with another nation. Imagine that the government of the nation with the political economy I have just described (which I will call the "home country") reaches an agreement with a foreign country such that for each small reduction in the home country tariff rate on good g, t_g, the foreign country will reduce its tariff rate on a home country commodity k, τ_k, by a small amount. Let us assume that this foreign country is large enough to affect the world price of good k, π_k. Furthermore, we will assume that the kth commodity is unbiased with respect to labor, as was the gth. The derivation is similar to the preceding results yielding the following real income changes from reciprocal liberalization.

For those specific factor owners in the gth industry:

$$B^i_{ggk} = Y(1 - \beta_g)\beta_g\lambda^i_g\hat{p}_g - Y\beta_k\beta_{\hat{g}}\lambda^i_g\hat{p}_k + Y\phi^i_g\beta_k(\hat{E}_k + \hat{p}_k). \tag{2.6}$$

For those in the kth industry—the export industry that receives greater access to overseas markets—the real income change is:

$$B^i_{kgk} = -Y\beta_g\beta_k\lambda^i_k\hat{p}_g + Y\beta_k(1-\beta_k)\lambda^i_k\hat{p}_k + Y\phi^i_k\beta_k(\hat{E}_k + \hat{p}_k). \tag{2.7}$$

Finally, for specific factor owners in any other industry h, where $h = 1, \ldots, n$, $h \neq g$, and $h \neq k$:

$$B^i_{hgk} = -Y\beta_g\beta_h\lambda^i_h\hat{p}_g - Y\beta_k\beta_h\lambda^i_h\hat{p}_k + Y\phi^i_h\beta_k(\hat{E}_k + \hat{p}_k). \tag{2.8}$$

All of the parameters have been described except $\hat{p}_k$, which is the percentage increase in the price of good k, and $\hat{E}_k$, which is the percentage increase in the quantity of exports as a result of the reciprocal trade agreement.

Each of the three results in equations 2.6 through 2.8 has three terms that have similar interpretations. The first term in these equations is exactly the same as the results for the unilateral case shown in equations 2.4 and 2.5, and it has exactly the same interpretation. It shows the effect of the small decrease in the price of good g from the liberalization of that good's market. As before, as long as the ownership shares in the various industries are roughly equivalent, the costs of this price reduction are concentrated on the owners of the gth specific factor, shown by the first term in equation 2.6. The first term in equations 2.7 and 2.8 shows that the benefits are spread across the kth and hth ($h = 1, \ldots, n$, $h \neq g$, and $h \neq k$) industries' specific factors—exactly the same as under unilateral liberalization.

However, under reciprocal liberalization this is not the only effect. The second term in equations 2.6 through 2.8 demonstrates one of the main theoretical points of this book. It captures the effects of the small increase in the relative price of the kth good from the liberalization of the foreign market for that product. Since $|1 - \beta_k| > |\beta_g|$ and $|1 - \beta_k| > |\beta_h|$ the costs of the price increase of the kth commodity are spread across the gth and hth ($h = 1, \ldots, n$, $h \neq g$, and $h \neq k$) industries, while the benefits are concentrated on the kth industry. This second term shows that reciprocal liberalization offsets the concentration of costs and dispersion of benefits of liberalization by concentrating the benefits on the industry that receives the foreign concession.

The third term in equations 2.6 through 2.8 shows an added benefit of reciprocal liberalization. The increase in exports from reciprocal liberalization increases Y, the aggregate size of the home country's economy. This third term is each individual's share of that increase in Y. The first and second terms of equations 2.6 through 2.8 capture the changes of each individual's share of the "pie" due to the relative price changes, while the third term is the increase in the size of the "pie" from increased exports.

We can use equations 2.6 through 2.8 to assess the greatest losers and gainers from the reciprocal trade agreement. The greatest losers are clearly the specific factors in gth industry. They lose on two counts and gain on one. They lose because of the reduction of the price of the product they produce and because of the increase in the price of the kth commodity. These losses are mitigated somewhat by their share of the increase in the aggregate economy from the larger exports of good k. The greatest winners are clearly those in the kth industry. They gain on all counts—from the decrease of the price of good g; from the increase in the price of their own product, good k; and from their share of the increase in the aggregate economy. The total effects on the remaining industries in the economy will continue to be small. They gain from the reduction of the price of the gth commodity and from their share of the increase in Y, but they lose slightly from the increase in the price of k. Appendix B illustrates the sensitivity of these conclusions to various values of the parameters in equations 2.6 through 2.8. Regardless of the parameters of those equations, though, the benefits of liberalization are always more concentrated in a reciprocal trade agreement than they are with unilateral trade policy.

III. The Effects of Real Income Changes on Trade Policy Lobbying

The preceding section discussed the underlying assumptions of a model of the real income changes that arise from reciprocal as opposed to unilateral liberalization. This section will describe the logic behind a model of the lobbying by interest groups that those income changes generate. Mayer (1984) assumed that tariff changes were set by referendum voting. This model will instead assume that they are set by a legislature that can be influenced by lobbying. The concentration of the costs of unilateral liberalization induces the protected industry to contribute to the lobbying effort to prevent the trade barrier reductions. Meanwhile, the diffusion of benefits makes it unprofitable for the beneficiaries of the unilateral liberalization to contribute at all because either marginal costs exceed marginal benefits or average benefits do not cover average costs. Under reciprocity, though, the benefits of liberalization to a particular export industry are increased so that members of that industry contribute to the lobbying effort. The extra lobbying by the export industry is not completely offset by an increase in lobbying by the protected industry in response, nor does the increase in lobbying by the export industry generally promote more free riding by the remaining proliberalization industries. In the end, the total net amount of proliberalization lobbying is increased.

A.   Voting Costs Models of Trade Policy Formation

Before describing the lobbying model, however, I will review Mayer's (1984) voting costs model of trade policy-making. To simplify the notation I will refer to the real income change of the ith member of the jth industry, which I derived in the last section as B_j^i. In his article, Mayer does not address the effects of reciprocity, but he does show the effect of the concentration of costs of unilateral liberalization for policy if the tariff rate t_g is set by a majority vote. Mayer argues that if there are voting costs, c, then each individual would vote only if $B_j^i \geq c$. As such, owners of the gth specific factor are more prone to vote than are factor owners in the hth industry because $B_g > B_h^i$.[2]

The problem is slightly more complicated than Mayer has let on, though. The expected net payoff of voting for a small change in t_g is actually less than $B_j^i - c$, since if i votes there is no guarantee that he will receive B_j^i. Instead the payoff from voting is $pB_j^i - c$, where p is the probability that voter i is pivotal to the electoral outcome. This is the familiar Downsian voting function (Downs 1957). For Downs, p was exogenous, which led to the "paradox of (not) voting"—in large electorates p is approximately zero so that for positive voting costs, c, no one would vote, but if no one votes then p is 1 so there is, once again, a reason to vote for a large enough B_j^i. More recent work has overcome this paradox by solving for p endogenously as a function of the strategic behavior of all the voters (Ledyard 1984; Palfrey and Rosenthal 1985; Hansen, Palfrey, and Rosenthal 1987). Although it complicates the simpler voting costs analyses, like Mayer's, somewhat, it does not change the qualitative result appreciably. In those cases where protected interests are less likely to vote because the outcome is fairly certain regardless of whether they vote or not, the remaining interests are less likely to vote, too, for the same reason.

---

2. Using the baseline numerical example for unilateral liberalization from appendix B, owners of the gth specific factor would be willing to vote at much higher costs of voting than would the $h \neq g$ specific factor owners—499 times higher. If, instead, we altered the ownership shares of each specific factor (the λ_j's in eqs. 2.4 through 2.8) then the hth specific factor owners would require an ownership share that was 499 times that of the gth industry. We could go through each of the parameters of equations 2.4 through 2.8 in this way but generally speaking, the conditions under which the hth specific factors are willing to vote are much more stringent than are those for the gth industry because the real income changes are much lower. This implies that the owners of the hth specific factor are less likely to vote than are the owners of the gth specific factor.

The important point is that the real income changes to the hth industry ($h = 1, \ldots, n$, and $h \neq g$) are lower than those of the gth industry so that $|pB_g^i| > |pB_h^i|$, and the specific factor owners in the hth industry will be more willing to avoid the costs of voting than will be those in the gth even when p is endogenous. To put it another way, as long as ownership share and sizes of the two industries are fairly equal, owners of the gth specific factor are willing to vote for much lower levels of p—that is, even when they are not particularly important to the outcome[3] Thus, despite these complications Mayer's point that the specific factor owners in protected gth industry will be more willing to participate than those in the many unprotected industries will be still holds.

In this voting costs model reciprocity will increase the incentives for those who own the kth specific factor to vote because their real income changes are much higher than under unilateral liberalization. Using the same type of analysis presented previously, owners of the kth specific factor would be willing to vote given higher voting costs, c. Alternatively they would be willing to vote for a smaller probability that they would be pivotal to the outcome, p. Therefore, under this type of model, liberalization has a much better chance of passage with reciprocal than unilateral liberalization.

B.   Lobbying Model of Trade Policy Formation

One criticism of Mayer's model is that it assumes that trade policy is made by referenda when in fact trade policy is usually made by pressure groups acting on a legislature or some administrative body (Conybeare 1991).[4] However, to make Mayer's model a lobbying model requires only a change of terminology. If rather than voting, constituents are assumed to make fixed contributions, c, to a pressure group's lobbying fund, and if we assume that the pressure group with the largest lobbying fund has its policy enacted then the model is exactly the same. Indeed, models of these "discrete public goods," as they are called, are

---

3. Specific factor owners are willing to vote as long as $p \geq c / B_j^i$. Using the assumptions from the baseline simulation in appendix B, the critical value for p for an hth specific factor would be 499 times higher than the critical value of p for an owner of the gth specific factor. Indeed, one of the results of this strategic voting literature is that the probability that a person will vote is negatively related to his or her cost-benefit ratio of voting—in this case c / B_j^i. Clearly, $c / |B_{hg}^i| > c / |B_{gg}^i|$ for similar size and ownership share, implying that the gth industry will have a higher probability of voting than will the owners of the hth specific factor (Ledyard 1984; Palfrey and Rosenthal 1985; Hansen, Palfrey, and Rosenthal 1987).

4. Verdier (1994) has argued persuasively that voters are much more important to trade policy outcomes than traditional theories have let on because they determine the political context—such as salience and divisiveness of trade issues—in which policy is made. However, even in Verdier's analysis trade policy is not made directly by referenda as Mayer (1984) assumed.

generally quite similar to models of voting behavior (see, e.g., Palfrey and Rosenthal 1984).

A more serious problem is the discrete nature of voting or of the contributions to the lobbying fund in Mayer's model—that is, the inherent assumption that constituents' only choice is to vote or not vote or to contribute c or nothing at all. If c was too large only those who owned the gth specific factor would contribute or vote and t_g would not be reduced. However, in such a scenario it may be in the best interests of each of the $h \neq g$ specific factors to pay one of the other $h \neq g$ specific factors to vote for a decrease in t_g or to contribute a value less than c to the lobbying fund. In fact, at first blush they should be willing to pay up to their marginal benefit, pB_j^i, to bring about the reduction of t_g. Furthermore, unless t_g is set below the "optimal" level, the sum of the gains to the $(n - 1)$ $h \neq g$ specific factors would, in total, be greater than or equal to the losses to the gth specific factor. Mayer's result that owners of one specific factor could resist a tariff reduction that was in the interests of the actual majority may simply be the product of his assumption that constituents' only choice is to not vote (if the costs outweigh the benefits), or vote otherwise, or (in the lobbying version) to contribute c or nothing at all. Does the result still hold if the public good is continuous?

There has been a great deal of work done on continuous public goods (Austen-Smith 1981; Chamberlin, 1974; Magee, Brock, and Young 1989, chap. 6 and appendix; Pincus 1977, chap. 5; Stigler 1974). These studies have generally shown that if there is declining marginal utility from the consumption of a public good individuals of a group will purchase less of it than if it were private. Also, contrary to the claims associated with Olson 1965, several studies have shown that there is no unambiguous relationship between the size of a group and the aggregate amount of a public good that the group provides. The intuition is simple—while each member of the smaller group contributes less, there are more of them, so that in total they may contribute more (Austen-Smith 1981; Chamberlin 1974). Olson's (1965) conclusion hinged crucially on the notion that smaller groups could more easily employ selective incentives to encourage their members to contribute.

Despite the ambiguity of the relationship between group size and total contributions to the group's efforts, I will show that Mayer's point and the views of Pareto and Schattschneider quoted in the first chapter still hold, even in the continuous case, under very plausible conditions. Since the benefits to the hth ($h = 1, \ldots, n$ and $h \neq g$) specific factors are considerably lower than those to the gth specific factor, specific factor owners in the hth industry will be more likely to drop out of the political process altogether, and make no contributions at all.

Even in cases where the hth specific factors would receive positive marginal benefits from a small contribution the average benefits of that contribution will not cover the average costs, and they will not have an incentive to contribute at all.

Let me begin by defining the net demand for liberalization faced by legislator l as:

$$D_l = \psi_l D_L + \omega_l D_P \tag{2.9}$$

where D_L is the total amount of lobbying in favor of liberalization, that is, the lobbying by all of the specific factor owners of the $(n - 1)$ $h \neq g$ industries and, under reciprocity, of the kth industry as well. D_P is the total amount of lobbying by the protected interest—that is, the owners of the gth specific factor. D_l is the net demand for liberalization, so the sign of D_P is negative. The weights ψ_l and ω_l capture the relative importance of lobbying by the gth industry as opposed to the kth industries in legislator l's district. D_l can take positive or negative values depending on the relative sizes of D_L and D_P and the weights ψ_l and ω_l. Let me further define d^i to be the amount of lobbying (or demand) contributed by person i and D^i as the total level of net demand for liberalization from everyone else in the political economy *except* person i.

Given these definitions a person deciding the amount to contribute to a lobbying effort has the following objective function:

$$F(d^i, D^i)B^i_j - cd^i \tag{2.10}$$

where c is the marginal cost of a contribution of one unit of lobbying. Since I assume no fixed costs, c is also the average cost. F is the probability that i's contribution will change the policy outcome. Furthermore, F has certain properties: First, the probability that i is pivotal to the outcome is higher the larger i's contribution. Therefore, F is an increasing function of i's contribution, d^i. Second, F depends on the contributions of the other individuals both allied with and opposed to i. If these contributions are such that the policy outcome is not likely to be enacted even if i contributes, i would not waste money on it. Similarly, if the contributions are such that the policy outcome is quite likely to be enacted, i will not spend money on something that i would probably receive anyway—a form of the familiar free rider affect. In other words i's contribution has the greatest probability of being pivotal when the policy outcome is too close to call (that is, it has about a 50 percent chance of passage).

Both of these features are captured nicely by a bivariate normal probability density function $f(d^i, D^i)$. For any given level of D^i the cumulative probability that i's contribution will decide the outcome is an increasing function of d^i. Furthermore, those contributions have the greatest chance of deciding the policy outcome when the contributions of the other constituents (both for and against i's preferred outcome) are closest to the mean of D^i. Finally, I have assumed that the equilibrium between the various potential contributors is a Nash equilibrium, so i assumes that the other interests in the political economy will set their values of d^i at their optimized levels and then i aggregates those contributions to determine the level of D^i. Just to be as clear as possible, D^i is indexed because it will take a different value for each individual, but it is fixed— it is not one of i's choice variables. The probability F in equation 2.10, then, is the cumulative probability $F(d^i,D^i)$ associated with $f(d^i,D^i)$, assuming this fixed level of D^i.

Any contribution by i must meet both marginal and average cost conditions to be an equilibrium. Differentiating equation 2.10 and dividing both sides by B^i_j yields the marginal cost condition:

$$f(d^i,D^i) = c\,/\,B^i_j. \tag{2.11}$$

Dividing average cost and benefit by B^i_j produces the following average cost condition:

$$F(d^i,D^i)\,/\,d^i = c\,/\,B^i_j. \tag{2.12}$$

The functions in equations 2.11 and 2.12 are plotted in Figure 2.1. The darker two curves are for a level of D^i, call it D', that makes i's contribution more likely to be pivotal. The two curves drawn in light gray are for a level of D^i, call it D'', that makes i's contribution less likely to be pivotal. The curves marked "$f(d^i,D')$" and "$f(d^i,D'')$" are simply two representations of the functions on the left-hand side of equation 2.11. I will call them marginal benefit curves throughout this discussion even though they are actually marginal benefit curves normalized by the real income change B^i_j. The curves marked "$F(d^i,D')$" and "$F(d^i,D'')$" are representations of the function on the left-hand side of equation 2.12 corresponding to the same two levels of D^i, D' and D''. I will call these curves average benefit curves even though they are average expected benefit divided by the real income change. The lines marked $c\,/\,B_1$, $c\,/\,B_2$, and $c\,/\,B_3$ are three examples of cost-benefit ratios from the right-hand sides of equations 2.11 and 2.12. Marginal and average costs are constant at c across individuals so the different levels of the $c\,/\,B$ curves correspond to different levels of real income changes resulting from the possible policy changes.

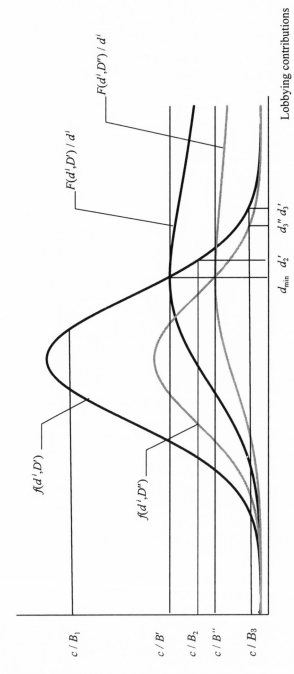

Fig. 2.1. The effects of the concentration of benefits on lobbying contributions: downward shift in the cost/benefit curves (c/B) and upward shifts in the average benefit curves ($F(d^i,D^i)/d^i$) and marginal benefit curves ($f(d^i,D^i)/d^i$)

Figure 2.1 illustrates several important points about these various curves. First, individuals with lower real income changes resulting from the proposed policy change will have higher cost-benefit ratios and therefore contribute less to the lobbying effort. For instance, looking at the darker marginal benefit curve marked $f(d^i, D')$ for the moment, a person with a very high real income change would have a cost-benefit ratio like c/B_3. Such a person will contribute d_3' to the lobbying effort of his or her cause. A person with a lower real income effect from the policy change would have a cost-benefit ratio like c/B_2 and contribute only d_2' to his or her preferred cause.

The other important point is that people with very small real income effects will not contribute at all, even if there is some positive marginal benefit to a contribution, because the average expected benefit from such a contribution would not cover average costs. For instance, a person with a low change in real income resulting from the policy change would have a high cost/benefit ratio like c/B_1. Such a person would not contribute at all because the contribution that meets average cost conditions does not meet marginal cost conditions and vice versa. In fact, any person faced with a level of $D^i = D'$ and with a cost-benefit ratio above c/B' would be in this position, and would not contribute at all. The minimum contribution, then, is d_{min}—a person must be willing to contribute at least that much or he or she will contribute nothing at all.[5]

Another important point is that the cutoff level of c/B for contributing changes with the values of D^i. This can be seen by comparing the darker and the lighter average benefit curves. If $D^i = D'$ (the darker curve), the maximum level of c/B that a person could have and still be willing to contribute is c/B'. If $D^i = D''$ (the lighter curve), though, the maximum level of c/B that would induce a contribution falls to c/B''. The intuition behind this fact is that anyone with a small stake in an issue (high c/B) would have to have a very large probability of being pivotal (the darker curve) to make it worthwhile to contribute. Alternatively, anyone with a very large stake in an issue (low c/B) would be willing to contribute even if his or her probability of being pivotal was not that high (the lighter curve).

By now the implications of this analysis for trade policy must be fairly obvious. As shown in the last section, the real income changes from a unilateral liberalization of the market for good g will be much higher for specific factor owners in the gth industry than for those in the rest of the economy. Producers of g will have cost-benefit ratios like c/B_3, while producers of other goods will

---

5. Because all equilibrium levels of lobbying contributions must fall to the right of the intersection between average and marginal costs at d_{min}, the second-order conditions for a maximum are always met in this model.

have cost-benefit ratios like c / B_1. The former will take costly political action to stop liberalization while the latter will do nothing, or at least very little.[6]

All of this changes with a reciprocal trade proposal, though. First, because reciprocity concentrates the benefits of liberalization on the export industry that receives greater access to foreign markets, exporters' cost-benefit ratios fall to around the level of the protected interests, c / B_3, and exporters increase their lobbying contributions accordingly. Second, as the contributions of all exporters rise due to reciprocity, D^i will increase and bring the probability of a proliberalization outcome closer to 50 percent. This in turn will increase the probability that i will be pivotal to the outcome. The exporters' average and marginal benefit curves will shift upward, something like a shift from the lighter to the darker curves. The magnitude of this latter effect will depend on increases in lobbying contributions by other groups, which I will discuss in the next several paragraphs. In the end, exporters' contributions will rise to a level like d_3'.[7]

Of course, once exporters increase their contributions, D^i will change for the other group members as well. Let's look at the effects of this change on members of the gth industry first. With the increase in lobbying by the export interests the probability of a liberalizing outcome increases and the probability of being pivotal rises for specific factor owners in the gth industry just as it does for those in the export industry. Therefore, those in the gth industry will increase their contributions as well. However, they will *not* increase their contributions so much as to totally offset the increase by the kth industry. This point has been proven in very general terms by others (see, e.g., Magee, Brock, and Young 1989, 278–84), so I will not reconstruct the proof here. Intuitively we can see why this would be the case, though: specific factor owners in the kth industry increased their contributions for two reasons—their probability of being pivotal in-

---

6. The result is actually going to be more extreme than is shown in figure 2.1, though. There, the gth industry's stake (B_3) is only about ten times larger than the hth industry's (B_1), but in the baseline simulation in appendix B the gth specific factor owner had a stake in the issue that was 499 *times* that of the other industries. Of course, as I show in appendix B it is possible that some specific factor owners in the hth industry might have very large stakes in an issue because their industry is abnormally large in the economy or they own a very large share of the specific factor in their industry. However if the gth and hth industries are on a relatively even footing on these other parameters the costs of liberalization will be much more concentrated on specific factors in the gth industry than the benefits will be on those in the hth industry, and the effects will be even more dramatic than those illustrated in figure 2.1.

7. For the second effect to operate, the probability of a liberalizing outcome before reciprocity is introduced—call it P_L—must be less than 50 percent and the increase in lobbying due to reciprocity cannot rise above $1 - P_L$. For example, if the probability of a liberalizing outcome without reciprocity was 10 percent and the probability of a liberalizing outcome with reciprocity was less than 90 percent, the argument I made will hold. If this condition does not hold the exporters marginal and average benefit curves will be *lower* under reciprocity than under unilateral liberalization.

creased *and* their stake in the issue increased by a great deal. The stake of those in the gth industry, on the other hand, does not change appreciably due to reciprocity. They increase their contribution only because they have a higher probability of being pivotal to the outcome.[8]

What about the specific factor owners in the remaining industries $h = 1, \ldots, n$, where $h \neq g$, $h \neq k$? When members of the kth industry increase their lobbying contributions they increase the probability of a liberalizing outcome, making all pro-liberalization interests—even those in the hth industry—more likely to be pivotal to the outcome. The specific factor owners in the hth industry will also see their marginal and average benefit curves shift up just as all the other interests do, say from the D'' (lighter) curves to the D' (darker) curves in figure 2.1. Therefore, there will be no increase in free riding by the rest of the proliberalization interests and they may even *decrease* their free riding (i.e., they bandwagon).[9] To show this I will assume that specific factor owners in the hth industry have the same real income gain from reciprocal liberalization as they do from unilateral liberalization.[10] There are three possibilities for specific factor owners in the hth industry. First, any person who contributes nothing under reciprocity—with a cost-benefit ratio above c / B' like c / B_1—would also have contributed nothing under unilateral liberalization, so there is no increase in free riding among these people—they do not contribute anything whether liberalization is unilateral or reciprocal. Second, there may be some people with cost-benefit ratios in the area between c / B' and c / B'' who did not contribute for a unilateral proposal but who would for a reciprocal proposal. Someone with a cost-benefit ratio of c / B_2 is an example. He or she would contribute nothing when $D^i = D''$ (lighter curve) but would contribute d_2' when $D^i = D'$ (darker curve). Such a person would actually free ride *less* (contribute more) under reciprocal as opposed to unilateral liberalization. Finally, if for some reason there was a person who contributed to a lobbying campaign for a unilateral proposal that person would contribute more for a reciprocal proposal. A person with a cost-benefit ratio of c / B_3 is an example. The contribution of such a person would rise from d_3' to d_3''. Again such a person would free ride less for a recip-

---

8. Again I assume $P_L < 0.5$ and that the probability of a liberalizing outcome does not increase beyond $1 - P_L$. If this assumption is not met, this result would be even stronger—the protected interest would actually *reduce* its contributions, because its chances of being pivotal would fall with the increase in exporter lobbying.

9. I am making the same assumptions about P_L that I made in footnotes 7 and 8.

10. Actually, as I show in appendix B, the hth industries will gain a little more from reciprocal compared with unilateral liberalization, shifting downward their cost-benefit curves and strengthening the results I present here.

rocal trade proposal than a unilateral one because of a higher probability of deciding the outcome. I do not want to make too much of these last two groups of people, since it would be rare indeed for a specific factor owner in one of the hth industries to have a cost-benefit ratio curve lower than c / B'. The benefits of liberalization are simply too dispersed over these industries. The point is that those in the hth industries will at least not free ride more and may free ride less.

In sum we are left with a large increase in lobbying by exporters as a result of reciprocity. Import competitors in the gth industry increase their lobbying somewhat in response but not by enough to completely offset the lobbying by exporters. Finally, the remaining interests in the hth industries who also benefit from liberalization do not reduce their lobbying contributions (i.e., they do not free ride more) in response to the increase in lobbying by exporters in the kth industry.

These results may beg the question "what about free riding?" Is it not one of the eternal truths of political economy? If lobbying is a public good how can we have a lobbying model in which people do not free ride and may actually bandwagon? First, free riding can occur in this model. For instance, if there was an exogenous increase in the amount of lobbying for protection in a unilateral bill all other protectionist group members would reduce their contributions— that is, free ride more—in the normal fashion. The exogenous increase in protectionist lobbying would increase the probability of a protectionist outcome by even more and would reduce the probability that any one member of the gth industry will be pivotal. Each would contribute less. Specific factor owners in the remaining hth industries would reduce their contributions to the liberalization side as well (if they had made any in the first place).

The more interesting answer, though, is that lobbying as I have described it here is not a regular public good. A typical public good exhibits decreasing marginal returns over its whole range of values. The more of it I can consume thanks to the contributions of others, the less I value more of it, so the less I contribute. Lobbying is not that kind of a public good.   The marginal benefit of lobbying is not always decreasing in the contributions of others in my group. In fact, if the contributions of others in my group bring the probability of an outcome closer to 50 percent the likelihood that I will decide the outcome will rise, so I will actually *increase* my own contributions. Compare this with the case described in the previous paragraph. There, increased contributions by members of the gth industry moved the probability away from 50 percent and *decreased* the probability that other members of the group will be pivotal, so they reduced their contributions. Generally speaking, the marginal benefits of an individual's contributions are *increasing* in contributions by others that bring the outcome *closer* to 50 percent (thereby increasing the probability that they will be pivotal) and *decreasing* in contributions of others that move the outcome *away* from 50 percent (thereby decreasing the probability that they will be pivotal). The lesson we should draw from this is that the marginal benefit structure of lobbying is not necessarily the same as that of typical public goods, so we should not directly translate conclusions from typical models of public goods to collective political action.

Having said all of this, even if lobbying was a typical public good, with decreasing marginal benefits over its whole range of values, my argument would still go through. Exporters in the kth industry will still increase their lobbying effort substantially because of the much larger stake in the issue that reciprocity provides. Import competers in the gth industry will increase their lobbying efforts in response, but not by enough to completely offset the increase in lobbying by the kth industry. Finally those in the hth industries cannot free ride more—that is, contribute less to the cause of liberalization—because they contribute nothing with unilateral liberalization. They cannot further reduce their contributions below zero.

Finally, I have made my argument here without resorting to any specific assumptions about Olsonian "selective incentives." To the extent that these exist they would make the argument offered here even stronger. If, as seems plausible, the gth industry could offer selective incentives that the many hth industries could not, the benefits to the specific factor owners in the gth industry of contributing to a lobbying effort would be even higher relative to the hth industries. These benefits might include avoiding ostracism from the group for instance. They would simply be added to the expected net benefits in equation 2.10, and the cost-benefit curve of those in the gth industry would be even lower than c / B_3 in figure 2.1. If export industries could also use selective incentives, their increase in lobbying contributions due to reciprocity would be larger as well.

IV. Conclusion

In section II, I used a simple Ricardo-Viner model of the effects of trade policy to show that unilateral liberalization concentrates the costs of liberalization on the protected interest and disperses the benefits over the rest of the economy. I then demonstrated that reciprocity concentrates the benefits of liberalization on the relevant export industry. In section III, I showed that specific factor owners in the export industry increase their lobbying contributions as a result. The protected interests increase their lobbying contributions in response but not by enough to offset the increases by the export industry. Finally, there is no increase in free riding by the remaining specific factor owners in the economy—contrary to the conventional wisdom about lobbying as a public good. If smaller, more concentrated groups can use selective incentives more readily than large dispersed groups can then the arguments I have offered here will be all the stronger.

As I discussed in appendix B, whether or not these changes promote more exporter lobbying than import-competer lobbying depends crucially on the size of the increase in benefits to the export industry. It is that increase that shifts the cost-benefit curves used in this chapter. It may also depend on the relative positions of the marginal and average benefit curves I discussed in section III. Still, one conclusion is clear: there will always be more concentrated benefits from reciprocal trade agreements as opposed to unilateral liberalization, and this always produces greater proliberalization lobbying with reciprocity compared with unilateral liberalization. In the next chapter I will discuss the *supply* side of trade policy—how the increase in the demand for liberalization is filtered through the political process and actually produces a change in trade policy.

CHAPTER 3

Reciprocity and
Congressional Delegation

Chapter 2 provided the first step of my argument—reciprocity gives exporters an incentive to lobby where they previously had an incentive to free ride because it concentrates the benefits of liberalization on them. The analysis was really a model of the *demand* for liberalization, particularly the effects of reciprocity on demand for liberalization. This chapter will take the next step in the argument by providing a model of the *supply* of liberalization by the government. Specifically, I will show how the increase in lobbying by exporters modeled in the previous chapter produced a shift in legislators' preferences in favor of freer trade and made deeper and deeper reductions in American protection possible. Reciprocity really created a "friendly cycle" of liberalization: each round of trade agreements encouraged more exporter lobbying, and, as more exporters became politically active, legislators became willing to allow deeper reductions in protection.

The argument in this chapter will rely heavily on the insights developed in the congressional dominance literature.[1] That literature has shown that, although policy making authority is often delegated by Congress to the executive, Congress still retains a great deal of control over policy outcomes. Congress grants authority to the executive because the executive is better able to provide services to congressional constituents (in this case exporters). However, Congress can still use its power of the purse, as well as the threat to reclaim any authority it has given the executive, to keep the executive in line. Furthermore, al-

---

1. Unfortunately, I cannot review all that this very large and interesting literature has to offer. In addition to the pieces cited in the text some good examples from this literature are Banks 1989; Bendor, Taylor, and Van Galen 1985, 1987; Calvert, McCubbins, and Weingast 1989; Fiorina, 1981; Gilligan, Marshall, and Weingast 1989; McCubbbins 1985; McCubbins, Noll, and Weingast 1987, 1989; and Weingast 1984. Noll 1989 offers a thorough review of the literature.

though the executive may have informational advantages over its congressional overseers, it cannot use these to set policy too much at odds with congressional wishes because constituents who are hurt by executive actions will pull "fire alarms," alerting Congress to executive abuses of power. Constituents, then, play a central role in congressional dominance theory. It is in order to provide better services to them that Congress delegates powers to the executive in the first place, and it is they who help Congress monitor the executive as it provides these services (McCubbins and Schwartz 1984; Weingast and Moran 1983). Therefore, I regard the effects of reciprocity on interest group behavior, which I modeled in the previous chapter, to be crucial in understanding congressional delegation and the liberalization of American trade policy.

The analysis in this chapter will also offer answers to several puzzles that are generated by existing explanations of the American liberalization that rely on delegation alone (Destler 1986; Lohmann and O'Halloran 1994; O'Halloran 1994; Schnietz 1993). These studies are concerned mainly with the effects of delegation on legislative-executive relations. As such they do not address the effects of delegation and reciprocity on interest group behavior, which I discussed in the last chapter, or the foreign policy aspect of Congress's delegation decision— the fact that Congress delegated to the president only the power to negotiate with foreign countries, not to set trade policy generally. My argument complements these works nicely because it addresses questions such as: "Why was Congress able to resist constituency pressures in creating trade policy-making institutions when it could not do so in creating trade policy itself?" and "Why did Congress choose delegation rather than some other institutional mechanism to escape its policy-making inefficiencies?" Furthermore, I will argue that without some shift in congressional and presidential *preferences* it is hard to see how trade barriers could have been reduced by as much as they were. My argument will help explain these puzzles and the shift in congressional preferences by means of the increase in exporter lobbying that reciprocity produced.

Central to my argument will be the increase in exporter demand for liberalization that I described in the previous chapter. In short, I will argue that Congress delegated for precisely the reason it said it did—to give the president the necessary authority to negotiate down *foreign*, not just American, trade barriers. Exporters who wanted to receive foreign trade concessions as part of a reciprocal trade agreement then lobbied the government more than they did under unilateral trade policy. This greater political activity by exporters (where there was previously rampant free riding) changed legislators' preferences on trade policy, and Congress, reacting to the greater proliberalizing lobbying, continued to delegate authority to the executive for deeper and deeper reductions in trade barriers in successive rounds of trade negotiations.

In the next section, I will illustrate this model of the supply side of American trade policy in greater detail. Section III will offer some implications of my argument for existing theories of American trade policy—particularly theories that rely predominantly on delegation to explain the liberalization of American trade policy over the last six decades. Section IV will conclude and offer some speculations about extensions of my argument to broader political economy issues.

II. The Effects of Reciprocity and Delegation on American Trade Policy

I will illustrate my argument on the effects of the reciprocal trade agreements program with the following form for each policymaker l's utility function:

$$u_l = -a_l(D_l, \mathbf{Z}_l)[t_l - t_l^*(D_l, \mathbf{Z}_l)]^2 + b_l(D_l, \mathbf{Z}_l)\,[\tau - \tau_l^*(D_l, \mathbf{Z}_l)]^2 \qquad (3.1)$$

although any quadratic-based spatial utility function will do. In equation 3.1, t is the home country's tariff rate under consideration, τ is the foreign country's tariff rate under consideration, and t_l^* and τ_l^* are respectively the policymaker's ideal home and foreign tariff rates. I have dropped the g and k subscripts for convenience of notation. Both t_l^* and τ_l^* are decreasing functions of D_l, the net demand for liberalization that policymaker l faces from his constituents, which I modeled in the previous chapter. In other words, a legislator's ideal points for the home and foreign tariff rate are lower the higher the net demand for liberalization from that legislator's constituents. These ideal points are also functions of factors besides demand, such as personal ideology and party, which I have lumped together in the vector $\mathbf{Z}_l$. Although these factors are undoubtedly very important in determining policy outcomes, I will not discuss them in any detail in this chapter in the interests of brevity. The parameters a_l and b_l capture how important or salient an issue the home and foreign tariff rates are for politician l. A value of a_l larger than b_l implies that the domestic tariff rate is a more important issue than the foreign tariff rate. These parameters are functions of the characteristics, $\mathbf{Z}_l$, and, of course, demand, since high net protectionist demand should make the home tariff rate a more important issue, and a great deal of lobbying by exporters in net should make the foreign tariff rate a more important issue.[2]

An example of an indifference curve from this type of utility function is

---

2. If $b_l = 0$, trade policy is unidimensional in t—actually not a bad assumption for the tariff history of the United States in the nineteenth century. It is also the implicit assumption of the studies I will discuss in section III of this chapter.

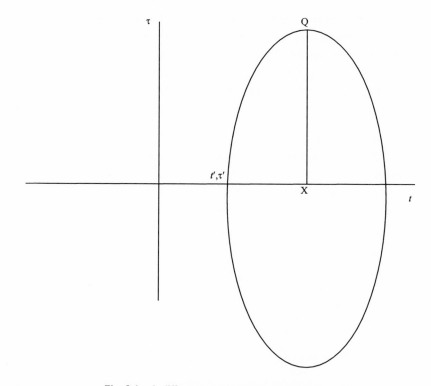

Fig. 3.1.   Indifference curve from equation 3.1

shown in figure 3.1. The curve plots all of the points that give the legislator the same utility as the status quo point Q. It is an ellipse taller than it is wide because I have assumed that the home tariff rate is a more important issue than the foreign tariff rate (i.e., $a_l > b_l$), so that it takes deeper reduction in τ to make the legislator as well off from a given reduction in t.

This figure offers several immediate implications for reciprocal trade policy as opposed to unilateral trade policy. For instance, if, as seems most plausible, the foreign tariff rate is higher than the ideal of a legislator, that legislator will be willing to vote for larger reductions in t if they are accompanied by concomitant reductions in τ. For instance, the legislator with the indifference curve in figure 3.1 has an ideal point for t and τ at X. Since this legislator's ideal value for t is the status quo, he would not be willing to vote for any change in t under unilateral trade policy (the one-dimensional case). However, the foreign tariff rate is higher than his ideal level, so he would be willing to vote for reductions in t all the way to t' as long as the foreign tariff rate was reduced to τ'.

Another important difference between reciprocal and unilateral trade policy is that Congress does not have direct control over τ. If Congress does not like the foreign tariff rate negotiated with the foreign government by the president it cannot set another level closer to its liking. Congress must rely on other countries if it wants to lower foreign trade barriers. This means that, since the president is constitutionally mandated to conduct relations with other countries, he will always have proposal power in trade policy as long as Congress wants foreign trade barrier reductions.[3]

Legislators from districts with high levels of D_l (low import competer lobbying and/or high exporter lobbying) will have ideal points and indifference curves farther to the southwest, and policymakers from districts with low D_l will have ideal points and indifference curves farther to the northeast.[4] Although in theory policymakers' ideal points could be anywhere in this policy space, a little intuition can help eliminate some configurations of legislators' ideal points. For instance, in figure 3.1, if Q is the status quo, it seems implausible that home

---

3. At first blush it may appear that there is some incentive here for the president to use information about the preferences of the foreign legislature strategically with Congress. If the president pretends that the foreign government is a tough bargainer he might be able to set lower levels of t than he could otherwise get simply by claiming that the foreign government "made him do it" in order to get lower levels of τ. It turns out that this is not the case. The president is typically assumed to prefer lower levels of both t and τ. Therefore, he has every incentive to get the best deal possible on τ for each reduction of t. In other words, for any given level of t that the president can get past Congress, he has every incentive to get the lowest possible level of τ from the foreign government. He has no incentive to squander his bargaining leverage with the other country. Of course, the president may have reason to lie to the *foreign* government about how tough his own country's legislature is in order to get a better deal from them. This point has been made by Putnam (1988) and many others. Modeling the bargaining process between the home and foreign government (in addition to the relationship between interest groups, Congress, and the executive, which I take up here) is beyond the scope of this book (if such a complicated game with so many actors is even really modelable to any worthwhile effect).

It is also tempting to use McKelvey's (1976) global cycling result to argue that reciprocity, by making trade policy two dimensional, combined with delegation to the executive gives the president more leeway in manipulating policy outcomes and thereby makes deeper cuts in t possible. However, McKelvey's result requires that legislative votes take place in a partyless, institutionless void. Furthermore, the president cannot offer any value of τ that he pleases to the legislature since the reductions of τ must be negotiated first with the foreign country. These two facts constrain the points in the policy space that the president as agenda setter can propose, and make McKelvey's result perhaps less applicable in the particular case I am discussing. In later work (1986), McKelvey himself showed that majority rule in several dimensions may not be as chaotic as his earlier work was thought to imply because, if the voters' ideal points are fairly centrally located, it would take many iterations of the voting cycle for the agenda setter to get a policy outcome far away from those ideal points (see Miller, Grofman, and Feld, 1989 for an intuitive treatment of this result).

4. Obviously, legislators' ideal points can be situated for other reasons as well, such as party and personal ideology and so forth, but these complications are not the subject of the present discussion.

country legislators would have ideal points to the northwest of Q, because these points would involve an increase in the foreign tariff rate and a decrease in the home tariff rate. Ideal points to the northeast of Q imply preferences for higher home and foreign tariff rates. These also seem fairly unlikely, although perhaps less so than points to the northwest of Q. Ideal points to the southeast of Q correspond to legislators who prefer higher home tariffs but lower foreign tariffs. These legislators are certainly a possibility. Finally, ideal points that fall in the quadrant to the southwest of Q correspond to reductions in both t and τ, also a likely configuration. The last two categories of points then—ideal points to the southeast and southwest of Q—are the only likely possibilities.[5] It also seems plausible that legislators would be closer to their ideal points on the t dimension than on the τ dimension since the legislature had more control over t than τ. Furthermore, τ is likely to be positive, and for some legislators the ideal level of τ will actually be negative—a foreign import subsidy. Finally, for similar reasons, the *foreign* legislators' ideal points can be expected to cluster within the quadrant southwest of Q with policymakers closer to their ideal points in τ than in t.

Now we are prepared to tell the story of the American liberalization of the last six decades. The argument is illustrated with a three-person home legislature in figures 3.2 and 3.3. The status quo trade policy is marked at point Q in figure 3.2. The legislators' ideal points are marked 1, 2, and 3. The president's ideal point is marked P. Consistent with the other studies in this literature I am assuming that the president has preferences for lower foreign and home tariffs because of his national constituency, so his ideal point is well to the southwest of that of the legislators. The foreign executive's ideal point is at point E for similar reasons. As was the case in 1934 when the first Reciprocal Trade Agreements Act was introduced, I have assumed that a majority of legislators wanted to reduce the U.S. tariff. Given this configuration of ideal points, the home legislature could unilaterally set trade policy at its median position, $\bar{t}$. The foreign legislature will also set its tariff at its median position $\bar{\tau}$, resulting in a policy at point A. When Congress considers whether or not to delegate to the president point A is the reversion policy since it is the policy that the home legislature can achieve without delegating to the president.

Figure 3.2 shows the relevant portions of the three home legislators' elliptical indifference curves centered on legislators' ideal points 1, 2, and 3. These curves plot all of the points that offer each legislator the same utility he or she would receive from setting trade policy unilaterally at point A, *given the utility*

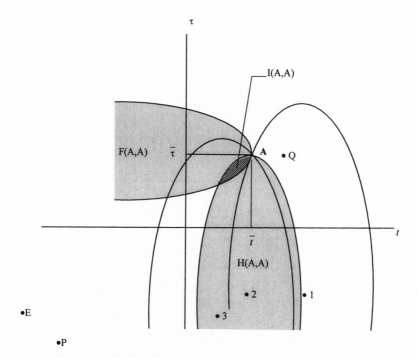

Fig. 3.2. The sets that beat policy **A** in the home and foreign countries, given the lobbying generated by policy **A** (H(A,A) and F(A,A) respectively), and the set of possible agreements with the foreign country given the lobbying generated by policy **A** (I(A,A))

functions produced by the lobbying for the policy at point A. Each point in the policy space corresponds with different levels of the home and foreign tariff rates. Therefore, each point produces different real income changes for exporters and import competers (the B^i_j in chap. 2), thereby generating different levels of net demand for liberalization, D_l, as modeled in the previous chapter. Each resulting level of D_l, in turn, changes the legislators' utility functions, as specified in equation 3.1, and therefore their indifference contours. I have not drawn the foreign legislators indifference curves to avoid cluttering the figure.[6]

The light gray shaded region marked H(A,A) is the set of points that beats point A—that is, they offer higher utility than point A does for a simple majority of legislators in the home legislature given the utility functions generated by the policy A. A similar set for the foreign legislature is shaded light gray and

---

6. Notice that since the indifference curves are ellipses I have made the implicit assumption that there is some salience attached to the foreign tariff rate, that is, $b_l \neq 0$ for all three home legislators in figure 3.2).

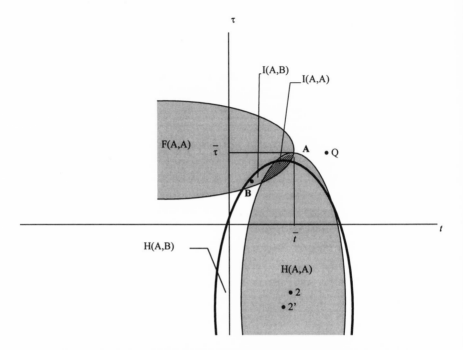

Fig. 3.3. Downward shift and "fattening" of the set that beats policy **A** due to the net increase in exporter lobbying for policy **B**, and the expansion of the set of possible agreements with the foreign country given the lobbying generated by policy **B** (**I(A,B)**)

marked F(A,A). The intersection of these two sets is the lens-shaped region marked with diagonal lines and labeled I(A,A). This is the set of points that makes a majority in both the home and foreign legislatures better off than they would be from unilateral trade policy at point A given the utility functions that are produced by that policy.[7] A policy X is an equilibrium if, given some reversion point R, X ∈ I(R,X). That is, a policy is an equilibrium if it is an element of the set of points that make a majority in both legislatures better off given the changes in legislators' utility functions that the policy generates. Perhaps more intuitively, a policy is an equilibrium only if it generates enough lobbying to create majority support for it in Congress and the foreign legislature.

---

7. The sets H, F, and I are not *win sets* in the way that term is used in the social choice literature because if any point in the set is chosen as a policy it would generate a different response from lobbyists and therefore different indifference curves changing the shape of the sets. As such, there are points not in I(A,A) that beat A because they change the lobbying behavior of exporters sufficiently to offer a majority in both the home and foreign legislatures higher utility than A does.

The shaded region I(A,A), then, represents the potential gains to Congress as a whole from delegating to the president rather than reducing trade policy unilaterally. Furthermore, Congress could expect to receive some of these gains. This is most obviously the case when Congress is needed to ratify the agreement that the president signs. In that case, the president must negotiate an agreement that can pass Congress.[8] But, because of the sunset provision, the president was also constrained by congressional preferences with the RTAA even though Congress did not have to ratify the trade agreements negotiated under its authority. Because the RTAA included a sunset provision by which the president's delegated authority would expire automatically if not renewed by Congress, the president had to give a simple majority in Congress at least a small increase in utility over what they could have given themselves with unilateral trade policy if he hoped to have his delegated authority renewed. In other words, he had to give a majority in Congress a slightly better level of utility than they received from setting trade policy unilaterally at point A.[9]

---

8. For instance, this is the case with the so-called "fast track" procedure which has been a feature of U.S. trade agreements negotiated since the Trade Act of 1974. Both Houses of Congress must pass the agreement by a simple majority in an up-or-down vote with no opportunities for amendment.

9. There are actually two complications in this statement. First, Congress requires a two-thirds majority to override a presidential veto, and, second, a congressional gatekeeping committee can keep policy proposals it does not like bottled up in committee. The first complication means that the president may not have to set a policy that makes a majority better off but only one-third of Congress better off. The second implies that the president may only have to make a majority of the *members of the committee* better off. I take up these two complications in appendix C. Here I will mention only that the formulation I use above is more plausible than if I had modeled these two complications because Congress included several provisions in the delegating legislation that helped prevent the president from setting policy that made a majority of Congress worse off. First, it included a sunset clause in the RTAA so that if a majority in Congress was made worse off by the reciprocal trade policy it could simply let the president's authority expire, as would occur automatically in three years. The president's veto power is useless against such a nonrenewal since he can only veto legislation that passes Congress—he cannot veto a congressional decision to *not* pass legislation. Of course, this would not allow Congress to reverse the policy set by the president since it would still be override proof, but if the president cares enough about maintaining his authority to negotiate future trade deals it would be a sufficient threat to force him to cater to the preferences of a majority in Congress. A second feature Congress added to the RTAA to prevent the president from liberalizing too much was to quantitatively limit the reductions the president could make. He was not authorized to reduce any tariff rate by more than 50 percent. This feature was included in all congressional delegation of trade policy authority until the Trade Act of 1974. Finally, since the Trade Act of 1974 Congress has given itself the authority to accept or reject any treaty the president negotiates under his delegated authority by an up or down vote—the so called fast track procedure—so that the president must negotiate a trade deal that is acceptable to at least a majority in Congress if it is to be enacted. Because of these safeguards I assume in the analysis that follows that the president negotiates a trade deal with the aim of pleasing a simple majority in Congress.

But this is only part of the story. Knowing that the president was constrained by congressional preferences, interest groups had every incentive to lobby Congress on treaties negotiated under RTAA authority. If exporters pulled more "fire alarms" than import competers did the president could negotiate deeper reductions in foreign trade barriers by offering deeper reductions in American trade barriers.   If import-competing groups could pull more "fire alarms" than exporters could the president would be severely constrained in the concessions he could make to foreign governments. Knowing that the president will not sign an agreement that does not improve the lot of a bare majority in Congress, and knowing that congressional utility is in part a function of their lobbying efforts, interest groups had strong incentives to lobby Congress on trade agreements negotiated under the RTAA, just as they did in later years when Congress had to ratify all foreign trade agreements.

Furthermore, as I modeled in the previous chapter, exporters have much stronger incentives to lobby with reciprocity than they did with unilateral trade policy because their real income gains are more concentrated and much higher. To use Olson's terminology, the group "exporters" was largely latent until reciprocity was adopted and gave them an incentive to lobby.[10] Of course, import-competing interests also have strong incentives to lobby against any reciprocal trade agreement that lowers their protection, but unlike in unilateral trade policy this was offset somewhat by the exporters' lobbying. Protected interests pulled "fire alarms," as they had in the past, but now Congress also heard "fire alarms" from exporters.

As exporters became politically active the net demand for liberalization (D_l) increased, and, as shown in equation 3.1, this affected legislators' utility in two ways. First, it lowered τ_l^*—legislators' ideal levels of the foreign tariff. That is, since exporters lobbied more, asking for more foreign trade barrier reductions than when Congress originally passed the legislation, legislators' ideal levels of the foreign tariff shifted downward. Second, the increase in exporter lobbying increased b_l. That is, the foreign tariff rate became a more important or salient issue for legislators because exporters who were free riding previously were now making the foreign tariff rate an issue that was important to legislators. Graphically, the decrease in legislators' τ_l^*s produces a downward shift in legislators' indifference curves, and the increase in legislators' b_ls "fattens" their indifference curves, making them somewhat more circular.

---

10. I say "largely" because, as I will show in the historical analysis in the next chapter, some exporters did lobby for reciprocity before 1934, but the degree was quite small compared with the amount of protectionist lobbying and the amount of exporter lobbying that followed 1934.

The effect of this increase in proliberalization lobbying as a result of the trade agreement on the set H(A,A) is shown in figure 3.3. Suppose that the president and the foreign executive propose the trade deal at point B. Suppose further that this agreement and the increase in exporter lobbying it generates would produce a southwest movement (e.g., legislator 2's ideal point moves from 2 to 2′) and fattening of legislators' indifference curves. I have removed the original indifference curves and assumed that the sets F(A,A) and F(A,B) are equivalent,[11] to avoid cluttering the figure, and included only the sets H(A,A), I(A,A), and F(A,A) from figure 3.2. The set marked H(A,B) and bounded by the heavy line in figure 3.3 is the set of points that beats A (the reversion policy) given the amount of lobbying generated by the agreement at point B. The set I(A,B) is the intersection of this latter set and F(A,B). Notice that A is not a member of the set H(A,B). To repeat the set H(A,B) is the set of points that makes a majority in Congress at least as well off as point A does *given the lobbying generated by the agreement at point B.* The trade policy at point B generates more exporter lobbying than the policy at point A does, so the policy at point A actually gives a majority of legislators *lower* utility with the lobbying generated by policy B, than it does with the lobbying generated by point A. As such, A is not a member of the set H(A,B). Point B, however, is. It is also a member of I(A,B), so it is an equilibrium trade policy.[12]

The result of this change in indifference contours, as shown in figure 3.3 is a southwesterly expansion of the set that makes legislators better off than unilateral trade policy does. The president can actually make trade agreements that are outside of the original lens-shaped region I(A,A) with deeper reductions in *t* because of the increase in exporter lobbying that those agreements create. The specific example in figure 3.3 illustrates a general point—since the increase in exporter lobbying shifts the legislators' indifference curves to the southwest and fattens them, there is always a policy outside the original set I(A,A), which still makes a majority in Congress better off than they would have been from their reversion level. Of course there is a limit to the reductions that the president can

---

11. Obviously, this simplifying assumption is not a very reasonable one. The trade policy B would change the utility functions of the foreign legislators as well as the home legislators and therefore change the set F as well as the set H. Including this change in Figure 3.3 would only further enlarge the set I(A,B).

12. I am not claiming that the two executives *would* set their respective tariff rates at point B, only that they *could* set them there and still be within the constraint imposed by the two legislatures' sets H and F. There is an infinite number of such points in the policy space. In reality, of course, the outcome of the negotiations would be a function of the bargaining between the two executives—a problem that is beyond the scope of the current analysis.

make in this way. Just any point in the space will not be an equilibrium. The president can only propose points that will make a majority of legislators better off by generating enough exporter lobbying in favor of the agreement to offset the import competing lobbying against it. If the president and foreign executive proposed a policy that included reductions in t that were too deep for the reductions that were made in τ, import competers would out-lobby exporters despite the increase in exporter lobbying that the agreement generated. The policy would not make a majority in Congress better off and would not be an equilibrium. However, as long as the president is mindful of the need to reach only agreements that generate enough exporter support to enhance the welfare of those in Congress, he is able to reduce trade barriers more deeply than would have been possible without reciprocity.

This downward shift and fattening of legislator's indifference curves can help explain why Congress was willing to continue delegating to the president even as American trade barriers were reduced to lower and lower levels. If the only effect of delegation and reciprocity was to capture the gains from the set I(A,A) associated with legislators' original indifference curves I suspect liberalization would have been very circumscribed indeed. I doubt the gains from the original set I(A,A) would have been sufficient to support over sixty years of reciprocal trade policy. But each iteration of delegation and negotiation led to more lobbying by exporters and a greater willingness among legislators to accept deeper reductions in American protection.

In short, it is in the best interest of a majority in Congress to delegate to the president because they know that the president must give them a trade agreement that makes them a little better off than their reversion level. Therefore, the president will only sign agreements that beat the reversion level. Whether or not a trade agreement beats the reversion level is a function of the lobbying for and against the agreement from interest groups. Knowing this, interest groups have every incentive to lobby Congress even when the trade agreement does not require ratification. If export groups out-lobby import-competing groups the president will be able to offer lower levels of t in order to get lower levels of τ. If import-competing groups out-lobby export groups the president will be severely constrained in the concessions he can offer his foreign counterpart in return for reductions in trade barriers overseas.

The story of the American liberalization, then, can be summarized as follows. The proliberalization New Deal Congress inherited the very high Smoot-Hawley tariff, at point Q in figure 3.2, and wanted to reduce it. Congress could have unilaterally reduced tariffs to $\bar{t}$—the ideal point of its median member in the t dimension. Similarly, the foreign legislature would set its tariff rate at its median value in the τ dimension at $\bar{\tau}$ with the resulting policy at point A in figure 3.2. However, rather than simply lowering the tariff to point A Congress delegated authority to the executive to negotiate foreign trade barrier reductions, expecting some greater political activity from the exporters, who wished to receive the preferential concessions in response. Exporters who were previously free riding now had an incentive to lobby Congress in order to ease the constraints of congressional preferences on the president's ability to strike a beneficial trade deal. Later (after 1974) exporters also had to lobby to get the trade agreement that the president signed through Congress on its "fast track" vote.

As exporters lobbied more strenuously, legislators' indifference curve shifted downward and fattened in the home country (westward and fattened in the foreign country), so that the executives in each country could negotiate deeper reductions. When Congress took up the issue of renewing the president's authority, it was willing to renew the legislation on the expectation that the president would be able to come up with an agreement that would elicit enough support from exporters to offset the protectionist reaction. It also knew that if the president did not—that is, if he came up with an agreement that did not make Congress at least as well off because it did not generate enough exporter support to offset the protectionist lobbying—it could always simply let the president's authority expire. So in the second round of negotiations the executives in the two countries could come up with an agreement that lowered trade barriers even lower, and the legislatures in each country would be at least as well off as they were with the status quo, which in the second round is point B.

As long as each iteration of the delegation-negotiation cycle brought more exporters into the political process (or at least more demand for foreign liberalization from those already in the political process) Congress had every reason to keep delegating to the executive. As soon as exporters failed to lobby sufficiently to cause the needed changes in at least a majority of legislators' utility functions Congress would have no reason to delegate. The president, then, would know that he must negotiate a deal that makes Congress better off than the status quo if his negotiating authority was to be renewed. This explains why Congress was continually willing to delegate to the president time after time. The key is the continual increase in exporter lobbying compared with import competer lobbying.

This argument may seem to have a hint of a "rational expectations" flavor to it—legislators' vote to delegate authority to the president expecting an increase in utility from increases in exporter lobbying, and in the end the president negotiates a trade deal such that Congress's expected increase in lobbying is realized. In fact, though, the argument works whether expectations are rational, merely reasonable, or wildly optimistic. Congress did not need to know the exact nature of future trade deals. It only had to know that the president was smart enough to realize that if he wanted to keep his authority he had to conclude only trade deals that made at least a majority of legislators slightly better off than they would have been without the trade deal.[13]

In short, the president continues to request trade policy negotiating authority from Congress and Congress continues to renew that authority because both have expectations that negotiated trade agreements will continue to make them better off. The program encourages exporters to come to the government to ask for foreign trade concessions (if they do not they do not get the foreign trade concessions). As they do, they increase the net demand for liberalization and progressively "fatten" and shift downward the intersection of the home and foreign legislatures' sets H and F.

III. Implications for Other Theories of American Trade Policy

The analysis just presented can also help clear up several puzzles that are created by existing studies of American trade policy. My intent here is not to be critical but merely to point out some of the puzzles that remain in explaining the American liberalization, despite these impressive studies. For instance, Destler (1986) lists many of the effects of the reciprocal trade agreements program on the American political economy—including a brief mention of its effects on exporter lobbying—but his main argument is that Congress delegated to the president to insulate itself from constituency pressures on trade policy. He writes:

> No longer did it [Congress] give priority to protecting American industry. Instead, its members would give priority to protecting themselves: from the direct, one-sided producer interests that had led them to make bad trade law. (14)

---

13. In this sense the relationship between Congress and the president is a little like a repeated prisoners' dilemma. A majority in Congress delegates to the executive as long as he "cooperates" by giving them agreements that make them better off. If he "defects" by giving them an agreement that does not do so, Congress does not renew his authority. Therefore, the president will always make sure that he does not reduce t by more than there is support for in Congress given the amount of exporter and import competer lobbying that the agreement generates. Some may raise the problem of a president at the end of his term. Why would he care whether Congress renewed his authority or not? And if he did not, wouldn't he simply set t wherever he liked? The way these sorts of problems have usually been dealt with in the political economy literature is to assume that the president cares about his party in future governments.

According to this argument, Congress is forced, against its wishes, to enact protectionist legislation by overwhelmingly protectionist constituency pressures. The president is assumed to have more liberal preferences and is less susceptible to lobbying pressures, so by delegating to the president Congress alleviates the pressure brought to bear on it by the army of protectionist lobbyists and insures that there will be a more liberal trade policy.

However, delegation could in no way insulate Congress from constituency pressures on trade policy. The main insight of the congressional dominance literature is that even when it has delegated its authority to the executive branch Congress maintains a great deal of control over policy outcomes. If this is the case, though, delegation to the executive cannot insulate Congress from protectionist pressures on trade policy. Congress still has ultimate control over trade policy. As we saw in figure 3.2, congressional preferences were crucial to the president and foreign executive's decision about where to set trade policy. If lobbying by interest groups affects legislators' ideal points, as I argue it does, then that pressure will indirectly be reflected in policy outcomes even when the president is actually setting the policy, because the president always must set a trade policy that makes a majority in Congress better off.

Furthermore, protected interests had every incentive to keep lobbying Congress if for no other reason than to urge it not to renew the president's delegated authority. If delegating to the president hurt protected interests, and if, for some reason, those interests have a higher probability of successfully influencing Congress than influencing the president (as Destler claims), then they should continue to lobby Congress in order to get it to take away the president's delegated authority. Delegating to the president was an institutional change that favored liberalization. Knowing this, protected interests had strong incentives to lobby Congress to reverse the institutional change.[14] Put in more game-theoretic language, even if Congress could credibly commit not to dabble in trade policy by delegating to the president it could not credibly commit to maintaining delegation to the president since it still retained control over that decision. Congress could *claim* that it was no longer in the business of setting trade policy, but protected interests, if they are rational, have no reason to believe it. Congress continues to have the power to act on trade policy whether it delegates or not. Protected interests are smart enough to know this, so if they

---

14. Riker (1980) made this point about institutions in general in his well-known criticism of the institutionalist literature: if institutions do impose equilibria on voting cycles the losers from any institutional setup will be able to gather enough votes for a different set of institutions that makes them winners. Cycling over policy outcomes is simply translated into cycling over institutional arrangements.

have a better chance of affecting policy by lobbying Congress they will continue to do so.

Congress could not simply divert constituency pressures on trade policy away from itself as Destler claims. In any case, Congress did not do so. When it delegated power over trade policy to the president it did it only for three-year terms, insuring that there would be a fight in Congress over trade policy at least that often—very strange behavior for a Congress seeking to insulate itself from constituency pressures on trade policy. The sunset provision also ensured that opponents of freer trade only had to muster a bare majority to take away the president's delegated authority; that is, they simply had to insure non-passage of the renewals of the authority with a 50 percent plus one vote against renewal. Since the president cannot veto a congressional decision to *not* pass legislation, Congress would not even have to muster enough votes to override the veto. Furthermore, O'Halloran (1994), who also argues that Congress did not legislate itself out of the business of making trade policy, shows that Congress still proposes and passes a large amount of legislation on trade.

In fact, delegation alone cannot explain why the RTAA and subsequent delegations of authority passed Congress in the first place. It cannot explain why Congress was able to resist protectionist pressures in creating trade policy institutions when it could not resist them when it set trade policy itself. Presumably protectionist interest groups are sophisticated enough to realize that delegation to the executive would lead to reductions in their protection. Therefore, they had every incentive to lobby against this institutional change. How is Congress able to resist these pressures in the institutional design stage and not in the policy creation stage?

My argument can help provide a solution to this puzzle, too. First, the problem does not arise in my analysis because I do not assume that Congress was unable to liberalize if it did not delegate. In my model Congress delegates in order to reduce foreign as well as American trade barriers, not because it is incapable of liberalizing otherwise. However, even if Congress did have problems dealing with constituency pressures my argument helps as well because reciprocity encourages more exporters to take political action and increases the amount of proliberalization lobbying Congress hears. In short, Congress is able to change the trade policy institution to reduce trade barriers, even when it could not reduce the trade barriers themselves because by changing the institution Congress generated more support for reducing trade barriers.

Lohmann and O'Halloran (1994) and perhaps in the greatest depth O'Halloran (1994) argue that Congress delegated to the executive in order to escape the universalistic logroll by which trade policy was made. In their model, trade policy is a multidimensional issue with the tariff rate on each product a different dimension. If Congress does not delegate it solves this multidimensional voting problem with a universalistic logroll in which each legislator votes in favor of protection for each other legislator's district in return for a vote in favor of protection for his or her district. Any legislator who violates this norm is punished by having protection for his or her district removed from the bill.[15] Each member of Congress is worse off under this arrangement than if the legislation had not passed, since the costs of protecting industries in all the other districts outweigh the benefits of receiving protection for one's own district. Congress delegates to the president in order to escape this highly inefficient logroll. The source of the problem for Congress in this model is universalism, and delegation cures the problem.

If universalism is the problem, though, this argument begs the question of why Congress chose delegation to escape it. Other institutional fixes to the problem would have allowed Congress to escape universalism and still maintain control over trade policy. For instance, Congress was able to liberalize substantially in the Underwood Act of 1913 without resorting to delegation to the president. Essentially, it was able to do this by drafting the legislation in the Democratic caucus and voting on it on the floor under a closed rule (Link, 1956). My argument deals with the problem effectively because Congress was not delegating simply to escape a universalistic logroll but because it wanted to reduce foreign as well as American trade barriers. No institution except delegating to the executive the power to negotiate reciprocal trade treaties could accomplish this goal.[16]

A third explanation for delegation avoids these problems. Schnietz (1993) argues that *Democrats* in Congress in 1934 delegated to the president. Democrats were able to resist protectionist pressures in both the trade policy creation and institutional design stages because protected interests were not part of their

---

15. Krehbiel (1991) has criticized, on empirical grounds, models which rely on universalistic norms. He showed that in several cases—including the paradigmatic case of Senator James Buckley's (Conservative-N.Y.) efforts to reduce pork barrel projects in 1973—universalistic norms were not enforced as the model suggests, and that legislators often had difficulty committing to such logrolls or devising procedures to facilitate them.

16. Neither O'Halloran (1994) nor Lohmann and O'Halloran (1994) offer a model of lobbying behavior by constituents that underlies their assumptions about legislators' preferences. However, there is reason to believe that collective action problems are also going to be particularly acute in their model. The costs of delegating are a reduction in protection for the protected interest in each representative's district (p_i for representative i in their model). The benefits of delegating are a reduction in the costs of protection for all other districts $j \neq i$, paid by *all* constituents in district i. Obviously the costs of delegation are much more concentrated than the benefits are—a reduction in protection for other districts paid by constituents.

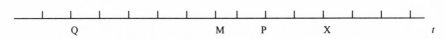

Fig. 3.4.   The effects of delegation on trade policy (Example from Schnietz (1993.)

political coalition. However, Schnietz argues, rather than simply reducing trade barriers, Democrats in Congress delegated to the president in order to commit future Congresses to lower trade barriers than they would have otherwise set.

Figure 3.4 illustrates her argument. Suppose that, after the Democrats took control of the government, they set trade policy at point Q in the standard way without delegation. If the Republicans took control of the government again the median Republican, with ideal point at M_R, would be able to make a closed rule policy proposal and raise the tariff all the way to X, the level of trade barriers that makes the median floor member, with ideal point at M, as well off as he or she was under the status quo. However, the Republican president is assumed to have more liberal preferences than the median Republican in Congress does. Therefore, if the Democratic Congress instead delegated to the executive in 1934, even in its "worst case" scenario of future unified Republican control of both Congress and the presidency, trade barriers would not be raised by as much as if Congress had not delegated. For instance, in such a case the president would have an ideal point, like P, and would set the trade policy at P—lower than X. Furthermore, the three-year sunset clause in the RTAA would not be a problem for the president because the median floor member is actually better off than if Congress had not delegated in 1934 since P is closer to his or her ideal point than both X and Q are. Therefore, when the president proposed them, RTAA renewals had no problem passing. In essence, the sole effect of delegation in Schnietz's view is the transfer of the power to make closed rule proposals away from the median legislator of the party in power to the president.[17]

Although the assumption that, before delegation, the median member of the ruling party could make closed rule policy proposals is somewhat unortho-

---

17. Schnietz (1993) also claimed that the president's veto power helped ensure renewals of the RTAA because Congress requires a two-thirds majority to override a veto: "Any President, even a Republican, would find it difficult to agree to a diminution of power and would probably veto a congressional attempt to reclaim tariff setting control" (22). Clearly, though, the president has no such power. The president can only veto legislation that *passes* Congress; he cannot veto legislation that does *not pass* Congress. All Congress had to do to "reclaim tariff setting control" was, in fact, nothing. The president's authority would have expired automatically. Of course, the president does not need to use the veto to keep his authority—as long as the president offers the median floor member at least as good a deal as he or she would receive from trade policy without delegation that member will always vote for renewals of the president's authority.

dox,[18] Schnietz's argument offers a powerful explanation for the American liberalization. Even more importantly, as I will discuss subsequently, Schnietz does a good job of explaining the *timing* of the American liberalization—why it did not occur before 1934. But what was striking about the American liberalization was not only that trade barriers were not raised by much, but that they kept coming down with each passing year. What is also striking is that, although they could not have known this in 1934, all the Democrats' fretting about future Republican governments was moot—Republicans eventually came to favor liberalization as much as the Democrats did. My argument can add to Schnietz's by explaining this remarkable transformation of preferences among policymakers.

Each of the explanations I have reviewed relies solely on delegation to explain the liberalization of American trade policy. They suggest that trade barriers should have been reduced to something closer to the president's ideal point and no further. Delegation was certainly necessary to bring about the liberalization, but was it sufficient of and by itself to explain a reduction of trade barriers as deep and prolonged as the one in the United States—a reduction in tariff rates from around 50 percent in 1934 to less than 5 percent today? I would argue that some change in congressional and presidential *preferences* was necessary to bring about liberalization of this magnitude.

Furthermore, there is a tension in each of these arguments that is common to all of them: all claim, in some way, that Congress delegated to the president and put up with lower trade barriers than it really wanted because it knew that if it did not do so it would get higher trade barriers than it really wanted (in Destler's case because of constituency pressures, in Lohmann and O'Halloran's case because of the universalistic logroll, and in Schnietz's case because of future Republican Congresses). These are compelling explanations of delegation, but as explanations of liberalization they are fairly limited—particularly a liberalization as prolonged and deep as the one in the United States. After all, American trade barriers are less than one-tenth what they were in 1934. If congressional fear of a protectionist binge is all that has driven delegation and liberalization one has to wonder how far trade barriers can be reduced before legislators begin to consider the cure worse than the disease. To foster liberalization

---

18. Trade policy was rarely considered under a closed rule before 1934, and if any group could be thought to possess closed-rule power it would be the House Ways and Means Committee, not the ruling party's caucus. The one exception of which I am aware is the Underwood Act of 1913. It was considered under a closed rule, under President Wilson's urging, to prevent special interests from attaching special protectionist amendments to it. Interestingly, Schnietz's assumption (1993) that the median legislator of the party in power makes the policy proposal is not a bad one for the Underwood Act. The bill was written in the Democratic caucus because the insurgent movement had dismantled the previous governance structures in the House (Link 1956).

as dramatic as the United States' it seems to me there must have been a shift in legislators' preferences on trade policy. In order to explain the American liberalization, then, we must explain this shift in preferences.

All of these explanations are correct in arguing that delegation was essential to the liberalization of American trade policy. But Congress did not delegate to insulate itself from constituency pressures—indeed, I would argue that it knew that would be impossible. Congress may have delegated to escape a universalistic logroll, but one has to wonder why it did not choose one of the many other institutional innovations that would do this. Democrats in Congress may have delegated to commit future Republican Congresses to smaller tariff increases, but while this can explain why trade barriers did not go back up it leaves open the question of why they kept coming down. I would argue that Congress delegated to the president for precisely the reason that it said it did—to increase exports by obtaining foreign trade barrier reductions. This simple fact can explain why Congress delegated, how the United States liberalized, and why congressional preferences became progressively more liberal on trade.

The important ingredient left out of the story told by those who see delegation as the primary engine of liberalization is that Congress did not delegate authority to the president to set just *any* trade policy; it delegated authority for him to set trade policy *reciprocally* with other countries. Reciprocity in turn produced an increase in exporter lobbying and created its own support base among constituents, as I discussed in the last chapter. This, in turn, generated more support for liberalization in Congress.

My argument also has implications for the analysis of Banks and Weingast (1992), who argued similarly, albeit in the different context of agency budget allocations, that interest groups are an important tool used by Congress to help them monitor the activities of government agencies. Banks and Weingast argued that because interest groups help monitor the activities of agencies Congress may be reluctant to delegate authority to executive agencies unless there is a dense network of interest groups to help them monitor the agency. In other words, Congress might not delegate authority to an agency, even though doing so would be beneficial to itself and its constituents, if the groups that would be needed to help monitor the agency face particularly severe collective action problems. The analysis presented here corroborates this argument with the added proviso that Congress may be able to recognize the latent potential of certain interest groups (in this case exporters) and design institutions (in this case reciprocity) that can help them overcome their collective action problems and aid Congress in monitoring the activities of the executive.

One potentially nagging question remains. If delegation has such wonderful effects, why did Congress wait until 1934 to do it? This is a question that plagues the arguments of Destler, Lohmann and O'Halloran, and O'Halloran and potentially my own. One of the more common answers to this question is that members of Congress learned from the disastrous consequences of the Smoot-Hawley Act that they were unable to set a responsible trade policy and delegated the authority to the president. (This is a common claim throughout the literature. A few examples include Baldwin 1985, Goldstein 1986, Goldstein and Lenway 1989, Pastor 1980, Pietro 1990 and Sundquist 1981.) Schnietz (1993) has persuasively shown the implausibility of this hypothesis. Of those legislators still in Congress in 1934 who had voted in favor of the Smoot-Hawley Act only a small minority exhibited this kind of learning by voting for the RTAA.

Schnietz's own answer to the question Why wait until 1934? is a compelling one. It is essentially a story about the process of institutional innovation by the Democrats, and it is equally applicable to my model of reciprocity as to hers of delegation. She argues that the only party that had an interest in liberalization did not really have a chance to use it until 1934. The seventy years between the Civil War and the Great Depression were a period of Republican hegemony in American politics. Democrats controlled both houses of Congress only twice, for a total of ten years during that period. Meanwhile, the Republican coalition that was in power during most of the period was built on a policy of protectionism. The Republican Party would have been cutting its own throat if it introduced real reciprocity and increased the chances of liberalization.

As such, the Democrats rarely had a chance to experiment with the effects of different institutions. In their first opportunity for reform, the Wilson-Gorman Act of 1894, they failed to bring about the kind of liberalization they wanted, and in any case, the act was simply reversed by the subsequent tariff bill. In their second opportunity they passed the liberalizing Underwood Act in 1913 and then attempted to institutionalize lower tariffs by creating the Tariff Commission in 1916, which was designed to make tariff setting less political and more scientific. Of course, when the Republicans took over again in 1921 they simply filled the Tariff Commission with their own commissioners, who favored high tariffs, and tariff politics as usual took over again. The Democrats would not be in power again until 1933. By then they had finally discovered the institutional innovation that would lock in future Congresses to lower tariffs whether they were Democratic or not—the RTAA. The short answer, then, to "why wait until 1934?" is simply that institutional innovation takes time, the Democrats did not have a chance until then, and the Republicans had no incentive to do it at all. Schnietz's explanation for the institutional innovation of

1934 is just as applicable to my own argument—except, of course, my explanation includes demand-side as well as supply-side effects.

Finally, I, and the other analysts of the institutional innovation I have discussed here, have assumed that the proposal must come from within the government—either the president or the legislature. But why couldn't a lobbyist from outside the government propose the institutional change? North (1981) has cogently argued that institutional change will usually come from within the state because collective action problems will prevent societal actors from making the proposal. In addition, no group, even if it could overcome these collective action costs, would have an incentive to waste resources on a proposal it thought had a very small probability of being enacted—and, as I will show in the next chapter, the type of reciprocity I modeled here was just such a proposal before 1934. There were some proreciprocity lobbying efforts before 1934, but these were weak in comparison with the post-RTAA period, and they did not get started until after the government proposed a form of reciprocity (much more circumscribed than the RTAA) in 1890. Furthermore, the quantitative estimates of the demand for liberalization that I will provide in chapter 5 suggest that lobbying for liberalization was insignificant before 1934. In short, we have both theoretical (North 1981) and empirical (chaps. 5 and 6) reasons for the assumption that the institutional innovation comes from within the state.

IV. Conclusion

This chapter has provided the last step in the main argument of this book by discussing the supply of trade policy by the government. It has shown how the increase in the demand for liberalization, which reciprocity itself fosters, encouraged legislators to submit to deeper reductions in trade barriers than they otherwise would have allowed. The analysis in this chapter complements existing models of American trade policy, which have explained liberalization with the use of delegation alone, by showing that, although delegation certainly facilitated a reduction of American trade barriers, reciprocity strengthened this effect by increasing the amount of pressure legislators received from exporters, thereby encouraging them to continue delegating to the president even after he had reduced trade barriers a great deal.

Finally, on a more speculative note, I believe the argument presented in the last two chapters has broad implications for the importance of the supply side in political economy literature in general. Although this study presents a theory of the effects of reciprocity on the *demand* for liberalization, it really has a great deal to say about the supply side, as well. In some theories of political economy, the supply side is just a mechanism for aggregating preferences. The government's desire for reelection prevents it from doing anything but the bidding of the strongest lobby. Policy is the result of the group that lobbies the hardest not the preferences of those in government. In the theory presented here, policy is also the product of the strongest lobby but with an important difference: the supply side, by concentrating the benefits and dispersing the costs of its policies, actually has a measure of *control* over which groups lobby the hardest. The theory presented here suggests that the supply side has a great deal of autonomy because by concentrating benefits and dispersing the costs of its preferred policies it can help determine the amount of demand for and against those policies.

Part 2
Historical Overview

CHAPTER 4

Reciprocity and American Trade Policy, 1890–1994

I. Introduction

In the title of a well-known article, Richard Cooper correctly remarked that "trade policy is foreign policy" (1972). However, this was not always the case, at least in the United States. Until the end of the last century trade policy was seen as a predominantly domestic issue—a question of government finance and industrial development. In the previous two chapters, I discussed endogenous tariff theory, which argues that tariffs may persist in part because the costs of reducing them are concentrated on a few producers while the benefits are spread over all the consumers in the political economy. That literature also treats trade policy as a purely domestic matter—ignoring the international political aspects of it and describing only the rent-seeking behavior of domestic actors. As such, the endogenous tariff literature treats trade policy in much the same way politicians of the nineteenth century did. Not surprisingly, then, the endogenous tariff literature does a remarkably good job of describing trade politics in the United States during that period.

However, the neglect of the international character of trade policy is one of my criticisms of that literature. I pointed out not only that "trade policy is foreign policy" but that the seemingly insurmountable collective action problems among the beneficiaries of liberalization may be overcome by internationalizing trade policy through reciprocity. In this chapter, I will illustrate the plausibility of some of these ideas with the tariff history of the United States. First I will show that before the use of the type of reciprocity that I modeled in chapters 2 and 3 there was no strong lobby in favor of liberalization. There was, however, a very strong lobby in favor of maintaining and extending protection. This pattern was true even in the one example of substantial liberalization during the period, the Underwood Act of 1913. Second, with the introduction of an earnest reciprocal trade agreements program in 1934 exporters became very politically active in order to urge the government to seek foreign trade barrier reductions on their products. This chapter will also provide some historical background for the quantitative analysis of major U.S. trade bills undertaken in chapters 5 and 6. Readers seeking a more in-depth treatment of American trade politics than I can provide here should turn to the many admirable histories of American trade policy (Stanwood 1903; Tarbell 1911; Taussig 1966; and Terrill 1973 are just a few of the better-known examples).

The next section will review the history of U.S. trade policy from 1890 through passage of the Smoot-Hawley Act in 1930, making the main point that there was a great deal of lobbying by protected interests and very little by consumers and exporters. Because this is a fairly uncontroversial point and because this history is fairly well known I will not dwell on this period. The next seven sections will review the history of U.S. trade policy since the launching of the United States' reciprocal trade agreements program in 1934. The main point of those sections will be to show that there was a large and growing exporter lobby throughout the period. Section IX will offer some conclusions and some evidence from hearings before the House Ways and Means Committee that suggests that demand by exporters for reciprocal liberalization did rise as a result of reciprocity.

II. A Brief Tariff History of the United States, 1890–1930

A. Major Trade Bills, 1890–1930

This section will review seven major trade bills from the turn of the century through the Smoot-Hawley Act in 1930. The first of these trade bills was the McKinley Act of 1890, named after House Ways and Means Committee Chairman William McKinley (R-Ohio). The Republican Party during this period was ardently protectionist. The Democrats in this period are commonly thought of as the free trade party; however, this is only partly true. There was a strong protectionist minority within the Democratic Party until 1888 when the Democratic president, Grover Cleveland, decided to run his reelection campaign on the tariff issue and moved the Democratic Party squarely behind tariff reform (Stanwood 1903; Tarbell,1911; Taussig 1966).

Lobbying on the McKinley Act fit the pattern of lobbying on other trade bills in this period both before and after it. The lobbyists were present, as ever, assuring their share of the increase in protection, but there was little if any opposition voiced by consumer interests. The wool and woolens lobby represented by the National Wool Growers Association and the National Association of Wool Manufacturers received substantial increases in protection. The alliance between these two interests was one of the most powerful forces in politics during this period (Stanwood 1903; Tarbell 1911; Taussig 1966; Terrill 1973). The American Iron and Steel Association, which had been particularly active in the presidential election of 1888, distributing over one million pamphlets and contributing large sums of money, was rewarded with the opportunity to virtually write its own duty schedules (Tarbell 1911, 193). The latter interest and a related group called the Tin Plate Association were also successful in having the duty raised on tin plate—a product that was not even produced in the United States—in order to encourage the creation of the industry (191–93).[1] The McKinley Act raised import duties to their highest levels since the Civil War.

The next major piece of tariff legislation was the Wilson-Gorman Act of 1894. Although it is not included in the quantitative analysis in the next chapter because of data limitations it is worthwhile discussing it for continuity and because it highlights the problems liberalization faced during this period of unilateral trade politics. The Democrats had unified control of both houses of Congress and the presidency on only two occasions (totaling ten years) between 1890 and 1932. The Wilson-Gorman Act was passed during one of these periods. Despite unified control by the party that had staked its reputation on tariff reform, appreciable liberalization was not possible. In fact, the politics of the Wilson-Gorman Act of 1894 were remarkably similar to that of its predecessors. Industrial interests were able to pressure their representatives in Congress to continue to protect them from foreign competition. James Wilson, (D-W. Va.) the new chair of the Ways and Means Committee, introduced his mildly reforming tariff proposal in December 1893, and the bill passed the House with little difficulty.

The Senate was an entirely different story. There a small contingent of Democrats, led by Arthur Gorman of Maryland and Calvin Brice of Ohio, was dissatisfied with the tariff reductions on several products and made it clear that they would defeat the bill if it were not changed. The Democrats did not have a large majority in the Senate in the first place, so the protectionist Democrats' threats were not empty. Furthermore, a Republican filibuster threatened to hold up legislation until several tariff rates were raised. James M. Swank of the Iron and Steel Association boasted that this tactic produced higher rates on "hun-

---

1. In 1886 the Tin Plate Association, under the leadership of John Jarrett, campaigned heavily against the reelection to the House of Representatives of William Morrison (D-Ill.), an ardent tariff reformer. With liberal use of funds the association managed to have Morrison removed from office (Tarbell 1911, 174).

dreds" of products, iron and steel and cotton manufactures reportedly being the largest beneficiaries (Tarbell 1911, 228–29). The House bill left the Senate with 634 amendments attached, mostly to increase the duties. In the conference committee the Senate refused to move from its position. Attempts by President Cleveland to make liberalization a matter of party loyalty only strengthened the senators' resolve. In the end the House accepted the Senate amendments, and the president let the bill become law without his signature. As a result of the legislation many duties were reduced somewhat compared with the very high McKinley duties; however, they were still higher than at any point before the McKinley Act (Stanwood 1903, 296–358; Tarbell 1911, 209–37; Taussig 1966, 284–320). Unilateral liberalization had failed.

Two months after the passage of the Wilson-Gorman Act, the Democrats were dealt a severe defeat at the polls. Large Republican majorities were elected to the House of Representatives. Two years later the Republicans won another resounding victory, taking both houses of Congress and the presidency. The Republicans had unified control over the government until 1911. Two tariff bills were enacted during this period—the Dingley tariff of 1897 and the Payne-Aldrich tariff of 1909.

The first of these bills when it was put forward by House Ways and Means Committee Chairman Nelson Dingley (R-Maine) was surprisingly moderate in its increases of the tariff, in many cases maintaining the rates of the Wilson-Gorman Act. The duties on iron and steel, for instance, were changed very little, if at all. Sugar, however, with beet sugar farming now a powerful interest in California, received protection that it had not received under the McKinley tariff, where it was free. The bill passed the House within two weeks. The Senate proved to be much more protectionist. There the bill was modified substantially on the floor after it was released by the Finance Committee. The powerful wool lobby was once again able to use its access to the system, call in its favors from the Republican campaign effort, and gain substantial protection (Tarbell 1991, 251–52). The lobby was strengthened by western Republicans who were swing voters on the tariff issue and willing to use their power to make sure that sheep ranchers in their districts received their share of the largesse. The duty on hides was also raised at the behest of these senators. After Senate consideration, the bill was substantially more protectionist than the House had wanted. In fact, due to increases in duties on raw sugar, wool, hides, and dozens of other products the Dingley Act actually raised the overall duty rate above the level set by the McKinley Act (Stanwood 1903, 360–94; Tarbell 1911, 237–58; Taussig 1966, 321–60).

Distrusted by fellow Republicans for earlier free trade leanings, Theodore Roosevelt left the tariff issue for his handpicked successor, William Taft (Baker

1941, 1–12). In the election of 1908, the Republicans pledged to reform the tariff, and two days after that election Sereno Payne (R-N.Y.), chairman of the Ways and Means Committee, began hearings on tariff reform. The legislative history of the Payne-Aldrich tariff is remarkably close to that of the Dingley Act. A moderately protectionist bill with reductions of various duties passed the House only to be substantially increased on the floor of the Senate. The Senate added 847 amendments, almost all of which increased the level of protection over the House version. Once again, wool was a major beneficiary. The National Association of Wool Manufacturers and National Wool Growers Association had met in Chicago shortly after Taft's election and agreed to jointly lobby for no reduction of their protection. As always the two groups had been heavy contributors to the Republican election campaign. The former group was politically very powerful in the East and the latter was very powerful in the West. The wool manufacturers' lobby also had special access and connections through its almost twenty year relationship with Senator Nelson Aldrich (R-R.I.) in part because of the textile mills in that state. Cotton manufacturers had a great deal of pull with Aldrich for the same reason. Despite the best intentions of President Taft the Payne-Aldrich Act failed to bring about tariff reform (Baker 1941, 77–122; Tarbell 1911, 297–331; Taussig 1966, 361–408).[2]

The Underwood Act of 1913 was the only case of substantial tariff reduction in this period. However, despite the fact that it was a case of liberalization it was still a *unilateral* bill and therefore interest group behavior was remarkably similar to such group activity with every other bill during this period—protected interests lobbied heavily with little opposition from consumer groups. Sugar and wool growers were particularly active, as always, and President Woodrow Wilson had to make special appeals to keep senators from wool-growing states in the west and the sugar-growing state of Louisiana in line (he failed in the case of Louisiana, as both senators crossed party lines and voted against the bill). Besides sugar and wool growers, cotton manufacturers, boot and shoe manufacturers, citrus fruit growers, and hundreds of other interests lobbied Congress vigorously to prevent reductions in their protection. Although the Underwood Act was a case of liberalization, the lobbying behavior was consistent with the theory presented in chapter 2.

---

2. This was a great disappointment to several midwestern senators and prompted the "insurgent movement" in Congress. The movement started with a few Republican Senators, mostly from the Midwest, crossing party lines on the Payne-Aldrich vote, but it eventually led to more widespread legislative reform and the stripping of the speakership of the House, then held by Joseph Cannon (R.-Ill.), of many of its powers. The insurgent movement was insufficient to change the legislative outcome, and the bill passed both houses of Congress, but the institutional changes it spawned did have important effects on the Underwood Act in 1913, as I will describe.

A series of fortuitous circumstances really helped Wilson achieve his aim of tariff reform despite interest group pressures to the contrary. The Progressive reform movement was at its apex during the first Wilson term, and, rightly or wrongly, high protection was associated with trusts, which the Progressives felt needed to be stopped. Second, there was no strong congressional leader to oppose Wilson. The insurgent movement had successfully removed much of the power of the Speaker, including the power to route legislation and make committee appointments. Decisions were made to a large degree consensually in the Democratic caucus, and there was no strong leadership there to challenge Wilson. Furthermore, there was a large Democratic majority in the House, and more importantly this majority was abnormally new (114 of the 290 Democratic congressmen were freshmen) and progressive in ideology. All of these factors helped Wilson control the tariff-making process in a way that had not been possible for previous presidents. Wilson also showed remarkable leadership of Congress. He called a special session of Congress for the sole purpose of tariff reform; he made a special personal appeal before Congress (the first presidential address made in person to Congress since that of Thomas Jefferson); he personally lobbied marginal senators, and he went "over the head" of Congress to bring public attention to lobbyists. All of these efforts were to some extent unprecedented at that time. Wilson successfully assumed the mantle of party, as well as national, leadership and helped the passage of the bill (Link 1956, 145–75).

The year after the Underwood tariff's enactment World War I broke out in Europe, substantially distorting world markets. American imports of manufactures from war-torn Europe plummeted while exports of war materials skyrocketed. Following the war the Republicans recaptured the government in 1920 and reenacted increases in protection with the Fordney-McCumber tariff of 1922. The familiar lobbyists such as those promoting cotton and wool textiles and raw wool were active. These interests remained major supporters of the Republican Party and were rewarded for their support with substantial increases in their level of protection from foreign competition. A new set of interests appeared on the political stage to lobby for protection—the "war baby" industries. "War babies" were industries that did not exist in the United States before the war but in the hothouse economic environment during the war had sprouted and quickly flourished. Following the war, European demand obviously fell while European supply rose again, threatening the profitability of these industries. These industries petitioned loudly for protection from the government and often received it. Taussig (1966) provided the dye industry as an example of a war baby industry that was able to garner protection following the war. The Fordney-McCumber Act was a "return to normalcy" for tariff politics

(447–448). It was even more protectionist in spirit than was previous trade legislation, though. Congress instructed the president to change tariff rates so as to equalize the costs of production at home and abroad. Had this actually been carried out the very basis of international trade would have been erased (Rhodes 1993, 42).

The final act of this period was the Smoot-Hawley tariff of 1930—certainly the most famous, indeed—notorious—tariff act discussed in this chapter. It is widely perceived to be the paragon of special interest politics run amok—a reputation that is well earned. Schattschneider (1935) is helpful on this point. He points to only one instance of a strong anti-protectionist lobby—an effort conducted largely by soap makers against a tariff on fats and oils (150–51). Later he tells the story of an unsuccessful surreptitious attempt by Coca-Cola and Hershey's to reduce the sugar duty (274–76). These were the only two instances that could be found in Schattschneider's very careful and thorough study of the passage of the bill. Thus, the Smoot-Hawley tariff provides further support for the collective action theory of trade policy.

B. "Reciprocity," 1890–1930

All of the bills enacted by Republican governments in this period contained so-called reciprocity provisions, although in none of the cases was there any serious attempt to trade access to the American market for access to foreign markets. In the McKinley and Dingley Acts, for instance, the president was not given the authority to negotiate down U.S. trade barriers for foreign trade barriers. Instead Congress placed several items not produced in the United States on the free list. The president was given authority to remove a country's exports of these products from the free list if he determined that that country discriminated against American products. In the McKinley Act this list of products included sugar, molasses, tea, coffee, and animal hides. In the Dingley Act it included coffee, tea, vanilla, tonka beans, certain liquors not produced in the United States, statuary, and works of art—hardly much leverage for American negotiators. The Dingley Act also authorized the president to negotiate tariff reduction on other products by as much as 20 percent in return for foreign trade barrier reductions, but these agreements had to pass *both* houses of Congress (Rhodes 1993, 23–37; Stanwood 1903; 281–93; Taussig 1966, 278–82, 352–54; Terrill 1973; 159–83, 200–201).[3]

---

3. Clearly this was not much of a delegation of trade policy-making authority to the president since the Constitution gives the president the authority to negotiate treaties with other countries, which become law with a two-thirds majority vote of the Senate.

The Payne-Aldrich Act contained similar "reciprocity" provisions with the innovation that Congress created two schedules: a minimum schedule, which would be used for countries that the president deemed worthy, and a maximum schedule for those countries that the president decided discriminated against U.S. products. Critics charged that the minimum schedule was where the maximum schedule should be, and there is some evidence that Congress purposefully raised the minimum schedule so that if the president did grant it to a country it would not harm protection to American products. The provision led to little in the way of liberalization or greater access of U.S. exporters to foreign markets (Rhodes 1993, 37–40; Taussig 1966, 403–7).

With the reciprocity provisions in the Fordney-McCumber Act the president was allowed to offer foreign governments concessions on an unconditional most favored nation basis for the first time in U.S. history. This seemingly liberal gesture was in fact empty because, as Rhodes (1993, 42) points out: "Congress at the same time *precluded any possibility of liberalizing the tariff*" (italics in the original) since in addition to raising duties it mandated that the president set tariffs to equalize costs of production at home and abroad. Finally, the Smoot-Hawley Act, like its predecessors, gave the president the authority to retaliate against foreign governments that discriminated against American products. Given that the Smoot-Hawley Act was the most protectionist legislation in American history this must have seemed like an empty threat to foreign governments—how much worse could retaliation possibly be? In the end Smoot-Hawley elicited not reciprocity but retaliation (Rhodes 1993; Jones 1934).

Clearly none of these so-called reciprocity provisions met the conditions described in chapters 2 and 3. Congress refused to allow the president to reduce American trade barriers in return for foreign trade barrier reductions. At best it set a minimum schedule (and this was generally quite high) and gave the president the authority to retaliate against foreign governments that did not come to some accommodation with the United States. Republicans in Congress had no desire to reduce protection on American products and therefore no real desire for reciprocal trade treaties. Rhodes (1993) concludes that "the history of this period reminds us that simply dubbing a policy reciprocal does not necessarily make it so" (52). Congress never allowed U.S. negotiators much latitude in reducing American trade barriers in return for foreign trade barrier reductions. Not surprisingly, foreign governments offered little in the way of access to their own markets in return, and American exporters had little reason to increase their lobbying efforts.

Despite this lack of meaningful reciprocity there was still some lobbying effort by exporters, but it truly paled in comparison with lobbying by protectionist groups during this period and the efforts of exporter groups after an earnest reciprocity program was introduced in 1934. One such group was the National Association of Manufacturers (NAM). The NAM was organized by a small group of manufacturers centered in Ohio in 1894 in part to pressure the government to use reciprocity to expand exports. NAM members were generally small- to medium-sized producers of manufactures that were competitive overseas who were interested in tapping into foreign markets to augment sales at home. Very large producers did not need reciprocity since they were usually able to gain access to overseas markets through foreign direct investment (Becker 1982, 48–68).

In 1902 a National Reciprocity League was formed. On its board of directors were manufacturers of iron and steel, agricultural machinery, processed grain, furniture, and locomotives—by then America's premier export industries, and likely candidates for foreign concessions in a reciprocity agreement (Ellis 1939, 9). In 1909 a third group, the American Manufacturers Export Association (AMEA) was formed. The companies that made up the AMEA were usually producers of specialized goods that exported a great deal of their production. The AMEA did not achieve the growth that the NAM did (Becker 1982, 64–68). Organizations like the NAM, the National Reciprocity League, and the AMEA show that there was interest in reciprocity. They also show that, even at this early stage, firms that were not interested in lobbying for *unilateral* tariff reductions *were* interested in forming lobbies for *reciprocal* trade treaties that gave concessions on their particular products.

However, the importance of these groups, at least during this period should not be exaggerated. The activities of these groups were insignificant compared with the activities of dozens of very powerful protectionist groups like the Tariff League, Joseph Wharton's Industrial League, the American Iron and Steel Association, the National Wool Growers Association, and the National Wool Manufacturers Association to name just a few. Furthermore, these three groups were completely outnumbered by the hundreds of protectionist groups and individual industries that pressured their legislators for protection from foreign competition. The AMEA and the National Reciprocity League never achieved much growth or political importance during this period. The NAM eventually grew to become quite influential, but, interestingly, it became infiltrated with protectionist interests and lost its proreciprocity purpose—it actually lobbied *against* the RTAA in 1934 because the legislation would have allowed the president to reduce an industry's protection without its permission (Committee on Ways and Means 1934)! It was not until after 1934 that exporters could be thought to be as politically active as were import-competing interest groups. The unilateral trade politics from 1890 through 1930 were dominated by protectionist groups, and there was little input from consumer and export groups, as the theory in chapters 2 and 3 would predict.

III.   The Reciprocal Trade Agreements Program, 1934–47

Before 1934 Congress had been very reluctant to give the president broad authority to negotiate trade treaties with other nations. In 1934 Congress did precisely that with the Reciprocal Trade Agreements Act. One of the reasons often cited in the literature for the shift in congressional willingness in 1934 was the Great Depression and the political realignment that followed it. Congress felt it was necessary to grant wide authority to the president to help him deal with the economic crisis. Most important, the Great Depression was responsible for a large turnover in Congress at that time. The massive political change—the New Deal realignment—meant that many members who had resisted granting presidential authority to negotiate liberalizing reciprocity agreements and had voted for the Smoot-Hawley bill in 1930 were not in Congress to resist the RTAA in 1934. Democrats who were committed to doing whatever it took to end the Depression replaced the resistant incumbents. Roosevelt had a new Congress that was willing to grant authority to the president and a very strong reason for doing so in the Great Depression. All of these factors helped in the passage of the landmark RTAA in 1934. This does not mean that the road to the RTAA was an easy one.[4]

Congressional hearings on the RTAA were dominated by defense of the legislation by administration witnesses. Both export interests that expected to be helped by the reciprocal trade agreements program and import-competing interests that expected to be hurt by it also appeared to lobby Congress. Familiar export groups such as the Chamber of Commerce and the AMEA appeared, as did some newer groups such as the Export Committee of the Automobile Chamber of Commerce. On the protectionist side, the Tariff League, various wool interests, and several other familiar protectionist groups also appeared.

---

4. The decision to ask for the new negotiating authority was itself the subject of disagreement within the administration. Some in the administration, including President Roosevelt, were far from being free-traders (Haggard 1988, 103–10; Kindleberger 1986, 197–229). However, Secretary of State Hull's continued appeals for international liberalization, the continued decline of exports, and the belief that exchange rates could be used to prevent severe import competition led the Roosevelt administration to seek reciprocity treaties that reduced trade barriers to American exports as a further means of recovery (Haggard 1988, 110–13; Steward 1975, 1–23). To this end, in November 1933, Roosevelt created the Executive Committee on Commercial Policy to draft legislation that would eventually become the RTAA (Sayre 1939, 54–57).

The NAM actually lobbied against the RTAA for granting the president authority to lower duties without giving business an opportunity to protest (Committee on Ways and Means 1934).

The RTAA faced stiff opposition in both houses of Congress. Congressmen did not like the idea of giving up their authority over trade policy. They also worried about the point raised by the NAM and others that businesses' protection could be reduced without consulting them. To allay the first fear, the legislation expired automatically after three years, giving Congress a measure of control through its renewal power. As I described in chapter 3 this sunset provision meant that the president had to negotiate agreements that would make at least a majority in Congress better off if he wanted his authority to be renewed. The latter fear was addressed by a Senate amendment requiring the State Department to notify the public of pending negotiations with particular countries to give business a chance to argue its case before the executive branch. The administration accepted the two amendments. Several other crippling amendments intended to keep certain products (particularly agricultural products) exempt from negotiations were defeated, and eventually, in June 1934, the RTAA as amended by the Senate was passed (Haggard 1988, 111; Sayre 1939, 57–59). Certainly the massive ideological shift had as much to do with the passage of the RTAA as did reciprocity, but, as I will show in the next chapter, reciprocity had its own strong effects independent of the ideological shift in Congress.

Following the passage of the RTAA, Secretary Hull and the State Department concluded treaties with twenty-eight countries (sixteen of which were Latin American) between 1934 and 1948, not including supplementary agreements with several countries. As per the Senate amendment, the State Department announced the countries with which it was planning to complete agreements, so there was some lobbying of the State Department by protected industries against provisions that would reduce their protection. For instance, when the State Department announced its intention to negotiate a treaty with Belgium in 1934, forty-eight groups opposed concessions on their products before the Committee for Reciprocity Information (a State Department organization that provided information to and received requests from the public on the reciprocal trade program). However, exporters also lobbied the State Department to include their products in any negotiations. In the Belgium case, twenty-one groups sought Belgian concessions (Haggard 1988, 116). In the various treaties with Latin American countries, many export groups were active, including the AMEA, the International Chamber of Commerce, the National Foreign Trade Council, the Automobile Manufacturers Association, and the Rubber Manufacturers Association, as well as several companies like General

Motors, and Chrysler, to name just two (Steward 1975). With the introduction of reciprocity, exporters were politically active in a way that only had been characteristic of import competers previously.

The State Department was very sensitive to the need to target gains to exporters in particular legislative districts in order to maintain the political viability of the reciprocal trade agreements program. Hull and Agriculture Secretary Henry Wallace tracked public opinion polls on the program and found that support was lagging in the agricultural regions of the Midwest and Far West (Kottman 1968, 217–19). Since the majority of treaties had been concluded with agricultural countries in the Western Hemisphere, agriculture had received few concessions compared with manufacturing, and farmers knew it. To remedy the situation the State Department sought a treaty with Britain—a major importer of U.S. agricultural produce. In a communication to U.S. Undersecretary of State William Phillips in Rome, Francis Sayre (Assistant Secretary of State) remarked:

> It is important from the standpoint of the situation in this country that we obtain improved export opportunities for American agriculture. As you know there has been a good deal of criticism in agricultural circles that we have heretofore negotiated to a disproportionate extent with agricultural countries, and, in consequence, that agriculture has been called upon to make sacrifices . . . for the benefit of increased industrial exports. If satisfactory concessions can be obtained for our agricultural exports in the important United Kingdom market, it will make it much easier to go forward with negotiations with agricultural countries. (Kottman 1968, 118–19).

In its negotiations with the British, the American negotiating team was insistent on gains for agricultural goods, including rice, lard, ham, and, most importantly, lumber. The lumber industry had lobbied the State Department heavily to prevent concessions in the Canadian pact of 1935. When the British negotiations came up, lumber lobbied equally heavily to reduce British imperial preferences for Canadian lumber. Particularly in light of the losses dealt to the American lumber industry as a result of the Canadian treaty the State Department was eager to help in the British treaty (Kottman 1968, 117–48, 246–67). Throughout the negotiation of the 1938 reciprocal trade treaty with Britain, exporters from other industries lobbied the State Department as well. For instance, the American film industry encouraged the State Department to press the British to ease quotas on American films (229–41).

If renewal of the RTAA is any measure, the State Department's efforts to create political support for the reciprocal trade program among exporters was a great success. The RTAA was renewed in 1937, 1940, and 1943—indeed, throughout the 1940s and 1950s until President Kennedy asked for all-new legislation in the Trade Expansion Act of 1962. In each case exporters came out in force to lobby Congress for the renewals, and, with the exception of the midwar 1943 renewal, the ranks of exporter lobbyists grew in number each time. At least in terms of the number of organizations testifying in favor of the legislation the response was considerably stronger than it was for the more limited reciprocity arrangements before the RTAA in which exporters had never outnumbered protected interests (Committee on Ways and Means, various documents).

IV. The Creation of the GATT and the Failure of the ITO

As part of the postwar settlement, the United States attempted to establish an international economic order based on the principles of liberalism and multilateralism espoused by Cordell Hull in the Roosevelt administration. The efforts of American and allied planners produced the International Monetary Fund (IMF), the World Bank and the GATT. However, at the time of its creation the GATT was merely an interim agreement meant to codify a set of tariff reductions until an organization with a more permanent character, called the International Trade Organization (ITO) could be negotiated and ratified.

However, after the war, the United States lost control of the negotiations on the new trade organization.[5] In the final draft of the ITO Charter, countries' rights to use quantitative restrictions for balance of payments disequilibria were maintained—even if these imbalances were the result of inflationary policy. No specific timetable was established to phase out the quantitative restrictions that were then in force. Lesser-developed countries (LDCs)at the conference asked for and received special authorization to use quantitative restrictions in their development strategies. The burden for balance of payments disequilibria was placed on surplus countries—read United States—and the charter suggested that full employment was a condition surplus countries owed to the rest of the world. Surplus countries were given the responsibility of inflating to correct the

---

5. Why the United States was less successful in achieving its goals in the ITO negotiations than it was in the Bretton Woods negotiations is speculative, but analysts have pointed to several factors. First, the Bretton Woods agreement was negotiated primarily between two countries—the United States and Great Britain—and presented to other members a fait accompli. The ITO was negotiated among many more countries, all with their own ideas about the ideal organization. Second, the Bretton Woods agreement was negotiated while World War II was still ongoing or had just ended so that the United States had greater bargaining leverage because Britain and other countries needed U.S. support in the war and during reconstruction. The ITO was negotiated later (Gardner 1980).

deficits of other countries. When the United States broached the subject of safeguards for foreign direct investments, the LDCs not only refused to grant them but even insisted on, and received, rights to interfere heavily in foreign direct investment (Gardner 1980, 361–68). Business's response to this disappointing charter was negative. There were signs that protectionism was increasing, particularly after the tariff reductions of the first GATT round (discussed subsequently) were beginning to bite, but the greatest blow to the ITO Charter was that those groups that normally would have supported it did not because of the litany of problems with the charter that I just mentioned. In the words of one well-known historian of the subject:

> Too much emphasis should not be placed on these symptoms of protectionist revival. The ITO might still have been saved had it not been for the defection of that critical portion of the American business community whose cooperation had made possible the passage of the Bretton Woods and British Loan agreements. By the time the American Congress finally began to hold hearings on the Havana [ITO] Charter all the business groups who appeared to have the greatest interests in foreign trade were arrayed in opposition—the National Association of Manufacturers, the National Foreign Trade Council, the U.S. Chamber of Commerce, and the U.S. Council of the International Chamber of Commerce. In view of the fact that their members were supposed to be the main beneficiaries of the project, the stand taken by these organizations greatly diminished the prospects for Congressional approval. (Gardner 1980, 375).

Given the likelihood that the charter would be rejected by Congress, the president, in December of 1950, announced that he would not resubmit it to the Senate for ratification. Without the support of the United States, no other country bothered to ratify it (375–80).

With the "stillbirth" of the ITO, all was not lost for international trade policy cooperation. During the negotiation of the ITO Charter in Geneva, a set of tariff reductions were agreed upon by the conference participants. The agreement was signed by twenty-three nations, making it the largest trade treaty that had ever been established. The United States reduced trade barriers on items that made up 1,766.5 million dollars in imports in 1939 (78 percent of total imports that year) and 1,192 million dollars in exports, bringing American tariff rates down to about the level of the Underwood tariff of 1913 (Gardner 1980, 360–61).

The failure of the ITO left the GATT as the only hope for international trade policy cooperation in the future. Without a secretariat or any organizational machinery to aid cooperation trade policy was disadvantaged relative to other policy areas such as international finance, which had the IMF. Still, American export interests preferred this thin reed of hope to the ITO, which bound them to policies with which they did not agree and gave foreign governments the right to discriminate against their products with quantitative restrictions and meddle indefinitely in their foreign direct investments. The demise of the ITO highlights the importance of the *nature* of the agreement for exporters' lobbying behavior—exporters do not lobby for any international trade agreement, only those from which they expect to get something. In the ITO case exporters lobbied against a proposal they felt would bring them absolute harm. Still, exporters had a great deal about which to be happy. Twenty-three countries had reduced tariffs substantially as part of the first GATT agreement, auguring well for exports in the future.

V.   The Trade Enhancement Act of 1962 and the Kennedy Round

The decade and a half following the failure of ITO continued to see tariff reductions and export growth under the auspices of the GATT. The GATT was given a more permanent character with a secretariat and staff in Geneva. Five rounds of GATT negotiations were conducted, culminating in the Dillon Round of 1962. The United States participated in all of these rounds under simple extensions of the RTAA. As a result U.S. tariff rates continued to be reduced. However, the RTAA was created to give the president authority to negotiate item by item reductions in bilateral negotiations. While this was fine when the GATT was a relatively small organization with a relatively clear objective—reducing the high interwar tariffs—it became clear that this approach to trade negotiations was losing its usefulness as the GATT became a larger organization, tariff barriers reached lower and lower levels, and national economies became more and more interdependent. A new mechanism was needed to continue U.S. participation in global tariff reduction and trade expansion (Evans 1971, 139–59).

An even more pressing development signaled the need for new negotiating authority for the president—the creation of the European Community (EC). As a result of the Treaty of Rome of 1958 the six members of the European Community began conducting their trade policies as a unit. The European Community gave the European powers a great deal more bargaining leverage in trade negotiations with the United States and posed some severe problems for American trade policy with Europe (Evans 1971, 139–59). The most severe problem arose in agriculture. As members of the EC harmonized their trade polices toward agriculture they took the opportunity to establish more protection for European farmers. This increase in protection for agricultural products—particularly on frozen poultry—triggered a trade war between the United States and the EC in 1962 called the "Chicken War." The "Chicken War" was never settled to the satisfaction of the United States, as the EC continued to restrict agricultural imports and subsidize agricultural production heavily (Evans 1971, 160–80; Conybeare 1987, 160–75). Indeed, the EC's Common Agricultural Policy (CAP) continued to be a major source of friction in U.S.-EC trade relations for the next three decades.

In response to these new threats President Kennedy asked for greater powers to negotiate trade treaties than had been granted under the RTAA and its various renewals. The Trade Expansion Act (TEA) of 1962, as the new law was called, granted authority to the president to reduce tariffs by means of a formula rather than forcing negotiators to trade concessions on particular products. It also gave the president authority to eliminate tariffs that were less than 5 percent. A major force behind the TEA was export interests, particularly in agriculture, hoping to maintain their market in Europe after the creation of the European Community's CAP. Manufacturing exporters were also active. In 1962 the United States was still very competitive if not the world's major producer of manufactured goods such as steel, automobiles, and electrical and industrial machinery. Thus, many manufacturing industry groups supported the TEA. Even the AFL-CIO, which would turn to protectionism in coming years, supported the legislation and the program of export expansion (Committee on Ways and Means 1962).

Of course, protectionist pressures were active, as always, particularly in claiming that the European Community was cheating on existing agreements. Some of the greatest threats to the passage of the bill were textile interests in the districts of powerful southern members of Congress that might have convinced those members to vote against the TEA. The Kennedy administration used a tactic that would be used by other presidents subsequently—it effectively detached the textile industry from the protectionist coalition by granting it special protection under a negotiated agreement with the major textile exporters. Thus, the textile interests were mollified and the southern congressional delegations were able to vote for the TEA (Evans 1971; Aggarwal 1985).

The TEA passed Congress easily, and subsequently the Lyndon Johnson administration went on to conclude the "Kennedy Round" of trade negotiations under the GATT. It was the most successful round of GATT negotiations up to that point. Agriculture was not liberalized, but tariffs were reduced substantially so that they were no longer an important means of trade restriction.

VI.   The Trade Act of 1974 and the Tokyo Round

After the Kennedy Round reductions, tariffs ceased to be a major impediment to trade, at least among developed countries. Instead, nontariff barriers became the new perceived threat to world trade. To deal with some of these stickier issues in world trade left over from the Kennedy Round, President Richard Nixon requested a new extension of trade policy authority in April of 1973. The Kennedy administration had not been given authority to negotiate nontariff barriers to trade by Congress in 1962, so Nixon made a point of requesting authority to address these issues.

It would be difficult to imagine a worse time for Nixon to request greater trade-negotiating authority. The competitiveness of the U.S. economy had declined substantially in the decade since the passage of the TEA. U.S. auto and electronics industries were already feeling the effects of substantial import competition from Japan, and, of course, the oil price shocks of October 1973 only made economic matters worse. The United States was losing manufacturing jobs in steel and automobiles, so that the AFL-CIO, which had lobbied *for* the TEA in 1962, came out strongly against the Trade Act of 1974. Indeed, the labor organization tried to kill the bill throughout its legislative history and instead supported the protectionist Burke-Hartke Bill. In addition to these protectionist pressures the Watergate scandal prompted legislators to question whether the president was worthy of greater negotiating powers, and the granting of most favored nation status to the Soviet Union, as part of détente, held up the legislation, as Senator Henry Jackson (D-Wash.) sought to force the Soviets to meet U.S. demands on Jewish emigration (Pastor 1980, 136–85).

It is a testimony to the strength of the post–World War II liberalization coalition that despite all of these pressures the Trade Act was able to pass, granting the president authority not only to negotiate tariff reductions, but to negotiate in new areas such as nontariff barriers and subsidies. All of this success cannot be ascribed to the strength of exporter lobbying, although exporters, particularly aircraft and computer manufacturers, did lobby heavily for the agreement. Some of the credit is due to the institutionalization of the trade negotiation process. Trade negotiations had become such an integral part of postwar economic policy that not participating was out of the question. The question was not whether the United States would participate or not, but what form that participation would take. Still, the United States had played its part in dismantling institutionalized postwar economic regimes before. Indeed, it is interesting that at virtually the same time that the United States was bringing about the destruction of the postwar balance of payments mechanism—the fixed exchange rate Bretton Woods system—it was extending the postwar trade system of trade liberalization to new areas such as nontariff barriers and subsidies (Pastor 1980, 136–85).

A new feature of the Trade Act of 1974 was "fast track" negotiating authority. The agreements negotiated by the president under the RTAA and TEA did not have to be approved by Congress. In the Trade Act of 1974, Congress reserved for itself the authority to accept the agreement that resulted from the negotiations; however, as part of the deal with the Nixon administration Congress could not make amendments. It could only accept or reject the agreement by an up or down vote. Thus, although the odds were in favor of the agreement due to the "fast-track" nature of the approval process, negotiators knew that any agreement reached would have to be acceptable to Congress (Pastor 1980, 167–71).

The Carter administration's trade negotiator, Robert Strauss, was aware of this need for congressional approval and was masterful at building domestic support for the agreement while it was still being negotiated. Much like the diplomats in the Roosevelt administration who wanted to ensure that agriculture received its share of the foreign trade concessions Strauss himself admitted that he sought foreign trade concessions for particular products to ensure that certain state delegations would vote for the agreement. One example that Strauss gave was the agreement on liberalizing trade in certain alcoholic beverages. The agreement harmed liquor producers in Kentucky, so Strauss made a special point of receiving foreign concessions on tobacco products—a major export of Kentucky. Strauss proudly reported that all members of the Kentucky congressional delegation were able to vote for the trade agreement because of this bargain (Strauss 1987).

In the end the trade agreement that resulted from these talks—the Tokyo Round of GATT negotiations—was a great success in Congress. It passed both houses of Congress as the Trade Agreements Act (TAA) of 1979 by wide margins with a great deal of support from exporter groups (*Congressional Quarterly* 1979; Committee on Ways and Means 1979). The agreement lowered tariffs even further than their already low levels. Furthermore, it began to address some of the more difficult issues in international trade. The agreement contained protocols on nontariff barriers and subsidies, although there is continued disagreement over whether the European Community has lived up to obligations under the subsidies code (Grieco 1988; Hudec 1990).

VII.   The Omnibus Trade and Competitiveness Act of 1988 and the Gephardt Amendment

The massive government budget deficit of the Reagan administration and the substantial appreciation of the dollar that accompanied it were devastating to the American balance of trade. American import competers were hammered with cheap foreign imports and exporters had a much harder time maintaining their access to foreign markets. Some in Congress blamed the problem on unfair trade practices abroad (particularly in Japan) and sought to do something about it (Bergstren and Noland 1993). The result was the Omnibus Trade and Competitiveness Act of 1988 and a policy that has been dubbed "aggressive unilateralism" (Bhagwati and Patrick 1990). The bill was truly a hodgepodge of trade measures, but certainly the most controversial aspect of the bill was its amendment of section 301 of U.S. trade law. Section 301 was originally created in the Trade Act of 1974 and was the U.S. law under which the president pursued complaints against trading partners in the GATT's dispute resolution and consultation procedures.[6] The Omnibus Trade Act's amendments to section 301, called "super-301," were designed to force the administration to take a stronger stand unilaterally against so-called unfair trade practices.

Super-301 changed current trade law in several ways. First, it moved the authority to conduct investigations under section 301 and proceed with negotiations and retaliation if necessary from the president to the U.S. trade representative (USTR). Congress believed it had more control over the USTR than the president, and it also felt that the president was too willing to give in to other countries on trade issues in return for concessions in other diplomatic arenas. Second, Congress mandated that the USTR must produce a report on countries that used unfair trade practices. Which countries and practices were included was determined unilaterally by the U.S. government. Furthermore, practices that were not illegal by current international trade standards—for instance, unfair labor practices or export targeting—were specifically mentioned in the legislation. Third, super-301 required mandatory retaliation according to a rigid time schedule if the offending country was unilaterally found to be in breach of so-called fair trade practices. The rigid time schedule all but ensured that the multilateral GATT dispute resolution process would not be followed (Bhagwati 1990; Hippler Bello and Holmer 1990).

Super-301 was actually a toned-down version of a much more aggressive procedure defined by the Gephardt Amendment, which passed the House by a

---

6. In practice section 301 was sometimes used in ways that were not strictly GATT legal, but the intent was that 301 would be used through the GATT (Hudec 1990).

very close vote in April 1987. The Gephardt Amendment would have required that countries with persistent trade surpluses with the United States voluntarily reduce them by at least 10 percent per year, or face trade restrictions by the United States to reduce them. The Gephardt Amendment also required that these trade deficits be reduced according to the schedule even if the so-called unfair trade practices that supposedly produced them were corrected. Furthermore, since the Gephardt Amendment was concerned only with the trade deficit, countries in "violation" of the Gephardt Amendment could have met its requirements by reducing exports—there was no guarantee (in fact, it was quite unlikely given that it is easier for countries to restrict exports than increase imports) that it would have led to expansion of U.S. trade. This amendment was eventually abandoned in conference committee for the less aggressive Senate procedure that became super-301 (Hippler Bello and Holmer 1990).

Gephardt defended his amendment as being far different from the Smoot-Hawley Act of 1930 (Berke 1987). But its reciprocity provisions, if they can even be called that, were remarkably similar. Like the Smoot-Hawley Act, the Gephardt Amendment—and even the less contentious super-301 procedure that was eventually enacted—would demand trade policy concessions from foreign countries and offer nothing in return except forbearance of retaliation. In fact, the Gephardt Amendment was even more draconian than the Smoot-Hawley Act in this regard because it would have required "retaliation" to correct persistent trade deficits even if they were not the result of protectionism overseas.

The Gephardt Amendment and the Omnibus Trade Bill were advertised as a means of promoting "fair trade" and of opening up markets abroad that were closed due to unfair trade practices. But an examination of the bill's supporters and opponents in the economy suggests that perhaps the bill was really protectionism in reciprocity's clothing. If the bill was truly about opening markets then exporters should have favored the legislation. In fact most opposed it, fearing retaliation if the provision was ever actually used as planned. Proexport groups like the Business Roundtable, which would also be very active in support of NAFTA and the Uruguay Round; the American Business Conference, a group of medium-sized export oriented firms; the Emergency Committee for International Trade; and the Chamber of Commerce, to name just a few, were successful in getting some of the bill's harsher anti-trade provisions watered-down (Rasky 1987a; Stokes 1987, 1988). Agricultural interests feared foreign retaliation if "super-301" were used as planned and to some extent legislative voting on the bills reflected this concern (Farnsworth 1987; Fuerbringer 1987). Last minute lobbying by these groups made passage of the Gephardt Amendment much closer than it otherwise might have been (Fuerbringer 1987). In addition, Wall Street was adamantly opposed to the bill (Rasky 1987b). The main supporters of the bill came not from exporters but from America's *import-competing industries*, and big labor. The AFL-CIO lobbied hard for the Gephardt Amendment, as did auto makers like the Chrysler Corporation (Farnsworth 1987; Milner 1990; Stokes 1987, 1988). Support for the legislation came from "industrial areas that have been devastated by import competition" (Fuerbringer 1987).[7] Milner concludes: "Most internationally oriented firms, however, have remained committed to multilateralism and the next GATT Round." and "[w]hile some global firms lent their support to toughening U.S. trade law, the main supporters . . . were organized labor and domestically oriented firms" (1990, 171–77). The Omnibus Trade Bill and the Gephardt Amendment demonstrate that reciprocity does not necessarily spell the end of protectionism, but the lobbying patterns on these bills do suggest that reciprocity has brought an end to the days when protectionism was virtually uncontested.

VIII.   Regional Reciprocity: The CUSFTA and NAFTA

The mid-1980s produced a new type of reciprocal liberalization in American trade policy—regional trade agreements. The first of these was the Canada-U.S. Free Trade Agreement (CUSFTA), which passed Congress in 1988 and took effect in 1989. Several groups lobbied behind the scenes on the agreement. Opponents seemed more concerned with what it left out than with what it included. A variety of Canadian subsidies—for wheat, uranium and other minerals, and textiles—were not eliminated by the agreement, and American producers of those products made their voices heard during the hearings on the agreement. Lumber interests complained that a building standard that excluded U.S. plywood from the Canadian market remained in effect, and in response the administration began working on eliminating it while the agreement was still under consideration. Supporters of the agreement included the NAM and the American Business Conference. The Reagan administration also assembled the "American Coalition for Trade Expansion with Canada," composed of five hun-

---

7. Milner (1990) has also speculated that support for the bill came from a new "third force" in American trade politics—export industries that exhibit increasing returns to scale and therefore would benefit from protection of their home market along the lines described by the strategic trade literature (Krugman 1986). However, Milner's evidence is anecdotal at best. She mentions certain high-technology firms with high research and development costs as an example but does not specify particular industries. Trade statistics from 1988 suggest that many of these industries were simply out-and-out import-competing by 1988 (*Import Data Bank*, 1988; *Export Data Bank*, 1988).

dred firms that lobbied for the agreement (*Congressional Quarterly* 1988). Despite all of this effort, the agreement was not particularly controversial (at least in the United States). Very little mention of it was made in the news at the time, and it passed easily through both houses.[8]

The same was not at all true for the next installment of North American regional integration, the North American Free Trade Agreement (NAFTA). This agreement, which extended the free trade zone to Mexico as well as Canada, was perhaps the most contentious piece of trade legislation of the twentieth century. Lobbying on both sides was extraordinarily heavy. The main core of the lobbying effort against the agreement was organized labor, which fed itself on horror stories of a mass migration of manufacturing plants to Mexico to take advantage of the cheap labor there. The AFL-CIO in particular lobbied heavily against the agreement by organizing letter campaigns and phone banks as well as advertising against the agreement, reportedly spending 3.2 million dollars on billboards and radio to defeat NAFTA (Kilborn 1993). The agreement caused a rift in relations between labor and the Clinton administration, which normally enjoyed the support of organized labor (Frisby and Harwood 1993).

Perhaps the heart of labor's efforts against the agreement was the United Auto Workers (UAW), which feared an acceleration of the trend of plants moving to Mexico to take advantage of cheaper labor (Toner 1993). The Teamsters Union (concerned about competition from lower-paid Mexican truckers) which "far out-pamphleted and out-demonstrated all other unions," also lobbied heavily against the treaty (Kilborn 1993). Various textile and apparel workers unions (which, like the UAW, were fearful of plant closures due to the agreement) pressured the government against the treaty as well (Saddler 1993; Brown 1993). However, not all of labor's response was from organized labor; nonunion textile workers in the South organized their own letter writing campaigns against the agreement (Kilborn 1993).

Labor's lobbying on the issue often took quite forceful directions, including direct threats by labor leaders that they would actively work against any legislator who voted for the agreement. Such threats, once they became public,

---

8. Alt, Frieden, Gilligan, Rodrik, and Rogowski (1997) speculate that this lack of controversy and lobbying activity may have been due to the fact that so much trade between the U.S. and Canada is *intra*industry trade, which does not have the stark distributional consequences that *inter*industry or endowments-based trade has. Elsewhere I have questioned the validity of this argument (Gilligan 1997), showing that intraindustry trade is in fact more contentious than interindustry trade is. My explanation is that intraindustry trade is characterized by monopolistic competition, which reduces firms' collective action problems and encourages greater lobbying despite the smaller real income changes caused by intraindustry trade.

prompted President Clinton to accuse organized labor of applying "naked pressure" to legislators against the agreement (Ifill 1993). Labor was particularly effective in keeping more Democratic legislators from supporting the president on the agreement, since many of them came from "rust belt" states where the effect of plant closings supposedly would have been most acute. Furthermore, these legislators received greater than average proportions of their campaign funds from organized labor. As a result, most of the Democratic support for the treaty came from the Southwest, which expected to see the greatest economic gain from closer trade ties to Mexico, and the Northwest, with its export-intensive, high-technology industries (Calmes and Harwood 1993; Harwood and Calmes 1993).

Labor was not the only force working against the agreement. Some business groups also lobbied against it, in particular clothing and textile manufacturers. Roger Milliken, the South Carolinian textile tycoon, expended a great many resources to pressure the government against the agreement behind the scenes. He contributed $400,000 a year to various protectionist think tanks and financially underwrote the lobbying activities of the "No-Name Group," an anti-NAFTA lobbying organization that included protectionist business interests, consumer advocate Ralph Nader, and conservative economists. Milliken personally called on legislators and other business leaders to take a stand against NAFTA (Ingersoll and Nomani 1993). Many apparel producers that were too small to relocate to Mexico also lobbied against the agreement; however, the apparel industry was somewhat split on the issue (Saddler 1993; Brown 1993).

Several groups not often involved in trade issues also took a stand against NAFTA. Some environmental groups feared a watering down of U.S. environmental regulations as the United States competed with Mexico, and some, like the Sierra Club, lobbied against the agreement. Interestingly, several well-known *consumer* groups came out against the agreement, despite the fact it would undoubtedly lead to some lowering of prices to consumers. In particular Ralph Nader's group, Public Citizen, took part in publishing full-page advertisements in The *New York Times* and The *Washington Post* against the agreement, fearing that the agreement might promote lower standards of consumer product safety. Consumers Union, the publisher of *Consumer Reports*, was in favor of NAFTA but had no resources to spend lobbying for it (Lagerfeld 1993). This evidence is consistent with the logic of collective action in the sense that consumer groups did not lobby in favor of the agreement, and in fact one major consumer group actually lobbied against it.

NAFTA was given greater salience and the protectionist side was given greater clout because of the involvement of the billionaire presidential candidate Ross Perot. He was personally against the agreement and used it as an issue in the 1992 presidential campaign to try to show that the candidates of both the major parties (both of whom favored the agreement in some form) were not working in the best interest of the American people. Perot's group, United We Stand America, was also heavily involved in the lobbying against the agreement, sponsoring letter-writing campaigns and phone banks and inundating "town meetings" with its members (Calmes and Harwood 1993). Perhaps the highlight of the legislative history of the bill was a televised debate between Perot and Vice-President Al Gore on NAFTA.

As with all other truly reciprocal trade agreements mentioned in this study, though, there was also substantial exporter lobbying. The pro-NAFTA lobbying effort was spearheaded by the group USA-NAFTA. The hard core of this lobbying effort was provided by the Business Roundtable, which was also active in the passage of the Uruguay Round agreement described subsequently. This group was composed of some of America's premier export industries. For instance, Lawrence Bossidy, the chairman of Allied Signal, served as chairman of USA-NAFTA (Mills 1993). Banks that expected to break into Mexico's financial service market, like Chemical Bank, Citicorp, and Salomon Brothers, helped in the effort. Pepsico and other consumer products giants like Proctor and Gamble also contributed (Mills 1993; Calmes and Harwood 1993). Caterpillar, which relies on exports for 50 percent of its earnings and is always active in reciprocal trade liberalization, also lobbied heavily for the agreement (Feder 1993). Medium-sized businesses that rely heavily on exports for their revenue but are too small to engage in a great deal of foreign direct investment often benefit the most from reciprocal trade treaties and lobby vigorously for them. NAFTA was no exception to this rule. Many owners of medium-sized businesses lobbied for the agreement, making special trips to Washington to speak to legislators about it (Saddler 1993).

Lobbying behavior over America's regional integration program conforms to the pattern we have seen with all the reciprocal trade proposals observed in this chapter and conforms as well to the theory suggested in this volume. Lobbying by exporters was quite heavy, in stark contrast to legislation earlier in the century that did not explicitly help open a foreign market. Furthermore, the proliberalization lobbying in this case was not done by the millions of consumers who benefit from greater liberalization through lower prices. Indeed, the benefit to consumers of the agreement was at best a side issue. Instead the impetus for lobbying came from specific industries that anticipated large economic gains from greater access to foreign markets.

IX. The Uruguay Round

The latest round of GATT negotiations, the Uruguay Round, began in 1986. After seven years of often difficult negotiations (indeed, there were serious threats that the negotiations would break down completely and fail to lead to an agreement) the round was concluded successfully in December 1993. As in previous GATT agreements, the Uruguay Round agreement further reduced tariffs on manufactured goods—in this case by one-third. However, the agreement was really a watershed in several ways. First, it included agricultural trade for the first time, reducing protection on farm products by 36 percent. Second, the agreement will eliminate quotas and replace them with tariffs that will then be progressively reduced—a dream of economists and trade negotiators in earlier rounds finally achieved. Third, the agreement included provisions to protect intellectual property, such as patents and copyrights, for the first time (Sanger 1994a, 1994b, 1994c)—although some firms like pharmaceutical companies, which lose billions a year in pirated drugs, believe these measures are to be phased in too slowly (Lueck 1993). Another major departure from earlier GATT rounds was the fact that the 1993 agreement created the World Trade Organization, which has an improved dispute resolution mechanism—long a goal of U.S. negotiators—that had been held up by European reluctance to create a stronger international trade organization (Sanger 1994a, 1994b, 1994c). With so many entirely new and controversial provisions it is not surprising that the Uruguay Round was the longest and most contentious to negotiate.

As in all previous GATT rounds lobbying by export companies interested in receiving greater access to foreign markets was quite significant. Indeed, exporters were politically active even while the agreement was still being negotiated in order to ensure that they gained sufficient access to foreign markets. For instance, a group of exporters composed prominently of IBM, Cargill, Caterpillar, Phillip Morris, and Hewlett-Packard kept representatives in Geneva expressly to lobby U.S. negotiators. They wanted the United States to water down an antidumping provision that was to be included in the final GATT agreement. These industries felt they would be the most likely victims of these provisions, which allow countries to place tariffs on imported goods that are sold in their countries at supposedly "less than fair value." Of course, the other side of the issue, comprising those industries that face stiff import competition, was also represented. A group made up of auto makers like Chrysler, semiconductor manufacturers like Motorola and Intel, and consumer electronics firms like Zenith, as well as Eastman-Kodak, kept representatives at the negotiations to lobby for the beefed-up antidumping provisions (Bradsher 1993; Nomani 1993).

Other groups sent representatives to lobby for their pet issues as well. Financial services firms like American Express and Citicorp sent representatives to Geneva to (ultimately unsuccessfully) garner greater access to foreign financial service markets (Nomani 1993; Lueck 1993). McDonnell-Douglas and Boeing sent representatives to Geneva to pressure U.S. negotiators to try to win reductions of Europe's heavy subsidies to Airbus (Lueck 1993; Nomani 1993). The American entertainment industry, particularly the Motion Picture Association of America, called in its campaign favors to the Clinton administration to secure an easing of European quotas on American television programs and movies (Calmes 1993; Lueck 1993; Weinraub 1993). Textile manufacturer Fruit-of-the-Loom sent its chief lobbyist to try to stop or at least slow down the dismantling of the byzantine system of quotas on textiles (Calmes 1993; Nomani 1993). Members of Congress themselves went to Geneva to try to secure benefits for their states' export industries, among them Senator Malcolm Wallop (R-Wyo.) who lobbied on behalf of his state's potash mining industry (Bradsher 1993).

After the conclusion of the deal in December 1993, the lobbyists moved to Washington to fight for passage or defeat of the agreement in Congress. The two sides of the antidumping issue continued their pressure in Washington to try to secure what they did not achieve or protect what they did achieve in Geneva, as did the entertainment and textile industries (Calmes 1993; Cooper 1994; Pasell 1994).

Spearheading the attack for passage of the GATT legislation was the Business Roundtable, a group of American business leaders that meets regularly with the president to advise him on business's position on issues. The Business Roundtable, with the help of the National Association of Manufacturers and the Chamber of Commerce, organized a lobbying group called Alliance for GATT NOW, which according to one report spent about two million dollars lobbying for the agreement. America's premier export companies, like Caterpillar and the others already mentioned, were contributors to the effort, as were other trade organizations like the Grocery Manufacturers Association and the Chemical Manufacturers Association. The Alliance's efforts were coordinated by Texas Instruments' chief Washington lobbyist and were run out of that company's Washington office. The administration's and the private sector's lobbying efforts were closely linked; indeed, they were jointly planned for maximum effect (Stone 1994). The core of the Alliance was composed of about 220 executives associated with the Business Roundtable who were asked by the administration to pressure legislators in person if possible. Most of the Alliance's work was in

Washington, although some grassroots support for the agreement was also created by Boeing, Monsanto, and Warner Lambert, the latter a chemical company. In addition to direct pressure on lawmakers and grassroots efforts in their districts the Alliance took out advertisements in major publications to build support for the agreement (Stone 1994).

Opponents of the agreement coalesced into two different groups, although they too were linked: Save Our Sovereignty (SOS) and the Citizens Trade Campaign (CTC). Both were alliances of businesses concerned about foreign competition, "America first" conservatives like Patrick Buchanan, and agricultural groups concerned about the dismantling of the United States' agricultural subsidization program. Ralph Nader's, group Public Citizen, and environmental groups like the Sierra Club were particularly active in the campaign against the Uruguay round agreement as they had been against NAFTA. They were concerned that the agreement's regulations, particularly given the stronger enforcement authority of the World Trade Organization, would overrule and weaken U.S. environmental and consumer protection regulations. CTC aired anti-GATT television spots with this message in a variety of agricultural states, although their efforts seemed less successful at building a grassroots movement against the agreement than they had been against NAFTA. United We Stand America, which had been extraordinarily active against NAFTA, also campaigned against the GATT, but its efforts were considerably more muted than they had been against NAFTA (Stone 1994).

This intensive lobbying effort by various interests once again confirms the logic of collection action. None of the export interests used the argument of greater efficiency to the economy as a whole or savings to consumers as a rationale for their support of the agreement, nor did they pressure U.S. negotiators for their various preferred provisions of the agreement on that basis. Instead, they lobbied with the health of their particular firm or industry in mind.

X. Conclusion

This chapter has shown qualitatively that proliberalization lobbying did in fact increase as the United States became involved in reciprocity in the 1930s. Although there were policies called "reciprocity" before 1934, they were hobbled by a highly protectionist Congress that did not want to lose its grip on trade policy. With the passage of RTAA in 1934 and the adoption of the aggressive reciprocal trade agreements program by Cordell Hull the balance of forces between protectionist interests and proliberalization interests was more even, as ex-

TABLE 4.1.   Witnesses before Trade Legislation Hearings, House Ways and Means Committee

Act	Year	Protectionist	Liberal	Questionable	n	Percentage Liberal
McKinley Act	1890	49	16	6	87	18.4
Wilson-Gorman Act	1894	46	11	2	63	17.5
Dingley Act	1897	46	15	2	63	23.8
Payne-Aldrich Act	1909	65	29	0	94	30.8
Underwood Act	1913	73	30	2	93	32.3
Fordney-McCumber Act	1922	48	14	1	63	22.2
Smoot-Hawley Act	1930	68	18	6	68	26.5
RTAA	1934	4	8	0	12	66.7
RTAA renewal	1937	2	6	4	12	50.0
TEA	1962	47	45	2	94	47.9

porters began to approach the government for their share of the concessions from other countries.

Table 4.1 gives some more concrete evidence of the increase in political activity on behalf of the RTAA and subsequent legislation. I took a random sample of witnesses from several of the major trade bills discussed in this chapter and coded them according to whether they testified in favor of liberalization or in favor of protection. Some witnesses' positions were unclear from their statements, and some even requested that their protection be increased while the protection of products that they used in their production be reduced. These are included in the "Questionable" column.[9] The table clearly shows that there was a sharp jump in the percentage of witnesses who appeared on behalf of liberalization after 1934. This jump is significant at any commonly used level of statistical significance. I have no independent measure of whether a particular witness was an exporter or not; however, most of the proliberalization witnesses after 1934 identified themselves as exporters although there were a few public interest groups as well. Before 1934 proliberalization witnesses rarely identified themselves as exporters, but instead claimed only to be consumers of the protected product. Thus, if testimony before Congress is any indication, political

---

9. Only witnesses who actually appeared before the committee were included in the sample. Letters and telegrams were not included since there was no way of counting letters sent to members of Congress and senators that were not published in the hearing report. Also witnesses from the administration and senators and members of Congress who testified were not included in the sample since they are not actually members of private sector interest groups. In shorter hearings (on the RTAA, RTAA renewal, TAA) all witness were included in the sample. The remaining hearings were quite long, so random samples of witnesses were selected from them.

activity in favor of liberalization did in fact increase after 1934. Notice also that, although the Underwood Act was a liberalizing piece of legislation, there were not significantly more witnesses in favor of liberalization than for other unilateral pieces of legislation, as is predicted by the theory. This finding would suggest that that episode of liberalization was due more to factors like party ideology and presidential leadership than to the demand for liberalization.

Other factors besides demand for liberalization and protection certainly had their role in the trade policy outcomes in other legislation as well. The "supply-side" factor of ideology was particularly prominent. Undoubtedly the switch from protectionism to liberalization in 1934 was in large part due to the massive ideological shift in Congress from predominantly Republican to overwhelmingly Democratic. However, despite the fact that reciprocity was not the only cause of liberalization after 1934 it did seem to bring about the predicted change in demand-side behavior. In all of the legislation studied in this chapter, export lobbies were clearly identifiable and politically active after 1934 in a way that they were not before 1934.

Part 3
Quantitative Evidence

CHAPTER 5

Estimating the Demand for Liberalization and Protection, 1890–1937

I. Introduction

In chapters 2 and 3, I laid out a theory that explains the dramatic postwar liberalization of American trade policy in a way that is consistent with the endogenous tariff and delegation literature. Reciprocity concentrates the benefits of liberalization on those particular export industries that receive reductions in foreign trade barriers as part of the international agreement. As a result, exporters have stronger incentives to lobby for reciprocal liberalization than they do for unilateral liberalization. This increase in exporter lobbying in turn changed legislators' preferences more in favor of liberalization and made deeper reductions in American trade barriers possible.

This chapter will use that logic to show that the demand for liberalization did indeed increase in the United States when it began to set trade policy reciprocally. I will compare U.S. trade policy in the period preceding widespread use of reciprocal liberalization with the early period of reciprocal trade policy in the United States. Specifically, I will compare demand for liberalization in eight pieces of U.S. trade legislation—the McKinley Act of 1890, the Dingley Act of 1897, the Payne-Aldrich Act of 1909, the Underwood Act of 1913, the Fordney-McCumber Act of 1922, the Smoot-Hawley Act of 1930, the Reciprocal Trade Agreements Act (RTAA) of 1934, and the first extension of the RTAA in 1937. As discussed in chapter 4, the RTAA and its various extensions were the first truly sweeping grants of congressional tariff-setting power to the president. Therefore, if the theory presented previously is empirically significant, we should see a marked increase in demand for liberalization in 1934 and after.

Unfortunately, for the period studied here demand for protection and liberalization is a largely unobserved phenomenon. Of course, there is information about which industries pressed their cases before congressional committees, and that evidence was used to some degree in the previous chapter. However, congressional testimony is not the only form of demand a representative faces. Equally important are private communications by powerful constituents and, of course, campaign contributions. Data on these less overt means of demanding protection or liberalization are not available for the 1890s through the 1930s. Second, whether or not an industry testifies is not merely a function of demand but also a function of whether it is allowed to testify by the congressional committee.

Because of these data limitations, in this chapter I will *estimate* the demand for protection and liberalization using available data and plausible assumptions about how legislators factor demand into their objective functions. I will assume that the higher the demand for liberalization a particular legislator faces the higher that legislator's utility from voting for liberalization or against protection, all else equal, and I will assume that legislators weight more heavily the lobbying by industries that are economically more important to their districts. From these two assumptions, as well as data on the economic characteristics of each state and legislators' votes in the eight trade bills, I will estimate the change in the demand for liberalization as a result of the reciprocal trade polices of the United States in 1934 and after. The rest of this chapter will show that, indeed, the estimates of proliberalization lobbying were higher for the two reciprocal pieces of legislation than for the previous unilateral legislation.

The following section will refine slightly the model developed in chapter 3 in order to test the empirical significance of the theory. Section III will discuss the data that I used in the analysis. The estimates themselves along with their substantive interpretations and some counterfactual simulations are presented in section IV. Section V concludes.

II.   The Model to Be Tested

The purpose of this chapter is to estimate the demand for liberalization in the eight pieces of legislation based on the plausible assumption that legislators are more likely to vote for liberalization the higher the demand for liberalization from their districts, ceteris paribus. In Chapter 2 the net demand for liberalization D_l was expressed:

$$D_l = \psi_l D_L + \omega_l D_P. \tag{5.1}$$

That is, legislators weigh more heavily the demand from industries that are more important to their districts. Therefore, demand for liberalization, D_L, is weighted by ψ_l, a measure of the importance of those industries lobbying for liberalization to representative l's district, and D_P is weighted by ω_l, a measure of the importance of those industries lobbying against liberalization to representative l's district. I will describe the measures used for these weights later.

To estimate the main prediction of the model, demand for liberalization, D_L, must be further specified as:

$$D_L = \gamma_0 + \gamma_1 R + \gamma_2 \mathbf{x}_l^L \tag{5.2}$$

where R is a dummy variable equal to one in reciprocal legislation and zero in unilateral legislation, and $\mathbf{x}_l^L$ is a vector of other variables that may affect the demand for liberalization from legislator l's district (to be described in greater detail subsequently). The demand for protection will be further refined to:

$$D_P = \gamma_4 + \gamma_5 \mathbf{x}_l^P \tag{5.3}$$

where $\mathbf{x}_l^P$ is a vector of variables that may affect demand for protection.

When a vote on trade policy arises, legislators are faced with a choice between the proposal and the reversion level (typically the status quo). I will call the trade policy couple for the more liberal of these two options (t^L, τ^L) and the policy couple for the more protectionist (t^P, τ^P). In other words (t^L, τ^L) is the reversion level and (t^P, τ^P) is the proposal when the policy proposal is protectionist and (t^P, τ^P) is the reversion level and (t^L, τ^L) is the proposal when the policy proposal is liberalizing. The policy under consideration could take one of two forms in this period: when trade policy was set unilaterally (as it was with the McKinley Act through the Smoot-Hawley Act) the policy under consideration would be the actual U.S. trade policy—that is, Congress set t directly. The foreign trade policy τ in that case would be the expected value of foreign trade barriers set unilaterally by the foreign country's policy process. In the RTAA and its renewal, on the other hand, Congress did not directly set the actual trade policy—it delegated to the executive. In those cases, the policy under consideration was actually the *expected* trade policy that would be negotiated by the president and foreign governments. As I discussed in chapter 3, because of the safeguards Congress placed in the reciprocal legislation, at least a majority of legislators could expect the president to negotiate a trade deal that made them slightly better off than they could have made themselves unilaterally.

Recall from chapter 3 that legislator l's utility from a particular trade policy (either the proposal or the status quo) was expressed as:

$$u_l = a_l(D_l,\mathbf{Z}_l)[t_l - t_l^*(D_l,\mathbf{Z}_l)]^2 - b_l(D_l,\mathbf{Z}_l) [\tau - \tau_l^*(D_l,\mathbf{Z}_l)]^2 \qquad (5.4)$$

where D_l is the net demand for liberalization from legislator l's district and $\mathbf{Z}_l$ is the vector of other characteristics that determine l's vote on trade policy. I will simplify the notation in equation 5.4 and call legislator l's utility from the more liberal of these options $u(t^L,\tau^L,D_l,\mathbf{Z}_l)$ and the utility from the more protectionist option $u(t^P,\tau^P,D_l,\mathbf{Z}_l)$. In other words, $u(t^L,\tau^L,D_l,\mathbf{Z}_l)$ is the utility derived from a liberalizing policy (the Underwood Act, the RTAA, and its renewal) or the reversion level when a protectionist bill is under consideration (the McKinley through Payne-Aldrich Acts and the Fordney-McCumber and Smoot-Hawley Acts); $u(t^P,\tau^P,D_l,\mathbf{Z}_l)$ is the utility derived from a protectionist policy or the reversion level when liberalizing legislation is up for a vote.

In estimating the demand for liberalization I will assume that legislators did not know with certainty the utility they would receive from the trade policies under consideration. This uncertainty would arise because they did know not for certain the economic conditions that would prevail in the future, or the effects of the tariff rates they were setting, or because they did not know with certainty the home and foreign tariff rates that the president would negotiate with the other countries, or for any number of other reasons. I will express this uncertainty as a random variable, η_l^L, for the stochastic component of utility for the more liberal outcome and η_l^P for the stochastic component of utility for the more protectionist outcome. In other words, $u(t^L,\tau^L,D_l,\mathbf{Z}_l)$ and $u(t^P,\tau^P,D_l,\mathbf{Z}_l)$ are each legislator's *expected* utility from liberalization and protection, respectively, and the utility that legislators actually receive is $u(t^L,\tau^L,D_l,\mathbf{Z}_l) + \eta_l^L$ for a relatively liberal policy and $u(t^P,\tau^P,D_l,\mathbf{Z}_l) + \eta_l^P$ for a relatively protectionist policy.

If we define a function v_l such that $v_l = 1$ when legislator l votes in favor of liberalization (or against protection) and $v_l = 0$ when legislator l votes against liberalization or for protection then clearly:

$$v_l = \begin{cases} 0 \text{ if } u(t^L,\tau^L,D_l,\mathbf{Z}_l) - u(t^P,\tau^P,D_l,\mathbf{Z}_l) & \leq \eta_l^P - \eta_l^L, \\ 1 \text{ if } u(t^L,\tau^L,D_l,\mathbf{Z}_l) - u(t^P,\tau^P,D_l,\mathbf{Z}_l) > & \eta_l^P - \eta_l^L. \end{cases} \qquad (5.5)$$

Typically the difference in utilities on the right side of (5.5) is expressed as a linear function of the utility functions' arguments:

$$u(t^L,\tau^L,D_l,\mathbf{Z}_l) - u(t^P,\tau^P,D_l,\mathbf{Z}_l) = \alpha_0 + \alpha_1 D_l + \alpha_2 \mathbf{Z}_l. \qquad (5.6)$$

To simplify the notation I will define the model represented by the right side of equation 5.6 as μ_l. Since t^L, τ^L, t^P, and τ^P are constant across legislators (they are all voting on the same piece of legislation), their effects are indistinguishable from the constant term, so I have dropped them from equation 5.6 and included only the constant term α_0. However, those parameters will vary from one piece of legislation to another, so in the estimations that follow in which several pieces of legislation are included I will control for these effects with bill-specific dummy variables. If we make the standard assumption that $\eta_l^P - \eta_l^L$ is distributed according to the standard normal distribution, then the probability that legislator l will vote for the legislation is $F(\mu_l)$, where F is the cumulative standard normal distribution function.

Equations 5.2 and 5.3 are substituted into equation 5.1, and equation 5.1 is plugged into equation 5.6. The parameters of this system are estimated easily with standard maximum likelihood procedures. Estimating the parameters for the Senate is a straightforward probit with each senator's vote as the dependent variable. The probability of observing an individual senator l's vote:

$$F(\mu_l)^{v_l}[1 - F(\mu_l)]^{1 - v_l}. \tag{5.7}$$

Assuming independence of the observations (a standard assumption for maximum likelihood techniques), the probability of observing the entire sample of votes is simply the product of the individual probabilities in equation 5.7:

$$\prod_{l=1}^{n} F(\mu_l)^{v_l}[1 - F(\mu_l)]^{1 - v_l} \tag{5.8}$$

where n is the number of observations in the sample. The likelihood that the model μ_l produced the data is proportional to the probability in equation 5.8. The maximum likelihood estimator chooses the parameters of μ_l that maximize this likelihood of observing the data.

Estimating the parameters for the House is no more difficult but is perhaps less conventional. Because I only have economic data at the *state* level, I could not use individual representatives' votes on these bills. The relevant dependent variable for the House is instead the state *aggregate* vote cast for liberalization (or against protection) in each bill. That is, there is one observation for each state, s, and the dependent variable can take on a value from $V_s = 0 \ldots N$, where N is the number of representatives in the state's delegation. The dependent variable, then, is the aggregation of each representative's individual voting decision. The probability of observing any given value of V_s is derived simply by aggregating the probabilities for the state's N individual representative's voting decisions using the binomial formula:

$$\frac{N!}{V_s!(N - V_s)!}F(\mu_I)^{V_s}[1 - F(\mu_I)]^{N-V_s}. \tag{5.9}$$

Notice that, although each observation is a state aggregate, we can still estimate the model μ_I for each individual representative; however, doing so requires that each representative in the state has the same probability of voting for liberalization, an admittedly strong assumption. As in the probit case, as long as the individual observations are independent, the probability of observing all n state votes in the sample is simply the product of the state's individual probabilities in equation 5.9:

$$\prod_{s=1}^{n} \frac{N!}{V_s!(N - V_s)!} F(\mu_I)^{V_s}[1 - F(\mu_I)]^{N-V_s}. \tag{5.10}$$

The maximum likelihood estimator chooses the parameters of μ_I to maximize this function. See King 1989 (117–21) for a fuller discussion of the binomial model.

The parameters of μ_I will allow us to reject or accept my hypothesis that the demand for liberalization rose in reciprocal as opposed to unilateral liberalization. To be consistent with the model's predictions the constant term, γ_0 in equation 5.2 must be small and statistically insignificant and the coefficient γ_1 on the dummy variable R in equation 5.2 must be positive and significant. These results would indicate that the demand for liberalization was small and insignificant in bills before the reciprocal trade agreements program and larger in the two reciprocal trade bills. Finally, it is impossible to estimate both the γs and α_1 from equation 5.6, so I set α_1 to one and estimated the γs.

III. The Data

A vote or announced pair against the five protectionist bills and for the three liberalizing bills was coded as a one. For the House the dependent variable was the total number of votes and announced pairs cast by each state delegation in favor of liberalization. For the district-specific "export dependence" weights, ω_I, I chose America's top net export industries which made up two-thirds of total U.S. exports respectively. Similarly, for the "import competition" index ψ_I I chose enough of those industries with the highest net imports to cover two-thirds of U.S. imports. The weights, then, are simply the total value of production for each state of these industries normalized by the total personal income of each state (gross state product figures are not available for this period).[1]

A wide variety of variables could be included in $\mathbf{Z}_l$—the matrix of variables that explain legislator l's vote besides demand. One obvious candidate is the political party of each legislator. The Republican Party was the party of protection from its beginnings until after World War II. Therefore, Republican senators should have voted more consistently protectionist than did Democrats, since it was more in keeping with their professed ideology and because of pressure from within their party. To control for these effects in the Senate specifications I included a dummy variable equal to zero if representative l was a Democrat and one if he was a Republican. For the House I included the total number of Republicans in each state's delegation. Third party candidates were excluded from the analysis. Each legislator's party was graciously supplied by Keith Poole, who cites Martis 1989. The expected sign on the party variable is negative since Democrats are expected to be more likely to vote for liberalization than are Republicans.[2]

Another control variable used in this analysis is the number of votes for liberalization cast by each state's delegation in the previous trade bill. This variable has not been used in other analyses of roll call votes on trade, largely because they have looked at only one bill. Since I include several different bills in my sample I included the variable to control for any stickiness in the way particular state delegations voted on trade bills. The sign on this variable should be positive—that is, a legislator from a state with a history of voting for liberalization should be more likely to vote for liberalization.[3]

Both Coughlin 1985 and MacArthur and Marks 1988 included a separate measure of each legislator's ideology such as the Americans for Democratic Ac-

---

1. It would not have been practical to use products with the highest exports as a share of production and highest imports as a share of consumption. There was no standard industrial classification during this period, so that trade and production statistics could not be reliably merged. In the end I doubt the list of products would have been far different in either case. Also the approach I chose maximized the coverage of U.S. trade.

2. Notice that the expected sign on the party variable is opposite what we might expect today. In fact, Coughlin 1985, MacArthur and Marks 1985, and Tosini and Tower 1987 all found that Democrats were significantly *more* likely to vote for protection in the bills they analyzed.

3. Ideally I would have included the individual *legislator's* last vote on trade policy to control for stickiness at the individual level, but unfortunately I could not. It would have been inappropriate for the House analysis since the dependent variable was actually the state aggregate vote for liberalization. Although it would have been appropriate for the Senate analysis where the dependent variable was each Senator's vote, it proved to be impossible because the substantial turnover in the Senate between 1929 and 1934. I simply had no observations for most Senators' previous votes on trade policy for the RTAA portion of the sample—the most important bill in the sample—because those Senators were not in office when the Smoot-Hawley Act passed. Luckily, the ideology score which I discuss next helped control for stickiness in individual Senator's votes.

tion (ADA) score or the *National Journal* rating. Both articles showed that the more liberal the representative the more likely he or she was to vote for protection. However, from the 1890s through at least the 1930s liberalization was a liberal position. Therefore, we should expect the more liberal representatives to be more likely to vote for liberalization. ADA ratings are not available for this time period, so I used an ideology measure developed by Poole and Rosenthal (1991). The measure captures the left-right dimension of ideology extremely well. It ranges from -1 (very liberal) to 1 (very conservative). For the Senate I used the individual senator's ideology score, and for the House I used the total aggregate of the scores of the states' representatives. The sign of the coefficient on the ideology variable should be negative since the more liberal the legislator the more likely he or she should have been to vote for liberalization.

I have included bill-specific dummy variables to control for any differences across the pieces of legislation in the liberalizing policy option (t^L, τ^L) as compared with the protectionist policy option (t^P, τ^P).

There is a large empirical literature that points to variables that may affect industries' abilities and incentives to organize for or against protection, which unfortunately I cannot review here.[4] In any case, thorough reviews have been completed elsewhere (Anderson and Baldwin 1987; Nelson 1988; Magee, Brock, and Young 1989; Odell 1990; Rodrik 1994). These variables are typically used to help explain differences in protection at the *industry* level. To my knowledge they have never been used in any analysis of congressional voting on trade policy where the unit of analysis is the individual legislator's vote. Legislative voting analysis requires using state aggregates of these variables, which may tend to dampen an individual industry's effects. Furthermore, most of the variables are rough proxies, and consequently their performance in the literature has been fairly spotty (see the reviews just cited). As such I do not expect their performance to be particularly good in this analysis. Still, the variables are included to control for other factors that might have influenced demand besides reciprocity (x_I^L and x_I^P in eqs. 5.2 and 5.3).

The first of these variables is labor share of value added. It has been shown that if an industry's labor supply is more elastic than its capital supply an increase in the price of a product will increase the incomes of its workers and capital owners relatively more the more labor intensive the industry (Anderson and Baldwin 1987). To control for this fact I have included this variable as a proxy

---

4. See Anderson and Baldwin 1987; Nelson 1988; Magee, Brock and Young 1989; and Rodrik 1994 for good reviews of the literature. See also Baldwin 1985; Cheh 1974; Finger, Hall, and Nelson 1982; Hansen 1990; Lavergne 1983; Pincus 1975; Ray 1981a, 1981b, 1987; Ray and Marvel 1984; and Reidel 1977.

for labor intensity in some of the following specifications. High labor share of value added in a state's export industries should induce more lobbying by those industries and increase the legislator's probability of voting for liberalization. High labor shares of value added in a state's import-competing industries should increase lobbying by those industries and reduce the legislator's probability of voting for liberalization.

The second variable is value-added share of value product. Price increases to a product will benefit its producers more the lower the value-added share of output; therefore, I have included this variable in the analysis. Higher value-added shares of value product in a state's export and import-competing industries may reduce those industries' incentives to lobby for and against protection respectively (Anderson and Baldwin 1987). Therefore, value-added shares of value product in the export industries of a legislator's district should be negatively correlated with that legislator's probability of voting for liberalization, and value-added share of value product in the import-competing industries of that district should be positively correlated with his or her probability of voting for liberalization.

Several studies have also found that declining industries have more of an incentive to lobby for protection (Baldwin 1985; Hillman 1982), and others have argued that protectionism rises and falls with the business cycle (Galarotti 1985; Cassing, McKeown, and Ochs 1986). Average wage per worker and value added per worker were included to control for this possibility in the results that follow. These variables also help control (along with bill-specific dummy variables) for changes in the economy due to the Great Depression since both fell substantially as a result. Lower values of these measures in the export industries of a legislator's district should increase that legislator's probability of voting for liberalization, and lower values in the import-competing industries of that district should reduce his or her probability of voting for liberalization.

Measures of economic concentration are also important to control for since more concentrated industries putatively find it easier to overcome the "free-rider" problems associated with collective action. Four firm concentration ratios are the usual variable of choice here but are simply not available for this period. Therefore, I have tried to control for economic concentration with average value product per firm, which should be positively correlated with concentration, and number of firms, which should be negatively correlated with concentration. I have also controlled for geographic concentration by including each state's share of total U.S. production of the export and import-competing industries. Higher levels of concentration in export industries and lower levels of concentration in import-competing industries should increase a legislator's probability of voting for liberalization.

Descriptive statistics for the dependent and independent variables are presented in table 5.1 for both the Senate and the House. The measures are presented for the whole sample and two subsamples—unilateral legislation and reciprocal legislation. Descriptive statistics for the same variables are slightly different between the House and the Senate because a few missing Senate votes means that some states are included more times than others in the averages. The variable labeled "same party as president" in table 5.1 will be described in the next section. The sources of all of these data are described in more detail in appendix D.

IV. Estimates of the Demand for Liberalization

A. Estimates from the Senate

The estimates of the model from Senate votes are presented in table 5.2. The table is divided by rows into three sections. The first section, marked "Supply-Side Variables" includes those variables that affect the senators' votes for liberalization besides demand. These include the senator's party, ideology, lag of the state delegation's vote, and dummy variables for each bill as well as a few interactions between these variables, which I will describe subsequently. The second and third sections, marked "Demand for Liberalization" and "Demand for Protection," include the estimates of the γs from equations 5.2 and 5.3. Notice that there are three "constant" terms in the table, one for each of the three sections, because each equation 5.2, 5.3, and 5.6 has a constant term.

The first column in table 5.2 provides estimates for the specification without the reciprocal trade legislation dummy variable. The supply-side variables all have the expected sign. The coefficient on the ideology score is large and highly significant, but the coefficient on party is not, probably due to multicollinearity with the ideology variable. The ideology coefficient confirms the prior expectation that more conservative senators were more likely to vote against liberalization (or for protection) than liberal senators were. The coefficient on the party variable is consistent with the expectation that Republicans voted against liberalization more than Democrats did, although not significantly less once ideology is taken into account. The coefficient on the lag of the state's vote for liberalization suggests that there is some stickiness in how state delegations vote for liberalization. Dummy variables for the various pieces of legislation were included, although only the significant dummy variables are listed to save space. Dummy variables for region of the country were also included but had no effect on the results and so are not reported.

TABLE 5.1. Means and Standard Deviations of Variables, 1890–1937

	Total Sample	Unilateral Legislation	Reciprocal Legislation
Senate Variables			
Vote for liberalization	0.5050	0.4460	0.6760
	(0.5003)	(0.4978)	(0.4693)
Party	0.4949	0.5667	0.2905
	(0.5034)	(0.4960)	(0.4553)
Ideology	0.0234	0.0807	−0.1397
	(0.5359)	(0.5686)	(0.3868)
Same party as president	0.1822	0.0000	0.7095
	(0.3863)	(0.0000)	(0.4553)
Export industries' share of state total	0.2103	0.2091	0.2138
personal income	(0.1948)	(0.1706)	(0.2517)
Import-competing industries' share of state	0.0925	0.0931	0.0909
total personal income	(0.1043)	(0.1089)	(0.0901)
Export industries' value-added share	0.4152	0.3641	0.5607
of value product	(0.4228)	(0.4630)	(0.2213)
House Variables			
Vote for liberalization	4.3351	3.7011	6.2105
	(5.3489)	(4.6175)	(6.5799)
Total votes cast by state delegation	7.9786	7.9963	8.1579
	(7.8808)	(7.6896)	(8.4215)
Party	3.7459	4.3820	1.9579
	(5.6604)	(6.0961)	(3.6754)
Ideology	0.3571	0.3415	0.4008
	(2.2113)	(2.2352)	(2.1538)
Same party as president	1.6408	0.0000	6.2211
	(4.3792)	(0.0000)	(6.5399)
Export industries' share of state total	0.2117	0.2104	0.2153
personal income	(0.1951)	(0.1703)	(0.2533)
Import-competing industries' share of state	0.0917	0.0917	0.0919
total personal income	(0.1028)	(0.1075)	(0.0889)
Export industries' average wage per worker	6.8570	6.1832	8.751
(in thousands of dollars)	(4.6818)	(4.6202)	(4.343)
State share of export industries' total	0.2447	0.2358	0.2696
U.S. production	(0.3060)	(0.2751)	(0.3804)
Import-competing industries' value-added	0.3976	0.4261	0.3175
share of value product	(0.1925)	(0.1971)	(0.1538)

Note: Standard deviations are in parentheses.

TABLE 5.2.   Demand for Liberalization and Protection Estimated from Senate Votes on Trade Policy, 1890–1937

			Supply-Side Variables		
Constant	−0.2935	−0.2945	−0.3416	−0.2215	−0.3018
	(0.2420)	(0.2585)	(0.3311)	(0.2699)	(0.2524)
Party (Republican = 1)	−0.1310	−0.1055	−0.0686	−0.3072	−0.1386
	(0.2780)	(0.2803)	(0.3231)	(0.4326)	(0.2813)
Ideology	−4.1042**	−4.0912**	−4.0986**	−4.0820**	−4.1704**
	(0.4280)	(0.4290)	(0.5086)	(0.5083)	(0.4386)
Previous state vote	0.4109**	0.4433**	0.4442**	0.4392**	0.4299**
	(0.1258)	(0.1281)	(0.1159)	(0.1121)	(0.1247)
Payne-Aldrich Act	0.7351**	0.7829**	0.7921**	0.8441**	0.8305**
	(0.3395)	(0.3466)	(0.3302)	(0.3635)	(0.3547)
Smoot-Hawley Act	−0.8772**	−0.7612**	−0.7491**	−0.7730**	−0.6853**
	(0.2856)	(0.3167)	(0.3045)	(0.3153)	(0.3131)
RTAA renewal, 1937	−0.5140*	−0.7327**	−0.7631**	−0.7294**	−0.7096*
	(0.2628)	(0.2950)	(0.3224)	(0.2796)	(0.2989)
Same party as president	—	—	0.0803	—	—
			(0.3471)		
Party × export dependence	—	—	—	0.4610	—
				(0.6955)	
Party × import competition	—	—	—	0.8198	—
				(2.1792)	

			Demand for Liberalization		
Constant	0.6197*	−0.0991	−0.0466	−0.2655	0.4318
	(0.4649)	(0.5956)	(0.5648)	(0.7105)	(0.7176)
Reciprocal trade legislation	—	1.3391**	1.2800*	1.2699*	1.6627**
		(0.7679)	(0.7405)	(0.7321)	(0.8320)
Value-added share of value product	—	—	—	—	−1.8266**
					(0.8468)

			Demand for Protection		
Constant	−0.0624	0.1944	0.2138	0.0272	0.2562
	(0.6823)	(1.0876)	(0.9234)	(0.9105)	(1.0016)
n	697	697	697	697	697
Mean log likelihood	−0.1627	−0.1606	−0.1649	−0.1646	−0.1567

Note: Standard errors are in parentheses.
*Significant at at least 5 percent in a one-tailed test.
**Significant at at least 1 percent in a one-tailed test.

In the absence of a dummy variable for reciprocal legislation the coefficient on the constant in the demand for liberalization equation is not significant but is the proper sign. This is not surprising given our theoretical prior expectation that demand for liberalization should have been low in legislation before the first RTAA in 1934. The coefficient on the demand for protection is also the proper sign but not significant. This is somewhat surprising since the demand for protection should have been high throughout the period, but it may be due to multicollinearity with the party and ideology variables since Republican conservative senators came from predominantly import-competing districts.

The specification in column 2 adds the dummy variable for reciprocal legislation. It is the proper sign and significant at the 5 percent level—suggesting that the demand for liberalization did in fact increase significantly in the Reciprocal Trade Agreements Acts of 1934 and 1937. As expected from the theory, the coefficient on the constant in the demand for liberalization fell substantially, suggesting that there was no significant demand for liberalization in the unilateral legislation in the sample. The coefficient on the demand for protection continued to be insignificant. The supply-side coefficients are very similar to the specification in column 1. This specification provides the first quantitative confirmation, then, that the demand for liberalization was higher in the reciprocal bills than in the unilateral legislation.

Columns 3 and 4 test for the presence of other political factors that may have influenced senators' votes on trade issues. First, since the RTAA involved a substantial delegation of authority to the president it seems likely that senators who were members of the president's own party would be more willing to delegate to the executive than would those of the other party. I tested for this effect by including the "same party as the president" variable. This variable is equal to one for Democrats in the votes on the RTAA and its extension and zero in all other cases. This should capture the greater willingness of Democrats to vote for the RTAA and its renewal simply because it was delegating trade policy authority to a Democratic president. The coefficient was not at all significant. This is an interesting result—Democrats were no more likely to vote for liberalization in the RTAA and its renewal than they were to vote for liberalization in previous legislation, ceteris paribus, even though it delegated authority to a president of their own party. Of course, Democratic (or more precisely, liberal) senators *were* more likely to vote for liberalization by virtue of their ideology. The ideology variable continued to be highly significant. The party variable remained insignificant, again, because of multicollinearity with the ideology variable.

Furthermore, Democratic senators (as well as Republican senators) were more likely to vote for liberalization in 1934 and 1937 because it was *reciprocal*. This is shown by the coefficient on the reciprocity variable. As in the other specifications in this table this coefficient confirms the theory by showing that the demand for liberalization was higher in the reciprocal bills than in the unilateral. The performance of the other variables in this specification is very similar to earlier specifications.

Column 4 tests for another political effect. It is often thought that the Republican Party at this time was supported by a coalition of import-competing industrialists while the Democratic party was supported by a coalition of mostly southern export-goods producers. If this is true, perhaps Republicans would re-act more to the economic importance of import-competing industries in their districts and less to the importance of exporting industries. To test for this I cre-ated interactive variables between the senator's party and the export depen-dence and import competition of the senator's district. That is, I multiplied the senator's party times the measures of ω_I and ψ_I for each senator's state. The coefficients on both variables should be negative—Republican senators should vote with less sensitivity to their states' export sectors and more sensitivity to their states' import-competing sectors than Democrats do. These expectations were not met, as is shown in column 4. Both variables were the wrong sign, al-though not significantly. There do not appear to be coalition effects, at least by these measures. The other results in the table remained similar to earlier speci-fications. In particular the demand for liberalization in the two reciprocal trade bills was still significantly higher than in the unilateral bills.

Finally, in column 5, I looked for the effects of some of the variables that measure labor intensity, industry concentration, and so forth. I tested for the importance of value-added share of value product, value added per worker, av-erage wage per worker, the state's share of total U.S. production, labor share of value added, average value product per firm, and number of firms. These vari-ables provided largely weak, although not particularly surprising, results. Only one of them was significant—value-added share of value product in export in-dustries. Its coefficient suggests that senators were more likely to vote for liber-alization if the export industries in their states were relatively low value-added industries. The other variables listed in column 5 performed similarly to the previous specifications, although the coefficient on the reciprocity variable grew somewhat and improved in significance.

The main point we should take from all of the specifications in table 5.2 is that voting patterns in the U.S. Senate suggest that the demand for liberaliza-tion was quite low and insignificant in unilateral trade bills but was larger and statistically significant in the two reciprocal trade bills. Next I will present the corroborating evidence from voting behavior in the U.S. House of Representa-tives.

B.   Estimates from the House

Table 5.3 presents the estimates from the House. The table is organized in the same way as table 5.2—each of the equations 5.6, 5.2 and 5.3 is given a separate section of the table marked "Supply-Side Variables," "Demand for Liberaliza-

TABLE 5.3. Demand for Liberalization and Protection Estimated from House Votes, 1890–1937

	Supply-Side Variables				
Constant	0.6303**	0.6892**	0.7922**	0.7028**	0.6018**
	(0.0855)	(0.0946)	(0.0799)	(0.0870)	(0.0886)
Number of Republicans	−0.0361**	−0.0334**	−0.0329**	−0.0095	−0.0309**
	(0.0055)	(0.0057)	(0.0057)	(0.0086)	(0.0057)
Ideology	−0.2336**	−0.2460**	−0.2469**	−0.2540**	−0.2399**
	(0.0192)	(0.0199)	(0.0201)	(0.0200)	(0.0202)
Previous state vote	0.0705**	0.0676**	0.0688**	0.0571**	0.0667**
	(0.0051)	(0.0052)	(0.0060)	(0.0053)	(0.0051)
McKinley Act	−0.7760**	−0.7647**	−0.8427**	−0.9613**	−0.8171**
	(0.1153)	(0.1163)	(0.1121)	(0.1134)	(0.1114)
Dingley Act	−0.6609**	−0.6465**	−0.7253**	−0.8811**	−0.8199**
	(0.1115)	(0.1131)	(0.1060)	(0.1088)	(0.1036)
Payne-Aldrich Act	−0.3755**	−0.3831**	−0.4693**	−0.5880**	−0.5224**
	(0.1066)	(0.1080)	(0.1000)	(0.1009)	(0.0962)
Fordney-McCumber Act	−1.2680**	−1.1678**	−1.2252**	−1.2424**	−0.9595**
	(0.1052)	(0.1122)	(0.1149)	(0.1134)	(0.1029)
Smoot-Hawley Act	−0.5179**	−0.4011**	−0.4348**	−0.4551**	—
	(0.0985)	(0.1088)	(0.1079)	(0.1085)	
RTAA, 1934	0.2357**	0.1635	—	—	—
	(0.0991)	(0.1043)			
Same party as president	—	—	0.0046	—	—
			(0.0062)		
Republicans × export dependence	—	—	—	−0.1456**	—
				(0.0250)	
Republicans × import competition	—	—	—	0.1094	—
				(0.0056)	
	Demand for Liberalization				
Constant	−0.1609	−0.6065	−0.7431	0.5148*	1.1404**
	(0.1297)	(0.2227)	(0.2141)	(0.3031)	(0.4480)
Reciprocity	—	0.6260**	0.7924**	0.4561*	1.8550**
		(0.2422)	(0.2497)	(0.2491)	(0.2628)
Average wage per worker	—	—	—	—	−0.2364**
					(0.0320)
Share of U.S. production	—	—	—	—	0.5104**
					(0.2157)
	Demand for Protection				
Constant	−0.1743	−0.3311	−0.5557	−1.3914**	−2.8413**
	(0.3373)	(0.3939)	(0.3794)	(0.4669)	(0.6162)
Value-added share of value product	—	—	—	—	6.5481**
					(1.4574)
n	373	373	373	373	373
Log likelihood	−3.7147	−3.7057	−3.7082	−3.6528	−3.5873

Note: Standard errors are in parentheses.
*Significant at at least the 5 percent level.
**Significant at at least the 1 percent level.

tion," and "Demand for Protection," respectively. The results have the same main substantive findings as with the Senate—particularly with regard to the importance of reciprocity in augmenting the demand for liberalization. Column 1 presents the specification that does not control for reciprocity. The supply-side variables all bear the proper sign and are highly significant. Republicans and conservatives are significantly less likely to vote for liberalization. Dummy variables for each piece of legislation were included, although I have reported only the significant ones to save space. Dummy variables for region were included. They were not significant and did not change the other results appreciably, so they are not reported. The demand for liberalization is not significant in this sample because it combines unilateral and reciprocal trade bills. The demand for protection was also not significant in this specification.

The specification in column 2 tests for an increase in the demand for liberalization in the two reciprocal trade bills. The estimates of the demand for liberalization did indeed rise in this specification, as was predicted by the theory. Furthermore, the results show that the demand for liberalization in the unilateral bills was insignificant. Demand for protection remained insignificant in this specification. The coefficients on the supply-side variables were largely the same as those in column 1, except for the first RTAA dummy variable, which was no longer statistically significant. The results from the House, then, confirm the theory, as did those of the Senate.

The remaining columns in table 5.3 test the robustness of the importance of reciprocity to a variety of political and economic factors. First, in column 3 I tested whether or not representatives were more willing to delegate to presidents of their own parties. Similar to the results in the Senate there appeared to be no increased willingness by Democratic members of Congress in this period to delegate to presidents of their own party. Again, to be clear, this does not mean that Democrats were not significantly more likely to vote for the RTAA than Republicans—in fact they were, as evidenced by the coefficients on ideology and party. Furthermore, all legislators were more likely to vote for the RTAA because of greater exporter lobbying, as shown by the reciprocity coefficient.

With the specification in column 4 I looked for the type of coalition effects that I did not find in the Senate. That is, I tested whether Republicans were more sensitive to import-competing interests in their districts than to export interests because the former were members of their political coalition while the latter were not. I used interactive terms between the number of Republicans in the states' congressional delegations and the export and import indexes, ω_i and ψ_i. The evidence is mixed. The interaction between party and size of a state's export sector was the proper sign and significant, but the interaction between party and the state's import-competing sector was not the correct sign. Since only one of the variables was the correct sign, I believe these two interactive variables were merely capturing the effects of the party variable (which has a negative effect on the probability of voting for liberalization) times the effects of the demand for liberalization and protection, and not the coalition effects. Therefore, in the remaining specification I removed both variables even though one was significant.

The final specification in table 5.3 tests for the effects of economic concentration, labor intensity, and so forth. Column 5 reports only the results of the variables from that list that were significant. These variables performed better in the House estimates than in the Senate—three were significant rather than just one. The average wage per worker variable suggests that members were more likely to vote for liberalization the lower the wage in their districts' export industries. The coefficient on state's share of total U.S. production shows that the congressional delegations of states with high percentages of the value product of America's export industries were more likely to vote for liberalization. Finally, state delegations were less likely to vote for liberalization if their import-competing industries had low value added as a share of value product.

A few other results in this specification were different from previous specifications in table 5.3. The dummy variable for the Smoot-Hawley Act was dropped from this specification because it was no longer significant. The constant in the demand for liberalization (which measures the average level of demand for liberalization in unilateral legislation) became even larger and more significant than in the last specification, but it still is only about one-third the size of the demand for liberalization in reciprocal liberalization. The demand for protection also became more significant once I controlled for these economic variables. Most important for our purposes, though, the estimates of the demand for liberalization in reciprocal trade bills was considerably higher than the demand for liberalization in unilateral trade bills. In fact, the results are considerably stronger in this specification than in any other in table 5.3—triple the size of the next largest coefficient in column two.

All of these robustness checks should not detract from the main point of table 5.3—in all of the specifications in the table the demand for liberalization was higher in *reciprocal* than in unilateral trade bills. These results were robust to a wide variety of specifications and actually became a good deal stronger once I controlled for certain economic characteristics of states' export and import-competing sectors in column 5. Between these results and those from the Senate we can be fairly confident that the demand for liberalization did in fact rise as a result of the reciprocal trade agreements program in 1934. Furthermore, because other factors were controlled for, we know the results were not due to other changes such as the massive supply-side changes in the composition of Congress as a result of the New Deal realignment or changes in the economy at the time.

C. Effects of Reciprocity on an Individual Legislator's Voting Behavior

Given these results we can determine the effects of each variable on a particular legislator's probability of voting for liberalization. These effects are shown in table 5.4. I used the specifications in the final columns of tables 5.2 and 5.3 for the Senate and the House, respectively. The first four rows are for a hypothetical "senator;" the remaining are for a hypothetical "member of Congress."

As a baseline for the senator, I set the values of the weights ω_l (degree of import competition) and ψ_l (export dependence) at their means (0.09 and 0.21, respectively). I also assumed that the senator was a moderate Republican, with an ideology score of 0.2, and that one senator in his state delegation had cast a vote for liberalization in the previous trade bill. The value-added share of value product was also set at its mean (0.415). Under these assumptions the estimated probability of a senator voting for liberalization is 18.48 percent. If the bill had been reciprocal the increase in demand for liberalization would have raised this senator's probability of voting for liberalization almost eleven points, as is shown in the first row of the second column.

The next three rows alter the various assumptions. In row 2, the senator's ideology was increased by one standard error to 0.75 (a highly conservative Republican senator). The probability of voting for liberalization fell to essentially zero. Reciprocal trade legislation raises this probability by a factor of three, but it was still very low—less than one percent.   In row 3 I changed the senator to an average Democrat with an ideology score of −0.44. The probability that this senator would vote for liberalization rose substantially to 81.85 percent. If the bill had been reciprocal it would have risen even further to 89.61 percent. In the fourth column I experimented with raising the export dependence of the senator's state by two standard errors, to 0.6, a very export-dependent state. Interestingly, a higher state export intensity actually leads to a small *reduction* in the senator's probability of voting for liberalization compared with the baseline. This is due to the interactive effect between the export industries' value-added share of value product and export intensity—higher export intensity produces a larger effect for value-added share of value product. This result has a problematic interpretation and suggests that the coefficient on value-added share of value product is spurious and perhaps should be removed (i.e., the specification in column 2 of table 5.2 is actually better since it does not contain this spurious

**TABLE 5.4.   Effects of Independent Variables on Individual Legislators'
Probabilities of Voting for Liberalization**

	Probability of Voting for Liberalization and Variance	
	Unilateral Legislation	Reciprocal Legislation
Senate		
Baseline[a]	0.1848	0.2921
	(0.0029)	(0.0060)
+1 s.e. (+0.536)	0.0009	0.0027
Ideology	9×10^{-7}	7×10^{-6}
Democrat, ideology score = −0.44	0.8185	0.8961
	(0.0022)	(0.0014)
+2 s.e. (+0.39) state export intensity	0.1495	0.2456
	(0.0069)	(0.0073)
+2 s.e. (+0.46) export industries' value-added	0.1415	0.2346
share of value product	(0.0029)	(0.0059)
House of Representatives		
Baseline[a]	0.6604	0.7899
	(0.0004)	(0.0005)
+1 s.e. (+0.536) ideology score	0.6118	0.7507
	(0.0004)	(0.0005)
Moderate Democrat, ideology score = −0.25	0.7137	0.8307
	(0.0004)	(0.0003)
+2 s.e. (+0.39) state export intensity	0.6082	0.9179
	(0.0023)	(0.0008)
+1 s.e. (+4.6979) export industries' average	0.5704	0.7157
wage per worker	(0.0005)	(0.0005)
+1 s.e. (0.306) state share of export industries'	0.6721	0.7993
total U.S. value product	(0.0004)	(0.0004)
+1 s.e. (+0.1043) in import competition	0.6424	0.7756
	(0.0013)	(0.0011)
+1 s.e. (0.193) import industries' value-added	0.7017	0.8217
share of value product	(0.0004)	(0.0004)

Note: Standard errors are in parentheses.
[a]See text for a description of the assumptions made for the baseline case.

variable). Despite this problematic result, though, reciprocity still has important effects on the senator's voting behavior—the senator's probability of voting for reciprocal liberalization rose almost ten percentage points to 24.56 percent. I do not show the effects of a different share of import-competing
industries in the state's total personal income because the coefficient on that
variable was the wrong sign. Finally, a two standard error higher value-added

share of value product (an increase of 0.46) reduces the probability of voting for liberalization to about 14 percent for unilateral liberalization and 23 percent for reciprocal legislation.

Turning to the House in the next eight rows of table 5.4, I looked at the effect of the variables on the vote of a single member of Congress from a state with only one. The legislator is a moderate Republican with an ideology score of 0.2 who voted against liberalization on the last trade bill. The bill-specific dummy variables were all set equal to zero. I set all other variables equal to their means: export dependence is 0.21, import competition 0.0925, average wage per employee 6.85, state share of total U.S. export production 0.245, and value-added share of value product 0.398. With these assumptions the baseline representative had a probability of voting for liberalization of about 66 percent.[5] In all of the results for the House reciprocity had a much larger effect than in the Senate. This is evident from the effect of reciprocal liberalization in the baseline case—the member of Congress's probability of voting for liberalization rose by almost thirteen points to almost 79 percent.

In row seven I increased the member of Congress's ideology score by one standard error to about 0.75. This produced only a small reduction in the legislator's probability of voting for liberalization to about 61 percent in unilateral legislation and about 75 percent in a reciprocal bill. Changing the member of Congress to a moderately liberal Democrat with an ideology score of −0.25 also had very small effects on his or her probability of voting for liberalization. They rose only a little over five percentage points, to 71.37 percent, for unilateral legislation and a little over four percentage points, to about 83 percent, in the reciprocal case.

Just as increasing the state's export dependence actually *reduced* the baseline senator's probability of voting for liberalization in row 3, so in the House the member of Congress's probability of voting for liberalization fell by over five percentage points from a two standard error increase (about 0.39) in his state's export dependence. This was due to the interactive effects between export dependence and the average wage per worker in export industries. (Again, it suggests the specification in column 2 of table 5.3 is superior.) The effects of reciprocity are most pronounced in a district with large export dependence,

---

5. It may at first seem strange that this *Republican* congressman's probability of voting for liberalization is greater than 50 percent; however, this is to be expected since the bill-specific dummy variables have been excluded. In the final specification there were bill-specific dummy variables for four of the five protectionist bills and none of the liberalizing bills. Including these would have reduced the baseline legislator's probability of voting for liberalization to below 50 percent.

though—reciprocity increased the representative's probability of voting for liberalization from about 61 to almost 92 percent in this case.

In rows ten and eleven I altered the assumption regarding two of the export industries' economic variables. A one standard error increase in the average wage per worker in the export industries reduced the probability that the member of Congress would vote for liberalization to about 57 percent in a unilateral bill. As always this probability was substantially higher in reciprocal legislation—about 71.6 percent. Increasing the state's share of total U.S. production in the export industries produced only meager effects on the probabilities that the legislator would vote for liberalization in both the unilateral and reciprocal cases—increasing it by about one percentage point in both cases.

Increasing the share of the import-competing industries in the state's economy reduced the probability that the member of Congress would vote for liberalization but not by much—only about three percentage points in the unilateral case and about one and a half in reciprocal legislation. Finally, an increase of one standard error (about 0.193) in the import-competing industries value-added share of value product increased the probability that the member of Congress would vote for liberalization by about four points in unilateral liberalization and about three points in reciprocal.

The main point we should take away from table 5.4 is that reciprocity increased the probability that legislators would vote for liberalization in all cases. In some cases the effects are smaller—for example, in row two, where the senator is quite conservative—and in other cases the effect is quite dramatic—for instance, in the House when the member of Congress's state has a highly export dependent district (row nine). Several other interesting patterns emerged. First, party and ideology seemed to make much more of a difference in the Senate than in the House. They were the most important variables in the Senate but hardly had any substantive effect at all in the House. Meanwhile, the economic characteristics of the state seemed to have much less effect in the Senate than in the House—in fact, they were among the most important variables in terms of their effects on voting behavior in the House. This is obviously speculative, but these estimates may be capturing the fact that senators can afford to vote their own ideology much more than members of the House can because they come up for election every six years rather than every two. House members, on the other hand, have to be much more sensitive to the needs and economic characteristics of their districts. Senators can ideologically "shirk," to borrow a term from the principle-agent model, while House members cannot, ceteris paribus. This may explain why ideological characteristics best explained Senate voting behavior while economic characteristics best explained voting behavior in the

House. Whatever the case we can be more certain now that reciprocity did in fact lead to substantially greater probabilities that legislators would vote for liberalization.

D.   Simulating Votes of the Whole House and Senate

The previous results showed the differences in *individual* legislators' probabilities of voting for liberalization in reciprocal as opposed to unilateral legislation, but they did not show the effects of reciprocity on the probabilities that liberalization would pass *the whole House and Senate* in each trade bill. Those latter probabilities are a combination of the probabilities that each legislator will vote for liberalization and would be too complex to find analytically. However, we can determine them by simulating the votes of the entire House and Senate in each bill using the results from tables 5.2 and 5.3. The specifications used for the simulations are from the last columns in each of those tables. The simulations were repeated ten thousand times.

The results of these simulations are shown in table 5.5 for the Senate and table 5.6 for the House. The numbers of proliberalization (or antiprotection) votes, the averages and standard errors calculated from the simulations, and the probabilities of a liberalizing outcome for each act are shown. Looking at columns two and three in both tables, it is clear that the average number of proliberalization votes jumped substantially after the Smoot-Hawley Act of 1930. Furthermore, as is shown in column 5 of both tables, a liberalizing outcome was a very unlikely event until 1934 (except, of course, for the Underwood Act of 1913), while in 1934 and 1937 the tables were turned—a protectionist outcome was quite unlikely.

There are many reasons for this dramatic change from 1930 to 1934, though. The argument here is that reciprocity was at least in part responsible for the large increase in the probability of passage of liberalizing legislation in 1934 and 1937. However, reciprocity was clearly only one factor. Also very important was the large ideological shift that occurred in Congress during those years from a Democratic minority to a substantial majority. To isolate the effects of reciprocity alone, I ran the simulations for the first six trade bills under the counterfactual assumption that they were reciprocal and the last two under the counterfactual assumption that they were unilateral. All other variables were kept identical to their factual values.

The results of these counterfactual simulations are presented in the last column of tables 5.5 and 5.6. They show that reciprocity would have increased the number of votes cast for liberalization in all cases, although the results are much

TABLE 5.5. Simulated Votes on Trade Policy Legislation, U.S. Senate, 1890–1937

	Sample		Simulations			
	Total Votes in Sample[a]	Liberal Vote[a]	Factual Mean Liberal Vote (st. dev.)	Counterfactual Mean Liberal Vote (st. dev.)	Factual Probability of a Liberal Vote[b]	Counterfactual Probability of a Liberal Vote[b]
McKinley Act, 1890	74	37	33.44 (1.21)	34.04 (1.31)	0.0005	0.0072
Dingley Act, 1897	72	31	31.31 (1.08)	31.85 (1.12)	0.0000	0.0006
Payne-Aldrich Act, 1909	92	38	37.88 (2.70)	39.47 (3.08)	0.0033	0.0189
Underwood Act, 1913	80	49	50.70 (1.80)	52.65 (1.85)	1.0000	1.0000
Fordney-McCumber Act, 1922	94	37	36.44 (2.45)	40.52 (2.99)	0.0002	0.0159
Smoot-Hawley Act, 1929	94	36	35.72 (3.56)	41.09 (4.29)	0.0000	0.0649
RTAA, 1934	94	61	60.55 (3.18)	57.22 (3.36)	1.0000	0.9958
RTAA renewal, 1937	85	60	60.17 (3.96)	53.53 (5.81)	0.9981	0.8493

[a]Number of votes in sample may be less than the actual number of votes cast due to missing data.
[b]Number of votes assumed needed to pass is the nearest integer greater than half of the total votes in sample in column 1.

TABLE 5.6. Simulated Votes on Trade Policy Legislation, U.S. House of Representatives, 1890–1937

	Sample		Simulations			
	Total Votes in Sample[a]	Liberal Vote[a]	Factual Mean Liberal Vote (st. dev.)	Counterfactual Mean Liberal Vote (st. dev.)	Factual Probability of a Liberal Vote[b]	Counterfactual Probability of a Liberal Vote[b]
McKinley Act, 1890	239	86	82.83 (8.17)	97.33 (8.38)	0.0000	0.0027
Dingley Act, 1897	325	128	127.87 (10.26)	155.09 (10.94)	0.0000	0.2169
Payne-Aldrich Act, 1909	385	187	187.73 (10.96)	206.57 (10.87)	0.2809	0.8833
Underwood Act, 1913	413	281	279.03 (9.78)	317.98 (9.21)	1.0000	1.0000
Fordney-McCumber Act, 1922	398	138	139.15 (10.72)	196.51 (14.46)	0.0000	0.3899
Smoot-Hawley Act, 1929	420	186	187.73 (9.64)	256.96 (11.85)	0.0072	0.9998
RTAA, 1934	401	298	294.70 (9.53)	255.00 (9.76)	1.0000	1.0000
RTAA renewal, 1937	395	313	292.28 (9.01)	211.31 (12.26)	1.0000	0.8536

[a]Number of votes in sample may be less than the actual number of votes cast due to missing data.
[b]Number of votes assumed needed to pass is the nearest integer greater than one half of the total votes in sample in column 1.

more dramatic in the House. As previously mentioned, senators seemed to vote much more in accord with their ideology than with the characteristics of their districts, so reciprocity seems to have had very little impact on the probability that any particular bill would have passed the Senate. The largest absolute effect was in the renewal of the RTAA in 1937. Had it not been a reciprocal trade bill the probability of its passage would have fallen by about fifteen percentage points, but it still would have passed with a probability of 85 percent. It appears then that, although reciprocity certainly has the effects posited in previous chapters, it did not have a large impact on legislative outcomes in the Senate—perhaps because of the ideological shirking that I discussed.

The picture in the House is entirely different, though. In two bills, reciprocity would have changed the historical outcome according to these results. The protectionist Payne-Aldrich Act—the act that spawned the insurgent movement—had about a 28 percent chance of failing without reciprocity. However, if passing the Payne-Aldrich Act would have meant reneging on a reciprocal trade agreement (with its concomitant loss of privileges overseas) it would not have passed at all with a probability of over 88 percent. The impact on the notorious Smoot-Hawley Act is even more pronounced. The bill was a shoo-in without reciprocity—it had less than a 1 percent chance of failure. But with reciprocity its probability of failure leaped to *almost one*—it almost certainly would have failed. About *seventy* more representatives would have voted against it than actually did. The results for a few other bills in the House were less dramatic but still worth mentioning. The Fordney-McCumber Act, for instance, would have gone from a sure thing to a nearly even chance of failing—about 39 percent with about sixty more members of Congress voting against it than actually did. Finally, under reciprocity the Dingley Act's probability of failure would have risen by about twenty-two percentage points, and, as in the Senate, the RTAA renewal would have had about fifteen percentage points less chance of passage had it not been reciprocal.

V. Conclusion

I have shown that the theory developed in previous chapters plausibly corresponds to U.S. trade history by estimating the demand for liberalization through its effects on legislators' voting behavior. Those estimates did increase significantly with the RTAA of 1934 and its first renewal in 1937—America's first serious attempt to use reciprocity on a wide scale—compared with the previous six major trade bills. These results were robust to a variety of specifications controlling for the legislators' ideologies, effects that were idiosyncratic to the particular bills, and various economic variables.

As expected, a wide variety of factors increased America's willingness and ability to liberalize in the mid-1930s besides the increase in demand for liberalization that the reciprocal trade agreements program created. The estimates provided here suggest that the massive change in the ideological makeup of Congress in the early 1930s as part of the New Deal realignment had a great deal to do with the liberalization of trade policy in 1934 and 1937. However, the effects of reciprocity alone—holding constant the large ideological changes in Congress—were considerable. The estimates implied that reciprocity would increase a given legislator's probability of voting for liberalization substantially. Furthermore, simulations showed that reciprocity alone would have produced substantial increases in the number of votes for liberalization in both houses of Congress. In fact, the Payne-Aldrich and Smoot-Hawley Acts would have had very little chance of passage in the House, and the Fordney-McCumber Act would have had a much more even chance of failure, even under the same Republican Party control of the House at that time.

These results suggest that the demand for liberalization did rise substantially with the advent of the reciprocal trade agreements program and that the increase in the demand for liberalization had a great deal to do with the liberalization of American trade policy in the 1930s. The next chapter will show that this phenomena continued in the post–World War II period as well.

CHAPTER 6

The Demand for Liberalization and Protection Today

I. Introduction

The last chapter provided the main evidence for the theoretical contention in this book—estimates of the demand for liberalization based on plausible assumptions about legislators' objective functions did indeed show that the demand for liberalization rose in 1934 and 1937 as opposed to earlier years. Simulations suggested that in the Payne-Aldrich and Smoot-Hawley Acts in particular reciprocity may have likely changed the historical outcomes—the bills would not have passed had exporters been as politically active as they became after the launching of the reciprocal trade agreements program.

It was important to show that the demand for liberalization was greater for the two reciprocal trade bills (1934 and 1937), which were closest to the unilateral bills in time and were passed before the United States took its leadership position in the world as hegemon. But readers will undoubtedly want to know if this pattern persists to this day. Does the demand for liberalization remain high or was the pattern observed in the last chapter an ephemeral characteristic of Roosevelt's leadership or the political economy of the 1930s? I offered some historical evidence from some of the postwar trade bills in chapter 4. I gave examples of the type of exporter lobbying for liberalization and against protectionism that has continued throughout the postwar period, right up to the North American Free Trade Agreement and the recently enacted Uruguay Round agreement that created the World Trade Organization.

In this chapter I will provide more rigorous quantitative evidence that the demand for liberalization has in fact remained strong throughout the post–World War II period, just as it was in the 1930s. To do this I have completed the same type of analysis that I did in the last chapter. In this chapter I will concentrate on a sample of four major postwar trade bills—the Trade Expansion Act of 1962, the Trade Act of 1974, the Omnibus Trade and Competitiveness Act of 1988, and the Canada-U.S. Free Trade Agreement of 1988.

II. Existing Evidence

In fact, a number of other researchers have unwittingly completed the task of this chapter. There is already a substantial body of evidence from a series of articles on legislative voting behavior in trade legislation, which show that exporter lobbying continues to be as strong today as it was when the reciprocal trade agreements program was launched. These articles were not written to provide evidence for my theoretical claims, but they in fact do. Most of them address the role of the export dependence of legislators' districts in determining those legislators' votes on trade issues. In all but one of the articles, the export dependence of a district was significantly negatively related to representatives' votes for protection or positively related to their votes for liberalization, and the one case which did not show a strong exporter lobby used a questionable measure for the districts' export dependence.

Tosini and Tower (1987) in their study of voting on a protectionist textile quota bill, and MacArthur and Marks (1988) in their study of voting in 1982 automobile domestic content legislation found that the higher the export dependence of a legislator's district—measured by the number of people in the district employed in industries directly producing products for export—the lower the probability that that legislator would vote for the protectionist legislation. Destler, Odell, and Elliot (1989) have carefully created a measure of antiprotectionist lobbying based on a variety of factors. They found that export industries were often quite active in opposing protectionist legislation that may have brought retaliation from foreign governments against them. For instance, U.S. soybean and wheat farmers lobbied heavily to prevent protection on European steel and Chinese textiles because those countries threatened retaliation against U.S. soybeans and wheat, respectively. The one exception to these findings is Baldwin's (1985) study of legislative voting on the Trade Act of 1974 in which he included a variable for the export dependence of each district—measured by employment in the district in "export-sensitive industries." The coefficient was not significantly different from zero in any of the specifications and it was generally not the proper sign.

One obvious reason for Baldwin's weaker results and the stronger results of Tosini and Tower and MacArthur and Marks is the different measure of the export dependence of legislators' districts used in each study. Tosini and Tower and MacArthur and Marks used employment in industries directly producing products for export as specified by the Commerce Department. Baldwin used employment in only *two* industries, computers and aircraft. Clearly, though, there were many other industries that had a stake in expanding exports. I have included the Trade Act of 1974 in my analysis. Contrary to Baldwin's results I found a strong positive link between the importance of exports in the economies of legislators' districts and the probability that those legislators would vote for liberalization or against protectionism. My estimates suggest that Baldwin's weaker results may indeed stem from the measure of export dependence that he used in his analysis.

III. Estimates of the Demand for Liberalization, 1962–88

The model I estimated in this chapter is exactly the same as the model used for the Senate and House in the last chapter. I have added a few new and different independent variables in these specifications to control for changes in the political economy of trade policy that occurred during this time period. In particular, I controlled for the changing role of ideology in the period covered in this chapter. Between 1962 and 1988 liberal Democrats changed from favoring relatively free trade to favoring protection of the domestic market, and Republicans dropped their previous support for protection of the domestic market and began to support a program of reciprocal liberalization. Other than that the variables used in this chapter will be the same as those used in the previous chapter and can be interpreted in the same manner. Descriptive statistics of these variables are presented in table 6.1.

A. Estimates from the Senate

The dependent variable for the following Senate specifications is the same as in the last chapter—individual senators' votes on the respective trade bills. A vote in favor of liberalization or against protectionism is coded as a one, so votes in favor of the Trade Expansion Act, the Trade Act of 1974, and the Canada-U.S. Free Trade Agreement and against the Omnibus Trade and Competitiveness Bill (with its "super-301" provisions)[1] are coded one. Table 6.1 provides summary statistics for the dependent and independent variables used in the analysis in this chapter.

---

1. I realize that coding a vote in favor of the 1988 trade act as protectionist may be controversial. There were many provisions in the bill besides "super-301," some of which were liberal. However, the super-301 sections were certainly the most salient of the international trade provisions of the bill. Indeed, parameter estimates using the votes on the Omnibus Trade Act alone were quite consistent with the estimates from the other postwar legislation, excluding the 1988 bill. Not surprisingly, then, excluding the Omnibus Trade Act from the analysis does not change the results appreciably.

TABLE 6.1.   Means and Standard Deviations of Variables, 1962–88

Senate Variables	
Vote for liberalization	0.7695
	(0.4215)
Party	0.4520
	(0.4981)
Ideology	−0.0606
	(0.4565)
Same party as the president	0.4927
	(0.5004)
Export industries' share of state total personal income	0.1975
	(0.2529)
Import-competing industries' share of state total personal income	0.1269
	(0.1526)
Export industries' value product per firm	6.1048
	(11.7044)
House Variables	
Vote for liberalization	6.2064
	(7.2571)
Total votes cast by state delegation	8.6744
	(8.6859)
Party	4.0029
	(5.0557)
Ideology	−0.0110
	(0.2592)
Same party as president	4.0484
	(4.6311)
Export industries' share of state total personal income	0.1993
	(0.2273)
Import-competing industries' share of state total personal income	0.1264
	(0.1482)

Note: Standard deviations are in parentheses.

Table 6.2 presents the estimates of demand for liberalization from the Senate votes. The specifications no longer include a separate dummy variable for "reciprocity" because all of the trade bills under consideration in this chapter are reciprocal bills or at least risked the loss of reciprocal benefits offered by another country. Therefore, we should see the same kind of high demand for liberalization that we observed in the RTAA and its first renewal in all of the bills in this chapter.

The baseline specification in column 1 reveals that the demand for liberalization, as estimated by this model, remained strong in the post–World War II period, as is shown by the constant term under "Demand for Liberalization."

TABLE 6.2. Demand for Liberalization and Protection Estimated from Senate Votes, 1962–88

	Supply-Side Variables				
Constant	0.8854**	1.3223	1.0158**	1.0084**	1.0115**
	(0.3552)	(0.2786)	(0.2824)	(0.3336)	(0.2426)
Party	−0.4063	−0.2824	0.6660	0.5088	0.7618
	(0.3358)	(0.5902)	(0.7365)	(0.7210)	(0.6171)
Ideology	0.5169	−3.9158**	−4.5234**	−4.8925**	−4.6104**
	(0.3491)	(1.0718)	(1.2420)	(1.4704)	(1.3422)
Previous state vote	0.1618	—	—	—	—
	(0.1724)				
Trade Act, 1974	0.7149**	0.0796	—	—	—
	(0.2951)	(0.2861)			
Omnibus Trade Bill, 1988	−2.1992**	−3.1584**	−2.9835**	−3.1229**	−3.0530**
	(0.2649)	(0.3504)	(0.3277)	(0.2899)	(0.2933)
Canada-U.S. Free Trade Agreement, 1988	0.3635	—	—	—	—
	(0.2835)				
Party × year	—	0.0214	−0.0416	−0.0329	−0.0461
		(0.0199)	(0.0332)	(0.0337)	(0.0296)
Ideology × year	—	0.1353**	0.1444**	0.1562**	0.1503**
		(0.0331)	(0.0367)	(0.0454)	(0.0410)
Same party as president	—	—	1.4288**	1.3894**	1.4615**
			(0.5815)	(0.4908)	(0.5142)
Party × export dependence	—	—	—	−3.8577*	—
				(2.0128)	
Party × year × export dependence	—	—	—	0.1365	—
				(0.0947)	
Party × import competition	—	—	—	5.8391	—
				(2.8807)	
Party × year × import competition	—	—	—	−0.2290	—
				(0.0976)	

	Demand for Liberalization				
Constant	1.6567*	2.3231**	2.8742**	3.2897*	2.4245**
	(0.9468)	(1.0571)	(1.1149)	(1.6656)	(1.0562)
Value product per firm	—	—	—	—	0.0013*
					(0.0008)

	Demand for Protection				
Constant	−1.2054*	−1.4411*	−2.0497**	−2.2423*	−2.0517**
	(0.6643)	(0.7601)	(0.8692)	(1.2389)	(0.6638)
n	372	372	372	372	372
Mean log likelihood	−0.3243	−0.2588	−0.2478	−0.2422	−0.2455

Note: Standard errors are in parentheses.
*Significant at at least the 5 percent level.
**Significant at at least the 1 percent level.

The demand for protection was also significant in this and all specifications in the table. Senators from states with a large share of import-competing industries in their economies were significantly less likely to vote for liberalization. This is consistent with the findings of most of the other studies of legislative voting on trade issues in recent years.

Two other patterns from the prewar sample are not corroborated in this simple specification for the postwar sample. First, according to the coefficient on the "previous state vote" variable there does not seem to be the consistency across time in the way particular state delegations voted on trade policy. Second, and perhaps more interestingly, ideology, which was quite a strong predictor of voting on trade bills in the prewar sample, was quite weak in its effects on the postwar sample. Party is also quite a weak predictor (although this is consistent with the prewar sample once the ideology variable is included).

These weak results for party and ideology are due to the parties' switching positions on trade policy during the period under consideration here. Conservative Republicans generally became supportive of relatively freer trade while liberal Democrats generally began to oppose it. Column 2 of table 6.2 highlights this point. The party and ideology variables are made interactive with year—a trend term. The coefficient on the ideology variable then became significant and negative, suggesting that conservatives were less likely to vote for liberalization in the early part of the period. The coefficient on the ideology variable interactive with year, though, is positive, suggesting that conservatives became increasingly more likely to vote for liberalization as the period wore on. For example, in the first year of the period, 1962, conservatives were substantially less likely to vote for liberalization than were liberals, but by 1988 there was no significant difference between the way liberals and conservatives voted on trade bills. The party variables were not statistically significant, although their coefficients were quite large. As in the prewar sample this is probably due to multicollinearity with the ideology variable.

The cause of this ideological switch by the parties probably had something to do with the declining comparative advantage of America's traditional "smokestack" industries and the importance of the highly organized blue collar workers in those industries to the Democratic coalition. Any answer as to why the parties decided to switch ideologies rather than form new coalitions would at this stage be speculative, but one possibility is that there are substantial fixed costs in creating new coalitions and it was simply cheaper in that sense to change ideologies rather than coalitions. That is, coalition membership may be "stickier" than ideology is.

The specification in column 3 of table 6.2 explores another pattern in party voting on trade policy in this period. As is often pointed out, with the RTAA in 1934, trade policy was no longer a strictly legislative issue. In fact, it really became a presidential responsibility. We might expect, then, that senators would be much more willing to delegate authority over trade policy to a president of their own party. Lohmann and O'Halloran (1994) and O'Halloran (1994) make this claim in their models of legislative voting on trade. There was no support for this proposition from the prewar results in the previous chapter; however, it *is* supported in the postwar sample, as is shown by the results in column 3. That specification shows that a senator of the same party as the president was significantly more likely to vote for liberalization than was a senator in the opposition party. Thus, Lohmann and O'Halloran's (1994) and O'Halloran's (1994) claim appears to be strongly supported by this analysis, at least for the post–World War II period.

In the specification in column 4 I looked for effects of strong party-industry coalitions on trade policy votes, as I did in the prewar sample. The export dependence and import competition of senators' states were made interactive with party and the party × trend interaction terms. The purpose of these variables is to show that, because they were part of the same coalition, Republicans should have been more sensitive to the demands of import-competing industries than Democrats were, and, because primarily exporting industries were not from the same coalition as Republicans were, Republican senators should have been less sensitive to the demands of those industries. However, these patterns should have switched as time went by and the economic characteristics of the parties' coalitions changed. In a way, then, this specification is a test of the "stickiness of coalition membership" argument that I just made to explain why the parties switch their positions on trade policy.

Both the party × export dependence and party × import competition interaction should be negative since Republicans should be less responsive to the export sectors in their districts and more responsive to the import-competing sectors in their districts. That is, they should be less likely to vote for liberalization for a given size of their export and import-competing sectors. Moreover, the interactions between party × export dependence × year and party × import competition × year should be positive as Republicans became more responsive to their export sectors and less responsive to their import-competing sectors over time.

This intuition was not borne out by the results in column 4. Indeed, the results are remarkably similar to those from the prewar sample—the coefficient on the party × export dependence interaction was the proper sign, but the coefficient on the party × import competition was not. As in the prewar results, I believe these variables are simply mirroring the significance of the demand for liberalization and protection. Similarly, the interaction between party $\times$ import competition $\times$ year was not the proper sign while the coefficient on party $\times$ export dependence $\times$ year was. I think that these variables are picking up the significance of the demand for liberalization and protection interactive with the switching of the parties' voting patterns on trade.

As in the previous chapter I tested for the effects of a variety of economic variables that may have affected industries' incentives and capabilities to take collective political action. These variables included value-added share of value product, the state's share of total U.S. production of the export and import-competing industries, and so on. In the interest of brevity I will not recount the rationale for each of these variables here but simply refer the reader to the discussion in section III of the previous chapter. In chapter 5 the performance of these variables was spotty at best—not a surprising result given their mixed track record in the literature and the fact that they have never been used in legislative voting analysis before, not to mention the fact that the variables are aggregates of many industries. The results in the postwar sample were lackluster, just like those in the prewar sample. Only one of the variables—value of product per firm—was the proper sign and significant at the 5 percent level. The results with this variable included in the specification are presented in column 5. This result is highly spurious, though. Higher output per firm is supposed to capture the effects of industry concentration on the ability of that industry to take collective action, but the variable is positively correlated with a state's export dependence weight, ψ_p and may simply be capturing the effects of the constant term in the demand for liberalization. Furthermore, the log-likelihood of this specification actually *declined*. Because its significance is so questionable I decided to leave the variable out of the final specification. In the end I chose to use the specification in column 3 as the final specification for the analysis in the next section.

Most important for the purposes of this monograph, of course, are the coefficients on the demand for liberalization variables. In all cases they remained positive and highly significant, showing that there was positive demand for liberalization in all of these trade bills, just as there had been for the Reciprocal Trade Agreements Act and its first renewal in the prewar sample. Indeed, the coefficients in the baseline specification of table 6.2 are quite similar to those in table 5.2, although the results in the other specifications of table 6.2 are actually stronger than in the prewar sample. These results corroborate those from the previous chapter, then. They show that demand for liberalization is as strong as (if not stronger than) it was when the reciprocal trade agreements program was first launched in 1934.

B. Estimates of the Demand for Liberalization in the House, 1962–88

The estimates of the model from House votes are presented in table 6.3. They generally corroborate the results just discussed from the Senate. Column 1 provides the coefficients from the baseline model. As in the Senate the estimated demand for liberalization in the House was positive and significant. The estimates of the demand for protection are also of the proper sign and significance. The coefficients on the ideology and party variables are, once again, not significant, just as in the post–World War II Senate sample. Again, the reason for this is the parties' changing positions on trade issues in this period, as is shown in column 2.

Column 2 of table 6.3 includes the party and ideology variables interactive with a time trend. The results are similar to those from the Senate, although in the House results the party variables are significant, as are the ideology variables. These coefficients suggest that in the Trade Expansion Act of 1962 conservative Republicans were considerably less likely to vote for liberalization than were liberal Democrats. The coefficient on the ideology × year interactive variable was positive and significant, showing that this relationship eroded throughout the period. By 1988, twenty-six years after the Trade Expansion Act, there was no significant difference between members of Congress with different ideological scores in the way they voted on trade issues. The coefficient on the party × year interactive term is very small and not significantly different from zero. This implies that the parties have not switched over the period, as the ideologies have, but this is obviously a ceteris paribus result, controlling for ideology, which is itself highly correlated with party.

The specification in the third column of table 6.3 adds a variable for the number of members of Congress in the state delegation who are of the same party as the president. As in the Senate, it was expected that members of Congress would be more willing to delegate trade policy authority to a president of their own party. Consistent with the postwar results from the Senate, the variable was significant. It appears that legislators in both the House and the Senate were more willing to delegate to a president of the same party in the postwar period than they were in the prewar period. Again this corroborates the claims of Lohmann and O'Halloran (1994) and O'Halloran (1994).

TABLE 6.3.   Demand for Liberalization and Protection Estimated from House Votes, 1962–88

	Supply-Side Variables			
Constant	0.3693**	0.3284**	0.3009**	0.3670**
	(0.1080)	(0.1104)	(0.1107)	(0.1230)
Party	−0.0192	−0.0219*	−0.0290*	−0.0028
	(0.0120)	(0.0118)	(0.0125)	(0.0181)
Ideology	0.1597	−2.6515**	−2.3933**	−2.4028**
	(0.2136)	(0.6723)	(0.6840)	(0.6818)
Previous state vote	0.0186**	0.0187**	0.0088	—
	(0.0037)	(0.0073)	(0.0088)	
Trade Act, 1974	0.3892**	0.4093**	0.4089**	0.2679**
	(0.1022)	(0.1049)	(0.1044)	(0.1148)
Omnibus Trade Bill, 1988	−1.8911**	−1.7571**	−1.7324**	−1.8534**
	(0.1148)	(0.1186)	(0.1193)	(0.1407)
Canada-U.S. Free Trade Agreement,	0.4923**	0.6444**	0.6696**	0.5452**
1988	(0.1102)	(0.1183)	(0.1190)	(0.1393)
Party × year	—	0.0000	0.0000	—
		(0.0001)	(0.0001)	
Ideology × year	—	0.0929**	0.0833**	0.0844**
		(0.0209)	(0.0215)	(0.0215)
Same party as president	—	—	0.0260*	0.0248*
			(0.0135)	(0.0118)
Party × export dependence	—	—	—	−0.1475*
				(0.0889)
Party × import competition	—	—	—	0.0273
				(0.1350)
Party × year × export dependence	—	—	—	−0.0010
				(0.0025)
Party × year × import competition	—	—	—	−0.0045
				(0.0059)

	Demand for Liberalization			
Constant	1.0536**	1.1887**	1.2251**	2.0381**
	(0.3768)	(0.4329)	(0.4319)	(0.6316)

	Demand for Protection			
Constant	−0.8003**	−0.7190*	−0.8367**	−1.3385**
	(0.3282)	(0.3325)	(0.3348)	(0.4590)
n	200	200	200	200
Mean log likelihood	−3.8854	−3.8345	−3.8252	−3.8166

Note: Standard errors are in parentheses.
*Significant at least the 5 percent level.
**Significant at least the 10 percent level.

Using the specification in column 4, I tested for the presence of the coalition effects previously discussed. If these effects were present import-competing industries should have been more important to Republican voting patterns and export industries should have been less important in the early part of this time period. However, these results should weaken over the course of the period. These expected patterns were not present in House votes in this period according to the estimates in column 4. The party × export dependence and party × import competition interaction terms are the proper sign, but only the former is significant at the 5 per cent level. These variables interactive with year are not statistically significant either and the party × export dependence × year interaction is not even the correct sign. These results suggest that Republicans in the House did not react to the economic characteristics of their districts differently than Democrats did in their voting behavior on trade legislation. All told, then, there is no evidence for the types of coalition effects discussed previously in either the prewar or the postwar sample or in either chamber of Congress. This preliminary evidence for stickiness of coalitions is not supportive.

Finally, I used the same economic variables included in some of the specifications in the last chapter and in the Senate specifications in this chapter: value added-share of value product, average wage per employee, share of total U.S. production, and so on. These variables have not performed well, and this case is no exception. None of these variables produced a significant coefficient in the estimates from the House votes. Therefore, I have omitted reporting them. The best specification for the House, then, is simply the one in column 3.

Of course, the main purpose of this chapter is to point out that the demand for liberalization remains strong to this day. All of the results in table 6.3 suggest that this is indeed the case. In all of the specifications the estimated demand for liberalization was strong, and in fact it became stronger as I controlled for more of the other determinants of legislators' trade policy votes. The demand for protection was also always statistically significant in the results in this table and became stronger with each specification. These results corroborate the argument I made in chapters 2 and 3 and the estimates presented for the prewar sample in chapter 5—the reciprocal trade agreements program seems to have empowered exporters to take political action that they did not take with unilateral trade legislation.

C. Substantive Interpretation of the Estimates

Table 6.4 presents some of the substantive implications of the estimates presented in tables 6.2 and 6.3 for an individual legislator's voting behavior. First,

TABLE 6.4.   Effects of Independent Variables on an Individual Legislator's Probability of Voting for Liberalization, 1962–88

	Probability of Voting for Liberalization (plus variance)
Senate	
Baseline[a]	0.8509
	(0.0047)
Moderate Democrat	0.9124
	(0.0014)
Republican president	0.9813
	(0.0001)
+1 s.e. (0.253) in export industries' share of state total personal income	0.9663
	(0.0021)
+1 s.e. (0.153) in import-competing industries' share of state local personal income	0.6808
	(0.0143)
Vote in 1962	0.6676
	(0.0064)
House	
Baseline[a]	0.6528
	(0.0012)
Moderate Democrat	0.6567
	(0.0015)
Republican president	0.6650
	(0.0011)
+1 s.e. (0.227) in export industries' share of state total personal income	0.7448
	(0.0017)
+1 s.e. (0.126) in import-competing industries' share of state total personal income	0.6043
	(0.0017)
Vote in 1962	0.4167
	(0.0047)

Note: Standard errors are in parentheses.
[a]See text for a description of the baseline assumptions.

with regard to the Senate, I assumed a baseline in which the senator is a Republican with an ideology score of 0.25. This moderate Republican senator comes from a district with the average level of export and import-competing production as a share of the state's total personal income (0.198 and 0.127, respectively). The president is assumed to be a Democrat. Finally, the bill under consideration comes up for a vote thirty years after the first bill in this sample, which is the Trade Expansion Act of 1962. The senator created from these assumptions would have an 85 percent chance of voting for liberalization.

Next I kept all of the baseline characteristics the same except that I made the senator a moderate Democrat with an ideology score of -0.25. Under these condition the senator's probability of voting for liberalization is slightly higher, about 91 percent. In the third scenario, I returned to the baseline moderate Republican but changed the president to a Republican as well. Under those conditions the senator's chances of voting for liberalization rose considerably to over 98 percent.

The economic characteristics of the senator's state had much more of an impact on voting behavior in the postwar sample than they did in the prewar sample. This is shown in rows 4 and 5 of table 6.4. In the fourth row, I changed the president back to a Democrat (so that the senator is an opposition party member) but increased the share of total personal income accounted for by exporting industries (ψ_i) in the senator's state by about one standard error. Raising ψ_i in this way increases the senator's probability of voting for liberalization from the baseline of 85 percent to 96 percent. In the fifth row, I examined the effects of increasing the level of the state's import-competing industries as a share of its personal income. Again I raised it by about one standard error. This increase reduced the senator's probability of voting for liberalization substantially—from 85 percent in the baseline example to about 68 percent. These results suggest that senators engaged in less ideological "shirking" in the postwar period than they did in the prewar sample—or the results may simply be a symptom of the breakdown of strong party discipline on trade issues.

Finally, if the same baseline senator—moderate Republican from an "average" district and so forth—had been voting at the beginning of this period, in 1962 rather than 1992, his or her probability of voting for liberalization would have been only about 67 percent—more than eighteen points lower than in 1992. This large reduction indicates the importance of the switch in ideologies by the parties.

Table 6.4 also illustrates some of the effects of the estimates from the House votes. I looked at the probabilities of voting for liberalization of a single legislator from a state with only one member of Congress. The baseline member of Congress is similar to the baseline senator. I assumed that he or she is a moderate Republican with an ideology score of 0.25 and an average share of state total personal income accruing from the export and import-competing industries. The president was assumed to be a Democrat, and the vote under consideration occurs thirty years after the Trade Expansion Act of 1962. This member's probability of voting for liberalization is a little over 65 percent. Changing the member of Congress to a moderate Democrat with an ideology score of -0.25 changes the member's probability of voting for liberalization almost imperceptibly to 65.7 percent. In the third scenario I assumed that the president was also a Republican. This raised the baseline legislator's probability of voting for liberalization a little over a point to 66.5 percent. None of these ideological and political variables, then, has a large substantive impact on House members' probabilities of voting for liberalization.

The economic characteristics of the states, on the other hand, *were* quite important, just as they were in the postwar Senate results. For instance, if the baseline member of Congress had come from a more export-dependent district his or her probability of voting for liberalization would rise substantially. I assumed that the state's share of total personal income accounted for by the export industries was 0.398, or about one standard error higher, and the baseline member's probability of voting for liberalization rose by almost ten points to 74.5 percent. Increasing the share of import-competing industries in the state's total personal income by about one standard error, to 0.29, did not have as dramatic an effect, although the member's probability of voting for liberalization did fall about four and half points to 60.4 percent. Finally, if this baseline, moderately conservative Republican member of Congress had been voting in 1962 rather than 1992 his or her probability of voting for liberalization would have been substantially lower—less than 42 percent, or a drop of more than twenty-three points. The parties' ideological switch during this period seems to be even more pronounced in the House than in the Senate.

IV. Conclusion

The following picture emerges from this analysis of postwar trade bills. First, the demand for liberalization as estimated by this model remains high to this day. In all specifications it appears that legislators with large export sectors in their districts have a significantly higher probability of voting for liberalization or against protection. This finding corroborates similar findings of others in the literature. Another interesting pattern has surfaced, though. Consistent with the conventional wisdom, trade policy has become less ideological over this period. As we saw, conservative Republican legislators had substantially lower probabilities of voting for liberalization in 1962 than in 1992 simply because of their party and conservative ideologies. Today ideology appears to play little or no role in voting on trade issues once factors like the economic characteristics of the state are controlled for. Another interesting difference between the postwar and prewar eras is that these economic characteristics, by contrast, *are* very important in determining legislators' votes on trade, even in the Senate where they were not that important before World War II. In short, we have seen a continued strength of the demand-side factors explored in the last chapter—particularly the demand for liberalization. Indeed, these factors have become more important, at least in the Senate. At the same time, there has been virtually a complete erosion of the ideological factors that were so important in the pre–World War II sample.

Finally, I should probably digress on the important issues of American hegemony and national security considerations. Many scholars have argued that politicians liberalized American trade policy after World War II either to stabilize the world economy as part of the U.S. role as hegemon, to shore up the economies of the nation's allies as part of the Cold War rivalry, or both. The argument suggests that all or at least most politicians felt an increased willingness to liberalize for national security reasons. These are really supply-side arguments—they suggest that the supply of liberalization shifted outward after World War II for national security reasons.

However, while the argument may be able to explain the liberalization of American trade policy after the war, it cannot explain two other pieces of evidence. First, it cannot explain why the United States began liberalizing seven years *before* its entry into World War II and even longer before it took on the role of hegemon. Second, it cannot explain why this *general* interest in national security and hegemony would manifest itself as a *differential* willingness by legislators to vote for liberalization. What is more, it cannot explain why that differential willingness would be correlated with the importance of export and import competing industries in the economies of the legislators' districts. It is precisely that correlation that was shown here.

None of this is to suggest that the national security and hegemony arguments are wrong. The argument is well known and somewhat obvious. Politicians during the period as much as said that this was at least one of the motivations for much of U.S. trade policy during the postwar period. I do suggest, though, that it is not a complete answer to the puzzle of America's liberalization after the war. The argument presented here is hopefully another piece of that puzzle.

CHAPTER 7

Conclusion

I. Summary of Results

A. Theoretical Conclusions

This study has argued that the reciprocal trade agreements program of the United States has brought about the dramatic liberalization of American trade policy not simply because it required delegating trade policy authority to the president, who has more liberal preferences on trade than Congress, but because it delegated to the executive in order to make reciprocal trade treaties with other countries. Furthermore these reciprocal trade agreements helped the U.S. government reduce trade barriers not simply because they forced the United States as a unitary actor to live by those international agreements but because they changed the balance of political forces *within* America's domestic political economy. By concentrating the benefits of liberalization on particular export industries reciprocity helped those export industries overcome their collective action problems and gave them more of an incentive to lobby for liberalization than they would have had for a unilateral trade bill. This increase in exporter lobbying actually changed legislators' preferences so that liberalization was more politically palatable to them, and they allowed presidents to liberalize more than they could have with delegation alone.

The theory has relied crucially on three concepts important in the literature that explain American trade policy: reciprocity, delegation, and collective action problems. All of these have been put forward as explanations of some aspect of American trade policy in the past. For instance, I have used many of the insights of the endogenous tariff literature—particularly where that literature has argued that it is the concentration of benefits and dispersion of costs of protection that makes protectionism such a powerful political force. Much of the

135

endogenous tariff literature has relied heavily on this argument, which was also made by Pareto (1927), Schattschneider (1935), Olson (1965), and many others. Empirically this point has been recognized for a long while by historians of American tariff policy, as was discussed in Chapter 4 (Stanwood 1903; Tarbell 1911; Taussig 1966; and Terrill 1973), and in the more quantitative studies of U.S. trade policy (Ray 1981a, 1981b, 1987; Ray and Marvel 1984; Lavergne 1983; Pincus 1975; Baldwin 1985; and many others). What these theories lack is an explanation for the opposite policy outcome—trade liberalization. By using the same collective action and concentration of costs and benefits argument this study has shown how reciprocity transforms the domestic political economy to one in which exporters who would benefit from international agreements have more reason to take political action and, therefore, have a greater voice in the political system.

I also built upon those theories that explain the American liberalization with the delegation of trade policy authority to the executive. There are actually a variety of arguments in this literature. Destler (1986) argued that delegation insulated Congress from constituency pressures and gave trade policy authority to the president, who is better able to resist these pressures. I argued that delegation did not and could not insulate Congress from constituency pressures since Congress retained ultimate control over whether the president's delegated authority would be renewed. Delegation did not *insulate* Congress from constituency pressures; rather, it *transformed* those pressures through the trade agreements that the president negotiated under his delegated authority. O'Halloran (1994) and Lohmann and O'Halloran (1994) claimed that delegation facilitated liberalization by allowing Congress to escape from the universalistic logroll by which it set trade policy. Schnietz (1993) argued that Democrats in Congress delegated in order to commit future Republican Congresses to lower trade barriers than they otherwise might set. My theory augments these compelling arguments by explaining why Congress chose delegation rather than some other institutional solution to America's protectionist bias and by explicitly taking into account the foreign policy dimension of the problem—the desire in Congress to reduce *foreign* as well as American tariff rates.

This study has also augmented some of the arguments of the international relations and international economics literatures on cooperation. Those literatures argue that countries are better off when they take into account at least some of the externalities imposed by their policies on each other. International institutions can aid in this process by reducing the transaction costs of international cooperation and changing international trade politics from a single play to a repeated game (Keohane 1984). However, these theories have been based on the untenable assumption that states are unitary actors with a single, well-defined set of preferences. In light of the century of historical work that suggests that domestic political considerations are extremely important in determining trade policy outcomes this assumption—and therefore the explanations that follow from it—need revision. I have argued that reciprocity and international institutions may very well facilitate international cooperation by reducing the costs of making international agreements and making cooperative commitments more credible, but in addition to those effects they reinforce trade policy cooperation by augmenting exporters' incentives to take costly political action *within* the domestic political economy, not only by changing the incentives facing unitary state actors.

My point is not that all of these literatures are wrong. On the contrary I believe they are all correct about the factors on which they focus. One of the contributions of this volume, I hope, has been to synthesize and enhance these diverse theories. This study has tried to reconcile these three literatures and provide an explanation that can help to account for both the postwar liberalization and the presence of strong domestic political forces that should have prevented it. Collective action problems continue to be important in determining trade policy outcomes in this explanation, but governments have been able to use these collective action problems to the advantage of liberalization with reciprocal trade policies that concentrate the benefits of liberalization on particular exporters.

The study has other, broader, implications for the study of political economy. Although this conclusion is speculative, I believe that, although this study presents a theory of the effects of reciprocity on the *demand* for liberalization, it also has important implications for the role of the supply side. In this model policymakers have a measure of control over policy outcomes even though they must do the bidding of the strongest lobby. This is so because policymakers can concentrate the benefits and disperse the costs of their preferred policies and to a certain extent *determine* the amount of lobbying for and against those policies. By exploiting the collective action problems of economic agents in society policymakers can increase the odds of achieving the policy outcomes they prefer.

B. Empirical Conclusions

I have provided two sorts of evidence for the general theoretical proposition of this book. First, in chapter 4 I reviewed the history of U.S. trade policy roughly from the turn of the century to the present. I argued there that the description of trade policy offered by this theory appears to be broadly consistent with the historical record. Before reciprocity, trade politics was very much like that described by the existing endogenous tariff literature. Import-competing producers were generally more active politically and provided more financial and organizational support for the party that supported their requests for protection, which in that period was the Republican Party. In the end, import competers asked for, and usually received, protection for their particular products. Consumer interests, on the other hand, were considerably less active, less well connected, and rarely heard from, and as a result, rarely heeded. A look at the hearings on several major trade bills from this period revealed that import-competing interests were more likely to request protection from Congress than consumers were to ask for lower tariffs. On occasion particular producer interests that used highly taxed goods intensively in the their production asked Congress for liberalization (some even had the audacity to ask for lower tariffs for their inputs and higher tariffs for their own products), but these producers were in a definite minority.

The result of this system was a long and steady string of protectionist legislation. Despite a general consensus that tariffs in the U.S. needed reform several attempts to lower them after the Civil War failed. Tariffs were not lowered and in some cases were even raised. The one exception was the Underwood tariff of 1913, which I explained by important changes in the party composition of Congress, the strength of the Progressive movement at that time, a power vacuum in Congress as a result on the insurgent movement, and a strong activist president who was willing to fill it. Indeed, the demand for liberalization in the Underwood Act—measured by the percentage of proliberalization witnesses before the tariff hearings—was remarkably close to that for other trade bills of the period. After World War I tariff politics "returned to normalcy"—that is, protectionism—in the Fordney-McCumber and Smoot-Hawley Acts. The latter act is often cited as the paragon of special interest politics run amok, but as we saw in chapter 4 the Smoot-Hawley Act was not an aberration. It was really just the last installment in a long series of highly protectionist trade legislation.

In 1934, however, the Reciprocal Trade Agreements Act changed all of this. Exporters became much more active in trade politics, requesting that import-competing industries' tariffs be lowered so that their products would receive preferential treatment abroad. The reciprocal trade agreements program lead to a substantial reduction of American tariff rates between 1934 and World War II. After World War II reciprocal trade policy continued under the auspices of the General Agreement on Tariffs and Trade, reducing tariffs even further and extending liberalization to other product areas like agriculture. Again and again Congress gave the president broad authority to reduce trade barriers in return for greater access to foreign markets, first under renewals of the RTAA, then, in 1962, under the Trade Expansion Act, and in 1974 under the Trade Act. If testimony before Congress is any guide, in all of these pieces of legislation, exporters and consumers were at least as active as import-competing interests were. Of course, today reciprocity continues not only under the GATT (and now the WTO) but also through regional agreements like the Canada-U.S. Free Trade Agreement and NAFTA.

The relative lack of exporter lobbying before 1934, and the increase in it after 1934, is consistent with the explanation offered here and suggests that the microfoundations used in this explanation of the great postwar liberalization were, in fact, operating. Other, more quantitative evidence for the theory was offered in chapters 5 and 6. Because exporters should not have been active in lobbying for unilateral trade bills, but should have been after the reciprocal trade agreements program became avowed U.S. trade policy, I argued that legislators' voting behavior on trade issues should not have taken into account the export dependence of their districts in unilateral trade legislation (because exporters did not lobby vigorously in such legislation) but should have after reciprocal legislation (because exporters did lobby in that type of legislation). In chapter 5 I used this logic to compare legislators' voting behavior in eight pieces of legislation. The estimates from this pre–World War II sample showed that, indeed, legislators did seem to take into account the export dependence of their districts in reciprocal trade legislation but did not in unilateral legislation.

Other factors were also shown to be very important in the different trade policy outcomes of 1934 and 1937 compared with the earlier, more protectionist legislation. Most important of these other factors was each legislators' party and ideological affiliation. As I already mentioned, party changes alone (along with a strong president and the Progressive movement) accounted for the liberalizing the Underwood Act, and estimates of the demand for liberalization were no higher in the Underwood Act than they were in the other unilateral legislation of the period. Party changes also account for a great deal of the more liberal legislative outcomes in 1934 and 1937. This is consistent with existing theories and evidence about the U.S. political economy of this period.

However, in addition to these well-known party and ideology effects reciprocity had a strong impact in its own right. Indeed, simulations revealed that if it would have meant reneging on reciprocal trade agreements the Payne-Aldrich and Smoot-Hawley Acts probably would not have passed the House—a reversal of the historical outcome—even with the Republican control of the

House at the time. The Dingley and Fordney-McCumber Acts would probably have passed but by much narrower margins. According to these estimates and simulations, then, if the Republicans had introduced earlier the kind of reciprocal trade agreements that I modeled in chapters 2 and 3 some of the protectionist legislation of that period might not have passed—a finding that helps explain why they did *not* introduce that kind of reciprocity even when they had the chance.

Chapter 6 extended the quantitative analysis up to the present and showed that the estimates of demand for liberalization continue to be as strong today as they were in the 1930s. This finding was consistent with other studies of legislative voting in the 1980s. The chapter also explored the changing role of ideology and party in legislative voting on trade. First, it seems to have become much less important as a predictor of legislators' votes than it was in the early part of this century. There has also been a switch of ideologies by the parties recently—Democrats becoming more protectionist and Republicans becoming more liberal on trade. The main point, though, was that the demand for liberalization, as estimated by this model, continued to be high in this period marked by many reciprocal trade agreements.

From both the qualitative and the quantitative evidence so far, it appears that the causal chain put forward by this study has some validity. Exporters did, indeed, seem to lobby more in reciprocal than in unilateral pieces of legislation, and legislators appeared to take this extra lobbying into account in their voting decisions since the RTAA in 1934 compared with earlier legislation. The implication, then, is that the effects of the RTAA and its successors may have helped the United States liberalize by increasing the incentives of proliberalization groups to lobby for liberalization *within* the domestic political economy. Perhaps politicians will be able use the example of reciprocity in international trade to skillfully devise other institutional structures that break apart suboptimal equilibria elsewhere in their political economies.

III. Agenda for Future Research

One of the main criticisms of my analysis will undoubtedly be that it stresses the importance of reciprocity but looks at only one country. Does the argument apply equally well to Britain, France, Canada, and other countries? I am hesitant to extend the analysis to other countries too quickly because domestic political institutions—particularly delegation of trade policy-making authority to the executive—played such an important role in my argument. In countries where the executive and legislative branches are not so distinct (such as parliamentary systems) the effects may not be as marked. This is precisely the point, though: these are interesting questions worth addressing more formally with the type of analysis completed in chapters 2 and 3. The analysis could incorporate the different institutional arrangements of other counties to see if the conclusions are still valid, and of course the same type of empirical analysis completed in chapters 5 and 6 could be applied to those other countries as well.

For instance, it may be interesting to extend the argument about U.S. trade policy making to the European Union. The Common Agricultural Policy was a very costly and inefficient policy that caused huge deficits in the Union's budget. However, the benefits of the program were highly concentrated on farmers, predominantly in France and southern Europe, and the costs were spread over millions of taxpayers and agricultural produce consumers throughout the Union. Perhaps one reason why policymakers in the European Union were able to begin dismantling the CAP in 1993 is that the issue was "internationalized" through the Uruguay Round negotiations. U.S. negotiators insisted on reductions in subsidies and protection to European farmers and made it quite clear that future reductions in American trade barriers would be contingent on a diminution of the CAP's role in European agricultural markets. In essence the costs of the CAP became concentrated on European exporters, who then lobbied for greater flexibility in the EU's bargaining position on the CAP. Obviously this story is highly stylized. Many other factors were very important in determining Europe's switch in agricultural policy (the Union's large budget deficit being foremost among them [Nugent 1994]), but the story does illustrate the way in which the analysis completed here could be extended to other countries.

A further avenue of research would be to study the negotiation process more explicitly. The framework I developed could be used to address *which* industries are liberalized. Clearly this is an entirely different dependent variable than the one addressed in this study, but the framework is amenable to studying it. Several scholars have already done some of this kind of analysis empirically, although without any strong theoretical background. Baldwin (1985), Reidel (1977), and Cheh (1974) all looked at the determinants of whether an industry was liberalized or not in the Kennedy Round negotiations.

The comparative statics presented in appendix B really offer a set of predictions about the characteristics of those industries a country would prefer to liberalize first and those industries it would ask the foreign government to liberalize first. In a nutshell each country should want its foreign counterpart to liberalize the industries that would elicit the greatest increase in lobbying from its own exporters. In return it would hope to liberalize the industries at home that would organize the weakest protest against the liberalization. In this way it could bring about the highest net increase in demand for liberalization. To really do this empirical analysis properly, though, poses a fairly complicated econometric problem. The industries that are actually liberalized are decided upon *simultaneously* between the countries through the bargaining process. To estimate this system of equations for two countries is simply a simultaneous equations problem estimable with two-stage least squares or maximum likelihood techniques—not all that difficult a problem in theory, assuming that the equations are identified (King 1989). But when looking at a large, multilateral negotiation between many countries the problem becomes a great deal more complicated. The only practicable solution may be the one Baldwin (1985), Reidel (1977), and Cheh (1974) chose: simply ignoring the international aspects of the problem.

The analysis in this volume could also be extended to a whole new set of issues. Reductions in barriers to trade in goods are only one of the major issues facing the United States and its trading partners—in fact, of all the issues in international trade today it is the one that has been addressed most successfully. Other important and perhaps stickier issues remain, such as codes of conduct on subsidies and countervailing duties, rights of labor to organize and child labor, and copyrights and other intellectual property rights. Will reciprocity be as successful an instrument in these problems as it was in reducing trade barriers?

Again I think the argument made here could be extended to address these issues. The argument suggests that the key to bringing about cooperation in these issues, as it was in fostering reduction of tariffs in the 1930s, is to ensure that the benefits of cooperation are sufficiently concentrated to encourage the beneficiaries to take costly political action on cooperation's behalf. In some cases this may not be particularly difficult. For instance, the main beneficiaries of tougher worldwide standards of copyright and intellectual property rights enforcement are a fairly concentrated group of recording and pharmaceutical companies. In some cases, though, the beneficiaries are less clear and more dispersed, as in the case of tougher international standards on workers' rights and child labor. If the United States is to press this issue in future negotiations there will have to be a group with powerful incentives to lobby for it domestically (perhaps unions in the industries where child labor and violations of workers' rights are particularly prevalent). This argument is speculative, of course, but again it illustrates the type of analysis that could be done in the future using my argument.

Finally, on an even more speculative note, what are the implications of this analysis for the future of U.S. trade policy? Certain developments do not augur well for a continued liberal U.S. policy: the heated rhetoric on trade policy in presidential primaries and elections, the brinkmanship between the United States and Japan or the European Union, or China on trade issues, and the fact that the Uruguay Round took longer than any previous GATT round and nearly broke down on several occasions. Are we to infer from these developments that America is becoming more protectionist and that its days of liberalization are coming to a close? The analysis presented here provides the opposite picture. Trade talks may stall and negotiations may slow as negotiators take up the more difficult trade issues that remain, such as nontariff barriers and standards on health, environmental protection, and fairness to labor. But the analysis suggests that the U.S. will not go back to the policies of protectionism it pursued in the past. Too many powerful interests—export interests—would be hurt by such a policy, and, thanks to the introduction of reciprocity in 1934, they have every incentive to fight tooth and nail to prevent it.

Appendixes

Derivation of Real Income Effects from Reciprocal and Unilateral Liberalization

This appendix will derive the main results of chapter 2 that were presented in equations 2.5 through 2.9. For convenience I will repeat equations 2.1 through 2.3 from the text:

$$U^i = U(p_1, 1, p_3, \ldots, P_n, y^i) \tag{2.1}$$

$$\phi^i_j = \frac{R_N + R_j V^i_j}{R_N V_N + \displaystyle\sum_{j=1}^{n} R_j V_j} \tag{2.2}$$

$$Y = \sum_{j=1}^{N} p_j X_j + t_g \pi_g M_g. \tag{2.3}$$

Equation 2.1 is individual i's utility given the prices of the n commodities p_1 through p_n (good 2 is the numeraire) and i's income y^i. Equation 2.2 specifies individual i's income in terms of his or her factor rewards. Equation 2.3 is the national income (i.e., GNP) of the home country under the assumption of a nonzero tariff on only one commodity—the gth. I also assumed that the gth and kth commodities were unbiased with respect to labor.

Given these assumptions, a small change in the tariff rate on the gth commodity, t_g, from its "optimal" level has the following effect on the ith person's utility:

$$\frac{\partial U^i}{\partial t_g} = \frac{\partial U^i}{\partial y^i} \left[\phi^i_j \pi_g \left(t_g - \frac{1}{\sigma_g} \right) \frac{\partial M_g}{\partial t_g} - Y \frac{\partial \phi^i_j}{\partial t_g} \right]. \tag{A.1}$$

Roy's identity[1] was used, as was the property of homothetic utility functions that the ith person's demand for a good j is the product of i's income share and the aggregate demand for good j (see Mayer 1984, 333, 341).

The first term inside the brackets in equation A.1 is i's income share, ϕ^i_j, times the change in aggregate income from changing the tariff. That is, the first term inside the brackets in equation A.1 is the ith person's share of the change in aggregate income that would result from moving t_g closer to or farther from the "optimal" tariff. Recall from the international trade literature that the "optimal" tariff when a country is large in consumption of a product is the inverse elasticity of the foreign country's export supply curve, or "offer curve," which is denoted by $1/\sigma_g$ in equation A.1 (Corden 1986, 167–68, 195–200). Because $\partial M_g / \partial t_g < 0$, the first term in brackets in equation A.1 shows that if t_g is less than the "optimal" tariff (i.e., $t_g - 1/\sigma_g < 0$) aggregate income will be increased from a small positive change in t_g. Similarly, if t_g is greater than the "optimal tariff" aggregate income would increase from a small negative change in t_g. Finally, if t_g is set at the "optimal" rate aggregate income will not be changed by changing t_g slightly, as we would expect from the envelope theorem.

Of course, changing t_g also changes relative prices and therefore changes the various R_js, as well. This in turn changes the ϕ^i_js. The second term in equation A.1 captures this effect. This change in income share for specific factor owners in any industry $h = 1, \ldots, n$ as a result of the tariff change can be expressed as follows:

$$\frac{\partial \phi^i_h}{\partial t_g} = \left(\frac{R_h V^i_h}{R_N V_N} \right) \left(\frac{\hat{R}_h - \hat{R}_N}{\hat{P}_g} \right) \frac{\partial P_g}{\partial t_g} \frac{1}{P_g} - \phi^i_h \left[\sum_{j=1}^{n} \alpha^j \left(\frac{\hat{R}_j - \hat{R}_N}{\hat{P}_g} \right) \right] \frac{\partial P_g}{\partial t_g} \frac{1}{P_g} \tag{A.2}$$

where

$\hat{R}_j$ is a percentage change in R_j,
$\hat{R}_N$ is a percentage change in the wage rate of labor, the mobile factor,
V^i_j is the amount of the specific factor used in industry j owned by i,
V_N is the total amount of the mobile factor, labor, in the economy,
$\hat{P}_g$ is a percentage change in the relative price of good g, and
α^j is the jth specific factor's distributive share of national income,

---

1. Roy's identity states that $-(\partial U^i / \partial p_j)/(\partial U^i / \partial y^i) = X^i_j$, where X^i_j is person i's demand for good j. See Varian 1984, 126–27.

or

$$\alpha^j = \frac{R_j V_j}{R_N V_N + \sum_{j=1}^{n} R_j V_j}$$

Furthermore,

$$\sum_{j=1}^{n} \alpha^j = 1 - \alpha^N$$

and

$$\alpha^N = \frac{R_N V_N}{R_N V_N + \sum R_j V_j}$$

where α^N is the income share of the mobile factor, labor. That is, the sum of the specific factors' distributive shares equals one minus the distributive share of the only remaining factor—the mobile factor, labor.

If the country was "small" in consumption of good g on the world market, $(\partial p_g / \partial t_g) / p_g$ would simply be $1 / (1 + t_g)$. However, we have assumed that the country is a large enough consumer of good g that it bids up the world price of good g, π_g, the more it buys, so that $\partial \pi_g / \partial M_g > 0$. This means that, by increasing imports of good g, the reduction of t_g increases π_g. So, instead of simply $1 / (1 + t_g)$, the value of $(\partial p_g / \partial t_g) / p_g$ would be $1 / (1 + t_g) + (\partial \pi_g / \partial t_g) / \pi_g$. This means that the reduction of p_g from lowering t_g is less than $1 / (1 + t_g)$.

The term in brackets in equation A.2 is the gth commodity's "bias" with respect to labor. A commodity is biased against labor if the relative change in the wage rate brought about by a change in that commodity's price is less than a weighted average of all other factor price changes. A commodity is biased in favor of labor if the relative change in the wage rate brought about by a change in that commodity's price is more than a weighted average of all other factor price changes. Naturally, then, a commodity is unbiased with respect to labor if the relative change in the wage rate brought about by an increase in the commodity's price is the average of the change in all other factor prices (Mayer 1984, 342–43; Ruffin and Jones 1977, 339). The average change of all the other factor prices is obtained by weighting each factor's relative price change by its share of national income (i.e., α^j). From these definitions it is easy to verify that the term in brackets in equation A.2 will be positive if the gth commodity is biased against labor,

$$\left(\frac{\sum_{j=1}^{n} \alpha^j \hat{R}_j}{\hat{P}_g} > \frac{\sum_{j=1}^{n} \alpha^j \hat{R}_N}{\hat{P}_g} \right),$$

negative if it is biased in favor of labor

$$\left(\frac{\sum_{j=1}^{n} \alpha^j \hat{R}_j}{\hat{P}_g} < \frac{\sum_{j=1}^{n} \alpha^j \hat{R}_N}{\hat{P}_g} \right),$$

and zero if it is unbiased with respect to labor,

$$\left(\frac{\sum_{j=1}^{n} \alpha^j \hat{R}_j}{\hat{P}_g} = \frac{\sum_{j=1}^{n} \alpha^j \hat{R}_N}{\hat{P}_g} \right).$$

Following Mayer 1984, I will use several equations from Jones 1975. For the reader's convenience, I will reproduce those equations here without deriving them. First, the percentage change in the wage rate of labor, $\hat{R}_N$, can be expressed:

$$\hat{R}_N = \sum_{j=1}^{n} \beta_j \hat{p}_j \tag{A.3}$$

and the percentage change in the return to the specific factor used in the jth industry, $\hat{R}_j$, is

$$\hat{R}_j = \left[\beta_j + \frac{1}{\theta_{jj}} \sum_{i \neq j} \beta_i \right] \hat{p}_j - \frac{\theta_{Ni}}{\theta_{jj}} \sum_{i \neq j} \beta_i \hat{p}_i \tag{A.4}$$

where

$$\beta_j \equiv \left(v_{Nj} \frac{\varsigma_j}{\theta_{jj}} \right) \Big/ \sum_i v_{Ni} \frac{\varsigma_i}{\theta_{ii}} \tag{A.5}$$

and

v_{Ni} is the share of the economy's total labor supply used in the production of good i,

ς_i is the elasticity of substitution between the specific factor i and the mobile factor, and

θ_{jj} is the cost share of factor j used in the production of good j, or $R_j V_j / p_j X_j$. Similarly, θ_{Nj} is the cost share of the mobile factor in production of good j.

If only the price of the jth commodity changes, equation A.5 shows that β_j can be thought of as the relative change in wage rate of labor as the jth commodity's price rises 1 percent. See Jones 1975 (5–6) for a fuller discussion of these equations and the roles that the parameters $v_{Ni}, \varsigma_i,$ and θ_{jj} have in changes in factor prices from a change in the price of a good.

Using these three equations, if the specific factor in question is the gth industry's, then the second term in parentheses in equation A.2 reduces to:

$$\frac{\hat{R}_g - \hat{R}_N}{\hat{P}_g} = \sum_{h=1, h \neq g}^{n} \frac{\beta_h}{\theta_{gg}} > 0. \tag{A.6}$$

Using equations A.2 and A.5, and the definition of bias shows that the gth specific factor will suffer a reduction in income share from a small decrease in the tariff if it is not biased against labor, or, if it is biased against labor, if that bias is relatively small. If the specific factor in question is the hth industry's ($h = 1, \ldots, n$ and $h \neq g$), then the second term in parentheses in equation A.2 reduces to:

$$\frac{\hat{R}_h - \hat{R}_N}{\hat{P}_g} = -\frac{\beta_h}{\theta_{gg}} < 0. \tag{A.7}$$

Once again, using equations A.2 and A.6 and the definition of bias shows that specific factors in the hth industry will enjoy and increase income share from a small decrease in t_g if the gth commodity is not biased against labor too severely.

I will assume, as did Mayer (1984), that the commodities are unbiased with respect to labor so that the term in brackets in equation A.2 is equal to zero. Furthermore, according to Ruffin and Jones (1977), when commodity g is unbiased with respect to the mobile factor, labor, then β_g is the domestic production of g's share of aggregate income—that is, $\beta_g = p_g X_g / Y$. It can also be expressed as the percentage of total factor income generated by the gth industry:

$$\beta_g = \frac{p_g X_g}{R_N V_N + \displaystyle\sum_{j=1}^{n} R_j V_j} . \tag{A.8}$$

This fact will further simplify the expressions that follow. Second, I will assume that the tariff rate on the gth industry was set at the "optimal" level (so that $t_g = 1 / \sigma_g$) before the small change studied here.

Under these assumptions, substituting equations A.6 and A.2 and the definition of unbiasedness into equation A.1 and dividing by the marginal utility of income shows that the effect of a small change in t_g on the gth specific factor's real income is:

$$B^i_{gg} = \frac{\partial U^i_g / \partial t_g}{\partial U^i_g / \partial y^i_g} dt_g = Y(1 - \beta_g)\beta_g \lambda^i_g \hat{p}_g . \tag{A.9}$$

To solve equation A.9 the property that

$$\sum_{h=1, h \neq g}^{n} \beta_h = 1 - \beta_g$$

was used. Completing a similar process by substituting equations A.7 and A.2 and the definition of unbiasedness into equation A.1 for the $n - 1$, $h \neq g$ specific factors, yields the following real income change:

$$B^i_{hg} = \frac{\partial U^i_h / \partial t_g}{\partial U^i_h / \partial y^i_h} dt_g = -Y\beta_h \beta_g \lambda^i_h \hat{p}_g \qquad \text{QED.} \tag{A.10}$$

Derivations of the real income effects of a reciprocal change in t_g in return for a change in τ_k are similar. I assumed that the kth commodity was unbiased with respect to labor, as was the gth. To derive the third term in equations 2.7 through 2.9 I used the fact that β_k is the kth industry's share of Y when it is unbiased with respect to labor.

Comparative Statics

Equations 2.4 through 2.8 in chapter 2 completed the first step of the theory of this study. They showed that the benefits of reciprocal liberalization are more concentrated than those of unilateral liberalization. This statement is true in all cases. However, whether or not reciprocity manages to give exporters a larger stake in the issue than importer competers depends on the various parameters of equations 2.4 through 2.8. For instance, the increase in exporters' stake relative to import competers will be smaller if there are very few different industries in the economy or if the ownership shares (the λs) of any particular industry are abnormally high. The increase will also be less dramatic if either the gth or the kth industry accounts for a particularly large share of the home country's economy (i.e., if β_k or β_g is very high). Table B.1 provides some numerical examples that should help illustrate the relationships between some of the parameters in equations 2.6 through 2.8 and show some of the differences between unilateral and reciprocal liberalization.

The columns of table B.1 consist of real income changes as a share of Y for each of the three groups (specific factors in the gth, kth and hth industries) under unilateral and reciprocal liberalization. The first two columns compare the real income changes between reciprocal and unilateral liberalization for the gth industry, the next two columns for the kth industry, and the fifth and sixth for the remaining h industries. The last two columns compare the ratio of the real income changes of the gth to the kth industries under unilateral and reciprocal liberalization. In the rows of table B.1, I have altered the various parameters of equations 2.6 through 2.8 to show the effects of different conditions within a political economy on the results derived in chapter 2. In a way, table B.1 provides a sort of numerical comparative statics analysis.

The first row of table B.1 contains the baseline case. I have assumed that there are five hundred equal-sized firms in the domestic economy so that $\beta_j =$

TABLE B.1. Effects of Various Parameters on the Concentration of Costs and Benefits of Liberalization (Change in real income as a share of GNP [Y])

	B_{gg}	B_{ggk}	B_{kg}	B_{kgk}	B_{hg}	B_{hgk}	B_{gg}/B_{kg}	B_{ggk}/B_{kgk}
Baseline[a]	−2E−06	−2E−06	4E−09	2.01E−06	4E−09	8E−09	499	0.99203
Fifty industries ($\beta_j = 1/50$)	−1.96E−05	−1.9E−05	4E−07	2.08E−05	4E−07	8E−07	49	0.92308
Five thousand industries ($\beta_j = 1/5,000$)	−2E−07	−2E−07	4E−11	2E−07	4E−11	8E−11	4,999	0.99920
Highly concentrated g industry ($\lambda_g^i = 1$)	−0.0020	−0.00199	4E−09	2.01E−06	4E−09	8E−09	499,000	992.0319
Highly concentrated k industry ($\lambda_k^i = 1$)	−2E−06	−2E−06	4E−06	0.002008	4E−06	8E−06	0.499	0.00099
10 percent reduction in p_g	−2E−05	−2E−05	4E−08	2.04E−06	4E−08	4.4E−08	499	9.76321
10 percent increase in p_k	−2E−06	−2E−06	4E−09	2E−05	4E−09	8E−09	499	0.09956
10 percent increase in exports of k	−2E−06	−2E−06	4E−09	2.04E−06	4E−09	4.4E−08	499	0.956947
g industry 20 percent of economy ($\beta_g = 1/5$)	−0.00016	−0.00016	4E−07	2.4E−06	4E−07	4.04E−07	400	66.38935
k industry 20 percent of economy ($\beta_k = 1/5$)	−2E−06	−1.6E−06	4E−07	0.00024	4E−09	4.04E−07	4.99	0.00639
h industry 20 percent of economy ($\beta_h = 1/5$)	−2E−06	−2E−06	4E−09	2.01E−06	4E−07	8E−07	499	0.992032

$^a\beta_j = 1/500, \lambda_j^i = 1/1,000, \hat{p}_g = 1, \hat{p}_k = 1, \hat{E}_k = 1.$

1 / 500 for all *j*. I have assumed that the ownership shares are all identical at 1 / 1,000. That is, one thousand people in each industry have equal-sized shares of the specific factors in their industry. All price changes, for both $\hat{p}_g$ and $\hat{p}_k$ are 1 percent, as is the percentage increase in the volume of exports, $\hat{E}_k$. Finally, I have assumed that each individual's share of income is simply his or her share of the specific factor used in his or her industry times the share of that industry in the economy, or $\lambda_j^i \beta_j^i$. This amounts to an assumption that returns to the mobile factor, labor, are an equally negligible share of each person's income.

For our purposes the most informative comparison is the one between columns 7 and 8. It shows that under the baseline assumptions unilateral liberalization produces a real income change in the *g*th industry that is 499 times higher than the real income changes of specific factor owners in other industries. Reciprocal liberalization, on the other hand, gives the *k*th specific factor a slightly higher stake than the *g*th industry. This is a consistent pattern in all of the results in this table. It happens because reciprocal liberalization mitigates some of the *g*th industry's losses from changing factor prices (share of the pie) with a gain from its share of the increase in the aggregate economy (the size of the pie). Meanwhile the *k*th industry gains on all fronts—its share of the pie increases along with the size of the pie.

In the second and third rows I altered the assumptions about the number of different equal-sized industries in the economy. We can think of this as changing the product diversification or differentiation in the economy. It is an important parameter because it changes the β_js in the equations. As is shown in column 2, a less diversified economy has fewer different industries over which to spread the benefits of liberalization, so that the problem of unilateral liberalization is not as severe. The ratio of industry *g*'s stakes to those of industry *k* falls to 49 under unilateral liberalization—still very high but less than the 499 times in the baseline case. With reciprocal liberalization the stakes are once again about even. Switching to a much more diversified economy in column 3 with five thousand industries shows the opposite effect. Under unilateral liberalization costs are much more concentrated than are benefits—4,999 times more concentrated. As before, though, reciprocal liberalization ensures that benefits to the *k*th industry are about even with costs to the *g*th.

Rows 4 and 5 experiment with the impact of concentration of ownership of the various industries. If ownership of the *g*th industry's specific factor is highly concentrated the costs of liberalization will be even more highly concentrated on it than before. If the *k*th industry's specific factor is highly concentrated the benefits of liberalization might be concentrated on it even in unilateral liberalization. In row 4 I assumed that the specific factor used in the *g*th industry was owned by one person—a very extreme assumption, to be sure, but an instructive one. Under this assumption, the losses to the gth industry under unilateral liberalization are the most concentrated of any in the table—499,000 times those of the specific factor owners of the kth industry. As always, reciprocal liberalization mitigates the problem but under such extreme conditions not by enough—the costs to the gth industry's specific factors are 992 times those of the gain to the kth industry's. If instead the specific factors in the kth industry were owned by one person the benefits even of unilateral liberalization would be sufficiently concentrated. The costs to the gth industry would only be half of the benefits to the kth, even under unilateral liberalization. Reciprocity strengthens the highly concentrated benefits so the losses to the gth industry are less than one-hundredth of 1 percent of the gains to the kth industry. While these assumptions are extreme they are informative because they show that if ownership of the gth specific factor is very highly concentrated even reciprocity cannot give liberalization a fighting chance in the political process. Furthermore, if ownership of the kth specific factor is highly concentrated the benefits of liberalization—even unilateral liberalization—would be so highly concentrated that liberalization would elicit more lobbying even without reciprocity.

The next set of parameters worth checking are the relative price changes of the gth and kth commodities. If the gth price reduction is much larger than the kth price increase the costs of reciprocal liberalization will be more concentrated on the gth industry than if the price changes are relatively equal. This is shown in row 6. I assumed that the price change of the gth good was ten times higher than the price increase of the kth good. The price of the kth good does not enter into equation 2.4 or 2.5, so this change has no effect on the relative stakes under unilateral liberalization—it is the same as the baseline case. However, the effect of reciprocal liberalization is much weaker in this scenario than in previous ones. Because the price reduction of the gth good is ten times higher than the increase of p_k, the costs to specific factor owners in the gth industry are over nine times higher than the benefits to the kth industry. Although the relative stakes are still much higher under reciprocity than under unilateral liberalization they are not as close as in other reciprocal scenarios. If, on the other hand, the change in the price of the kth good was ten times higher than that of the gth good, as shown in row 7, the situation is reversed. Again, this does not affect unilateral liberalization, but with reciprocity the losses to the gth industry are only about one-tenth the gains to the kth industry. These two examples show the importance of negotiators getting a "good deal" from their foreign counterparts. If the relative price reductions of the liberalized home market are too much larger than the price increases of the export good the benefits of liberalization will not be sufficiently concentrated and even reciprocal liberalization may not survive the political process.

Simply for the sake of completeness, in row 8 I have included an example in which the volume of exports rises more sharply than in previous examples— by 10 rather than 1 percent. Obviously this has no bearing on unilateral liberalization where there is no increase in the volume of exports. Even in reciprocal liberalization it has only a small effect, particularly considering the magnitude of the change. The benefits to the kth industry become slightly higher compared to the costs with the gth industry because the larger increase in exports produced a larger aggregate change in Y. This means that the kth specific factor owners received a larger share of a slightly larger pie.

The next two rows provide more significant results. I altered the assumptions about the size of the gth and kth industries in the economy. In row 9 I assumed that $\beta_g = 1 / 5$, that is, the gth industry made up a very large share of the economy. In the tenth row I made the same assumption for the kth industry. Under unilateral liberalization with the gth industry very large the ratio of costs to g and benefits to k is 400—still quite large but lower than in the baseline case. As shown in columns 1 and 3, the costs to g and the benefits to k of reducing the protection are both larger in this case than in the other, but the benefits are larger by more. Reciprocal liberalization helps concentrate the benefits of liberalization as always, but its effects are less dramatic than in previous scenarios. Changes that effect larger industries have a larger impact on the economy as a whole, and changes in the economy as a whole have a larger impact on larger industries. In row 9, the kth industry is small in the economy relative to the gth industry. Therefore, changes in p_k have a small effect on factor prices while changes in p_g have large effects. This means that the reduction in factor rewards to the gth industry are much larger than the increase to those in the kth industry when the gth industry is very large. Row 10 reverses the situation—the kth industry is very large in the economy. When the kth industry is larger in the economy than other industries are, the reduction in p_g has larger aggregate benefits to it. To put it another way the kth industry gets a larger share of the benefits of liberalization because it accounts for a larger share of the aggregate economy. Because of this the costs of unilateral liberalization to the gth industry are only about five times as large as benefits to the kth industry from unilateral liberalization—1 percent of the baseline ratio. As always reciprocity concentrates benefits even more, so that the costs to the gth industry are about two-thirds of a percentage point of the benefits to the kth industry. These results suggest that even reciprocity might not help enact liberalization if the industry to be liberalized has too large a share of the aggregate economy. Meanwhile, if export industries are a very large part of the aggregate economy reciprocity might not be necessary for liberalization at all.

Before closing the discussion it might be worthwhile to mention the effects of reciprocal as opposed to unilateral liberalization on the rest of the industries in the economy, what I have called the hth industries. We have seen in equation 2.5 that liberalization of the gth industry was beneficial to those in the hth industries but only to a very minor extent. This was the essence of their political problem, as recognized by Pareto, Schattschneider, and others. Equation 2.8 showed that reciprocal liberalization had a somewhat ambiguous effect on them. They gained from liberalization of the gth industry and from the increase in Y, but they were harmed by the increase in p_k.

Columns 5 and 6 of table B.1 help illustrate some of these contradictory effects in a variety of scenarios. In all cases the hth industry is better off under reciprocal liberalization than unilateral liberalization, but the changes in real incomes to the specific factors in the hth industry are always quite small. Often in the reciprocal scenarios in table B.1, the gains from liberalization of the gth industry are canceled out by the losses from the price increase of the kth industry, and in the end the factor owners in the hth industry only gain their share of the increase in Y. These gains are always larger than those from unilateral liberalization, but they are still quite small, so according to the "logic of collective action" members of the hth industries can still be expected to be relatively minor political players. Columns 5 and 6 should at least assure us that those in the hth industry do not have *less* of a stake in reciprocity than they do in unilateral liberalization.

To sum up, I have shown that with reciprocity the benefits of liberalization are more concentrated than they are under unilateral liberalization. Although this statement is always true, whether or not the real income changes to exporters are larger than those to import competers depends on the conditions in the political economy. If there is a very small number of different industries in the economy, if ownership of the specific factors in the protected or exporting industries is highly concentrated, if the reduction of the price of the protected good is much larger or smaller than the increase in the price of the export good in question, or if the protected or export industries comprise a very large share of the aggregate economy, then reciprocity will still concentrate the benefits of liberalization, but it will be less politically significant. In those situations even the benefits of unilateral liberalization may be highly concentrated, or the costs of reciprocal liberalization may still be relatively much larger than the benefits.

Effects of Two-Thirds Majority
and Gatekeeping Power

The story about the effects of delegation and reciprocity that I told in chapter 3 is complicated by two facts of American politics: Congress requires a two-thirds majority to override a presidential veto, and committees in Congress often have gatekeeping power, so that they can prevent legislation they do not like from reaching the floor for a vote. The effects of these two features of American politics are shown in the one-dimensional case by Ferejohn and Shipan (1990). The two-dimensional case of U.S. trade policy, which I will discuss here, actually has very similar results. The effects of both the two-thirds majority and gatekeeping power described in the main text are deeper potential reductions in trade barriers. However, as I mentioned in the main text, Congress took certain precautions to help ensure that the equilibria I describe here would not occur.

I will use a five-person legislature in figure C.1 to illustrate the effects of these two complications to my argument. The reversion level is point A, as it was in the main text. Five indifference curves to this point, centered on legislators' ideal points 1, 2, 3, 4, and 5, are shown in thin black lines. The sets H(A,A), and F(A,A) are shown in gray, as they were in Figures 3.2 and 3.3. These are sets of points that make a *simple majority* in the home and foreign legislatures, respectively, better off than point A does given the amount of lobbying generated by point A. The set I(A,A) shaded with diagonal lines is the intersection of these two sets.

In the text I argued that the president had to negotiate a trade deal that would make at least a simple majority better off than they would have been from the reversion level if he expected to have his negotiating authority renewed. However, if the president did not care about renewals of his negotiating authority he could in fact set an even more liberal trade policy than a majority in Congress preferred without Congress changing it because Congress requires a

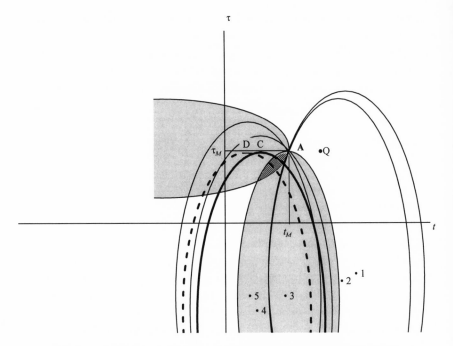

Fig. C.1.   Delegation with two-thirds majorities and gatekeeping power

two-thirds majority to override a presidential veto. In other words the president only has to make one-third of Congress better off than they would be under the reversion level because that one-third will vote against any congressional attempt to change the policy set by the president.

In figure C.1 the legislator required to override a presidential veto is legislator 4. Assuming that the foreign legislature maintains its policy at its median level τ_M, the best policy that a majority in Congress can offer legislator 4 is the policy at point C. Therefore, C is the relevant reversion level in this case. The set bounded by the heavy solid line is the set that offers legislator 4 higher utility than does point C, given that C is the policy proposal. Call this set V(C,C). If a majority in Congress instead offered legislator 4 a policy closer to point A this would give legislator 4 lower utility from the reversion level than point C and the president would be able to reduce tariffs by even more and still make that legislator better off. However, it would make a majority in Congress worse off. In other words, if a majority in Congress offered legislator 4 a policy closer to point A the set V would be even larger, making a majority in Congress even worse off from the president's veto-proof policy. Moving the reversion level C farther away from A than it is in figure C.1 would have the same effect, making both legislator 4 and a majority in Congress worse off. In short, point C is the best policy a majority in Congress can offer legislator 4; Congress has every incentive to offer legislator 4 precisely this policy since if it offers a different policy the president will be able to set a veto-proof policy that makes a majority in Congress even worse off. Clearly the set V(C,C) includes lower levels of *t* than the set H(A,A). Completing the same argument I made in the main text, a negotiated deal B (not shown in figure C.1) would be an equilibrium if B ∈ F(A,A) ∩ V(C,B). If the president negotiated some deal B with the foreign country it would generate more exporter lobbying and allow deeper reductions than would be allowed by V(C,C), and even deeper reductions than those allowed by the set H(A,B), which I discussed in the main text.

If the gatekeeping committee in charge of trade policy has even more liberal preferences than does legislator 4 the president would have even more leeway in reducing trade barriers, as is shown by the heavy dashed line in figure C.1. The gatekeeping committee will not "open the gate" on trade legislation if it knows that a majority in Congress will set a trade policy that makes it worse off. Therefore, the president can effectively use the committee's gatekeeping powers to set lower trade barriers knowing that the committee will not allow legislation that would change the policy he set to reach the floor for a vote. As an example, let us assume that legislator 5 is the member of a one-person gatekeeping committee in charge of trade policy. The best policy that a majority of Congress can offer this legislator is point D, and, as I just discussed in the context of the veto override, the majority in Congress has every incentive to offer that policy to him since if it does not the president would be able to reduce trade barriers even further. Therefore, the set of points that makes legislator 5 better off than D, which I will call C(D,D), is the set bounded by the dashed line. The intersection of this set and F(A,A) is even larger than the sets V(C,C) and H(A,A). A negotiated deal B (not shown) would be an equilibrium if B ∈ C(D,B) ∩ F(A,A). Since deal B would generate more exporter lobbying we would expect it to allow even greater reductions than the set C(D,D) would. Obviously, if the committee's preferences are not more liberal than those of the legislator needed to override a veto, this analysis will not apply, and the president will be constrained by the legislator needed to override his veto.

In summary, the requirement of a two-thirds majority to override a presidential veto and gatekeeping committees (if their preferences are sufficiently liberal) allow the president to reduce trade barriers by even more than I suggested in the main text. However, if the president negotiated a trade policy at some point in F(A,A) ∩ V(C,B) or F(A,A) ∩ C(D,B) that made a majority in Congress worse off, Congress would not renew the president's policy-making authority. It would be unable to change the policy set by the president because it would not have enough votes to override his veto or because the gatekeeping committee would not allow the legislation to reach the floor, but it could prevent the president from engaging in negotiations in the future. As I argued in the text I regard this threat as sufficient to keep the president from negotiating a deal that makes a majority in Congress worse off. Furthermore, in all delegating legislation since the Trade Act of 1974 Congress has included fast track provisions in legislation that delegates to the executive so that a majority in Congress can accept or reject the negotiated agreement on an up or down vote. As such the agreement must make a *majority* in Congress at least as well off as it would be from the reversion level if it is to pass that vote. Because of these provisions I regard the assumptions I made in the main text as the most plausible.

Data Sources

By far the most time-consuming task in this project was gathering the data for the tests in chapters 5 and 6. The vast bulk of that time and effort was spent constructing the data series for the period before 1972 since no machine-readable sources of data before that period exist. Constructing the data for the pre-1972 period involved several steps. First, I entered into the computer by hand U.S. trade data from published sources. I then used those data to determine which industries to include in the analysis. As was described in the text I used America's top import and export industries, calculated as those industries with the highest net imports and exports, respectively. I used a sufficient number of these industries to cover two-thirds of U.S. trade in each of the respective years. The two-thirds cutoff point was not chosen because it had any substantive significance—only because it represented the most data I could enter in a reasonable period of time. Extending the cutoff point to, say, three-fourths of U.S. trade would have required entering data for hundreds more industries and simply would have been impossible given the resources at my disposal. For instance, in 1934, a typical year, extending the coverage to three-fourths of U.S. imports would have increased the number of industries included from twenty-seven to fifty-nine. The next step was to concord the categories from the trade series with those from the production series. Once this was completed I photocopied the production data from various economic censuses and other sources and entered the production data for each state by hand into the computer.

Data on production of manufacturing industries were taken from the *Census of Manufactures* for some years (U.S. Department of Commerce, Bureau of the Census 1913b, 1919, 1933a, 1967, 1975b, 1993; U.S. Department of the Interior, Census Office 1895a, 1902b) and from the *Biennial Survey of Manufactures* for others (U.S. Department of Commerce, Bureau of the Census 1926, 1938, 1939). Manufacturing data from 1890 through 1963 were entered into the computer by hand. Data from 1972 were taken from a computer tape purchased from the National Archives. I purchased the *1987 Census of Manufactures* on CD-ROM from the Census Bureau. The availability of all of the manufacturing data series I used was remarkably good all the way back to 1890. If data existed for value of production they also existed for value added (or costs of materials from which value added could be calculated), workers' wages, numbers of firms, and numbers of workers, plus a variety of other measures not used here. Thus, the series for these measures are notably complete even for the 1890–1937 period.

Data on mining industries' production were taken from the *Census of Mineral Industries* (sometimes called the *Census of Mines and Quarries*) (U.S. Department of Commerce, Bureau of the Census 1913c, 1933c, 1944, 1967b, 1975c, 1993; U.S. Department of Commerce and Labor, Bureau of the Census 1905; U.S. Department of the Interior, Census Office 1892). I purposefully avoided using data from the 1919 *Census of Mineral Industries* because its values were still artificially inflated due to World War I. Therefore, for the Fordney-McCumber Act of 1922 I used some figures that were available from the 1922 statistical abstract (U.S. Department of Commerce, Bureau of the Census, various years). In cases where those figures where unavailable I interpolated values from the 1910 and 1929 censuses. I used the 1910 census for the Underwood Act of 1913 since it contained the temporally closest available data. For similar reasons I used the 1939 census for the RTAA renewal in 1937. I interpolated figures between the 1929 and 1939 censuses for the RTAA in 1934. As with the *Census of Manufactures* all mining data for 1890 through 1963 had to be entered by hand. The 1972 and 1987 censuses were available in machine-readable form. Like the *Census of Manufactures* the data series were remarkably complete for the entire period—including data series for costs of materials from which value added could be calculated, workers' wages, numbers of firms, and numbers of workers (as well as other measures that I did not use) all the way back to 1890.

Data on agricultural products were taken from the *Census of Agriculture* (U.S. Department of the Interior, Census Office 1895b, 1902a; U.S. Department of Commerce, Bureau of the Census 1913a, 1933b, 1937, 1943, 1968, 1977, 1990). I did not use the *Census of Agriculture* for 1920 for the same reason I did not use the *Census of Manufactures* for 1919—values were inflated due to the war. In my analysis of the McKinley Act of 1890, values for wool and sugar were created by multiplying production figures from the *Census of Agriculture, 1890* by prices of those goods for 1890 taken from *Historical Statistics: Colonial Times to 1970* (U.S. Department of Commerce, Bureau of the Census 1975a). The agricultural production data for the Underwood Act of 1913 were taken from the temporally nearest *Census of Agriculture* in 1910. The *Census of Agriculture* does not include the same data series as the *Census of Manufactures* and *Census of Mineral Industries.* There were no series for value added, wages, or numbers of workers. The only series available were value of production and numbers of farms. For crops (as opposed to livestock) acreage figures were also generally available, but I did not use them in my analysis. Therefore, the measures that included these variables in chapters 5 and 6 do not include agricultural production. Although the number of data series was more limited for the *Census of Agriculture* than for manufactures and mining, the data series that were available were quite complete for the entire period, going all the way back to 1890. That is, both value of production and numbers of farms were available on all agricultural data series.

Matching production data from the economic censuses with trade data for the 1890–1937 period was unfortunately a subjective process. International trade data for the 1890–1937 period were taken from the annual series *Commerce and Navigation of the United States* for the years in which the legislation I discussed was passed (U.S. Department of the Treasury, Bureau of Statistics 1890, 1898; U.S. Department of Commerce and Labor, Bureau of Statistics 1912; U.S. Department of Commerce, Bureau of Foreign and Domestic Commerce 1924, 1932, 1935, 1940). These data predate the Standard Industrial Classification (SIC) codes, and since different bureaus of the Commerce Department produced the economic censuses and the international commerce statistics the match between trade and production statistics was rarely perfect. Therefore, I had to develop my own concordance of the trade and production data for this period. In most cases the match was fairly obvious. I tried to be as consistent as possible throughout the period, but the Commerce Department was seldom consistent in the way it classified data from census to census, or even year to year, in its reporting of trade data.

Starting in 1958 the Commerce Department became more conscientious about the problem of comparing trade with production data and began publishing the annual *United States Commodity Export and Import as Related to Output,* which is still published today. This volume listed America's exports and imports by SIC code and allowed for a somewhat less subjective concordance between trade and production data. Trade data by SIC for 1962 and 1974 were taken from this series (U.S. Department of Commerce, Bureau of the Census 1967a, 1979). Trade data for 1988 were taken from computer tapes entitled *Export Data Bank, 1988* and *Import Data Bank, 1988* (U.S. Department of Commerce Bureau of the Census 1989a, 1989b), which I purchased from the National Archives. These trade statistics were matched with production data using a computerized concordance file purchased from the National Archives.

State personal income statistics were taken from the Commerce Department's *State Personal Income* time series (U.S. Department of Commerce, Bureau of Economic Analysis 1989). Values for total state personal income before 1929 were found in Kuznets, Miller, and Easterlin 1960. This latter source offered total personal income values only at twenty-year intervals starting in 1880, so values for 1890, 1909, and 1913 were interpolated from the adjacent figures.

Finally, data on the political variables party and ideology were quite easy to come by and very trustworthy. The ideology scores that I used are Poole and Rosenthal's (1991) ideology scores. These data, which were supplied very generously by Keith Poole, also contained each legislator's party. Roll call votes were taken from *Congressional Record* (1889–90, 1897–98, 1909, 1913, 1921–22, 1929, 1934, 1937) for the pre World War II sample, and from *Congressional Quarterly* (1962, 1974, 1988) for the post–World War II sample.

All data are available from the author upon request.

References

Aggarwal, Vinod K. 1985. *Liberal Protectionism*. Berkeley: University of California Press.

Alt, James E., Jeffry Frieden, Michael J. Gilligan, Dani Rodrik, and Ronald Rogowski. 1997. "The Politics of International Trade: Enduring Puzzles and an Agenda for Inquiry." *Comparative Political Studies* 29:689–717.

Anderson, Kym, and Robert E. Baldwin. 1987. "The Political Market for Protection in Industrial Countries." In A. M. El-Agraa, ed., *Protection, Cooperation, Integration and Development*. New York: Macmillan.

Austen-Smith, David. 1981. "Voluntary Pressure Groups." *Economica* 48:143–53.

Baker, Richard Cleveland. 1941. *The Tariff under Roosevelt and Taft*. Hastings, Neb.: Democrat Printing.

Baldwin, Robert. 1985. *The Political Economy of U.S. Import Policy*. Cambridge, Mass.: MIT Press.

Banks, Jeffrey. 1989. "Agency Budgets, Cost Information, and Auditing." *American Journal of Political Science* 33:670–99.

Banks, Jeffrey, and Barry Weingast. 1992. "The Political Control of Bureaucracies under Asymmetric Information." *American Journal of Political Science* 36:509–25.

Bauer, R. A., Ithiel De Sola Poole, and Lewis A. Dexter. 1963. *American Business and Public Policy: The Politics of Foreign Trade*. New York: Atherton.

Becker, William H. 1982. *The Dynamics of Business-Government Relations: Industry and Exports 1893–1921*. Chicago: University of Chicago Press.

Bendor, Jonathan, Serge Taylor, and Roland Van Galen. 1985. "Bureaucratic Expertise vs. Legislative Authority: A Model of Deception and Monitoring in Budgeting." *American Political Science Review* 79:1041–60.

———. 1987. "Politicians, Bureaucrats, and Asymmetric Information." *American Journal of Political Science* 31:796–828.

Bergsten, C. Fred, and Marcus Noland. 1993. *Reconcilable Differences? United States-Japan Economic Conflict*. Washington, D.C.: Institute for International Economics.

Berke, Richard L. 1987. "Gephardt Defends Trade Plan." *New York Times*, October 30, D5.

Bhagwati, Jagdish.1990. "Aggressive Unilateralism: An Overview." In Jagdish Bhagwati and Hugh T. Patrick, eds., 1990. *Aggressive Unilateralism: America's 301 Trade Policy and the World Trading System.* Ann Arbor: University of Michigan Press.

———, and Hugh T. Patrick, eds. 1990. *Aggressive Unilateralism: America's 301 Trade Policy and the World Trading System.* Ann Arbor: University of Michigan Press.

Bradsher, Keith. 1993. "U.S. Politicians Turn into Lobbyists over GATT." *New York Times,* December 11, A39.

Brown, Ken. 1993. "Trade Pact Divides New York's Garment Industry." *New York Times,* November 9, D1.

Calmes, Jackie. 1993. "World Trade Talks: No NAFTA-like Battle Seen in Congress over Pact." *Wall Street Journal,* December 15, A6.

———, and John Harwood. 1993. "The Battle over NAFTA: As Congress Begins Hearings Agreement Faces Uphill Climb." *Wall Street Journal,* September 15, A.18.

Calvert, Randall, Matthew McCubbins, and Barry Weingast. 1989. "A Theory of Political Control of Agency Discretion." *American Journal of Political Science* 33:588–610.

Canzoneri Matthew and JoAnna Gray. 1985. "Monetary Policy Games and the Consequences of Noncooperative Behavior." *International Economic Review* 26:547–64.

Cassing, James, Timothy McKeown, and Jack Ochs. 1986. "The Political Economy of the Tariff Cycle." *American Political Science Review* 80:843–62.

Chamberlin, John. 1974. "Provision of Collective Goods as a Function of Group Size." *American Political Science Review* 68:707–16.

Cheh, John H. 1974. "United States Concessions in the Kennedy Round and Short-Run Adjustment Costs." *Journal of International Economics* 4:323–40.

Committee on Ways and Means, U.S. House of Representatives. 1890. *Revision of the Tariff,* Hearings before the Committee on Ways and Means, 51st Cong. 1st sess., 1889–90. Washington, D.C.: Government Printing Office.

Committee on Ways and Means, U.S. House of Representatives. 1893. *Tariff Hearings before the Committee on Ways and Means,* 53d Cong., 1st sess., Misc. Doc. 43. Washington, D.C.: Government Printing Office.

Committee on Ways and Means, U.S. House of Representatives. 1897. *Tariff Hearings,* 54th Cong., 2d sess., 1896-97, H. Doc. 338, vols. 1–2. Washington, D.C.: Government Printing Office.

Committee on Ways and Means, U.S. House of Representatives. 1909. *Tariff Hearings,* 61st Cong., 1st sess., 1909, H. Doc.1505, vols. 1–9. Washington, D.C.: Government Printing Office.

Committee on Ways and Means, U.S. House of Representatives. 1913. *Tariff Schedule Hearings before the Committee on Ways and Means, House of Representatives,* 63d Cong., 3d sess., H. Doc. 1447. Washington, D.C.: U.S. Government Printing Office.

Committee on Ways and Means, U.S. House of Representatives. 1921. *Hearings on General Tariff Revision before the Committee on Ways and Means, House of Representatives,* 66th Cong., 3d sess., vols. 1–7. Washington, D.C.: Government Printing Office.

Committee on Ways and Means, U.S. House of Representatives. 1929. *Tariff Readjustment, 1929,* Hearings before the Committee on Ways and Means, 70th Cong., 2d sess. Washington, D.C.: Government Printing Office.

Committee on Ways and Means, U.S. House of Representatives. 1934. *Reciprocal Trade Agreements*, Hearings before the Committee on Ways and Means on H.R. 8430, 73d Cong., 2d sess., March 8–14, 1934. Washington, D.C.: Government Printing Office.

Committee on Ways and Means, U.S. House of Representatives. 1937. *Extending the Reciprocal Foreign Trade Agreement Act*, Hearings before the Committee on Ways and Means on Joint Res. 96, 75th Cong., 1st sess., January 21–26, 1937. Washington, D.C.: Government Printing Office.

Committee on Ways and Means, U.S. House of Representatives. 1962. *Trade Expansion Act of 1962*, Hearings before the Committee on Ways and Means on H.R. 9000, 87th Cong., 2d sess., March 12–April 11, 1962. Washington, D.C.: Government Printing Office.

Committee on Ways and Means, U.S. House of Representatives. 1979. *Hearings on S1376 (Trade Agreements Act of 1979)*, 96th Cong., 1st sess. Washington, D.C.: Government Printing Office.

Congressional Quarterly. 1962. *Almanac*. Vol. 18.

———. 1974. *Almanac*. Vol. 30.

———. 1979. *Almanac*. Vol. 35.

———. 1988. *Almanac*. Vol. 44.

Congressional Record 1889–90. 51st Cong., 1st sess. Washington, D.C.: Government Printing Office.

Congressional Record. 1897–98. 55th Cong., 1st sess. Washington, D.C.: Government Printing Office.

Congressional Record. 1909. 61st Cong., 1st sess. Washington, D.C.: Government Printing Office.

Congressional Record. 1913. 63rd Cong., 1st sess. Washington, D.C.: Government Printing Office.

Congressional Record. 1921–22. 67th Cong. 2d sess. Washington, D.C.: Government Printing Office.

Congressional Record. 1929. 71st Cong., 1st sess. Washington, D.C.: Government Printing Office.

Congressional Record. 1934. 73d Cong., 2d sess. Washington, D.C.: Government Printing Office.

Congressional Record. 1937. 75th Cong., 1st sess. Washington, D.C.: Government Printing Office.

Conybeare, John, A. C. 1987. *Trade Wars: The Theory and Practice of International Commercial Rivalry*. New York: Columbia University Press.

———. 1991. "Voting for Protection: An Electoral Model of Tariff Policy." *International Organization* 45, no. 1:56–81.

Cooper, Helene. 1994. "Politics and Policy: Corporate America Finds Devil is in the Details as Its Lobbyists Press Congress to Change GATT." *Wall Street Journal*, June 27, A14.

Cooper, Richard. 1972. "Trade Policy is Foreign Policy." *Foreign Policy* 9:18–36.

Corden, W. M.. 1986. *Trade Policy and Economic Welfare*. New York: Oxford University Press.

Coughlin, Cletus. 1985. "Domestic Content Legislation: House Voting and the Economic Theory of Regulation." *Economic Inquiry* 23:437–48.

Currie, D. and P. Levine. 1985. "Macroeconomic Policy Design in An Interdependent World." In W. Buiter and R. Marston, eds., *International Economic Policy Coordination*. New York: Cambridge University Press.

Currie, D., P. Levine, and N. Vidalis. 1987. "International Cooperation and Reputation in an Empirical Two Block Model." In R. Bryant and R. Portes, eds., *Global Macroeconomic Policy Conflict and Cooperation*. London: Macmillan.

Destler, I.M. 1986. *American Trade Policy: System under Stress*. Washington, D.C.: Institute for International Economics.

———, and John Odell, with Kimberly Ann Elliot. 1987. *Anti-protectionism*. Washington, D.C.: Institute for International Economics.

Downs, Anthony. 1957. *An Economic Theory of Democracy*. New York: Harper Row.

Ellis, L. Ethan. 1939. *Reciprocity, 1911: A Study in Canadian-American Relations*. New Haven: Yale University Press.

Evans, John W. 1971. *The Kennedy Round in American Trade Policy: The Twilight of the GATT?* Cambridge: Harvard University Press.

Farnsworth, Clive. 1987. "Counting Ways to Open—and Close—Markets." *New York Times*, June 21.

Feder, Barnaby J. 1993. "Caterpillar Sees Free Trade Boon." *New York Times*, September 21, D1.

Ferejohn, John and Charles Shipan. 1990. "Congressional Influence on the Bureaucracy." *Journal of Law, Economics, and Organization* 6:S1–S20.

Finger, J. M., H. Keith Hall, and Douglas R. Nelson. 1982. "The Political Economy of Administered Protection." *American Economic Review* 72:452–66.

Fiorina, Morris. 1981. "Congressional Control of the Bureaucracy: A Mismatch of Incentives Reconsidered." In Lawrence C. Dodd and Bruce Oppenheimer, eds., *Congress Reconsidered*. Washington, D.C.: CQ Press.

Frieden, Jeffrey. 1988. "Sectoral Conflict and U.S. Foreign Economic Policy, 1914–1940," In G. John Ikenberry, David A. Lake, and Michael Mastanduno, eds., *The State and American Foreign Economic Policy*. Ithaca: Cornell University Press.

Frisby, Michael K., and John Harwood. 1993. "Clinton Picks Up New Support for NAFTA, But Is Assailed by AFL-CIO's Kirkland." *Wall Street Journal*, November 16, A3.

Fuerbringer, Jonathan. 1987. "Tough Retaliatory Measure Wins by 4-Vote Margin in the House." *New York Times*, April 30, A1.

Galarotti, Giulo. 1985. "Toward a Business Cycle Model of Tariffs." *International Organization* 29:155–88.

Gardner, Richard. 1980. *Sterling-Dollar Diplomacy in Current Perspective*. New York: Columbia University Press.

Gilligan, Michael J. 1997. "Lobbying as a Private Good with Intra-Industry Trade." *International Studies Quarterly* (December, forthcoming).

Gilligan, Thomas, William Marshall, and Barry Weingast. 1989. "Regulation and the

Theory of Legislative Choice: The Interstate Commerce Act of 1887." *Journal of Law and Economics* 32: 35–61.

Goldstein, Judith. 1986. "The Political Economy of Trade: Institutions of Protection." *American Political Science Review* 80:161–84.

Goldstein, Judith and Stefanie Lenway. 1989. "Interest and Institutions: An Inquiry into Congressional-ITC Relations." *International Studies Quarterly.* 33:303–27.

Grieco, Joseph. 1988. *Cooperation among Nations.* Ithaca: Cornell University Press.

Grossman, Gene, and Elhanan Helpman. 1994. "Protection for Sale." *American Economic Review* 84:833–50.

Haggard, Stephen. 1988. "The Institutional Foundations of Hegemony: Explaining the Reciprocal Trade Agreements Act of 1934." *International Organization* 42:91–120.

Hamada, K. 1976. "A Strategic Analysis of Monetary Interdependence." *Journal of Political Economy* 84:677–700.

Hansen, John Mark. 1987. "Choosing Sides: The Creation of an Agricultural Policy Network in Congress, 1919–1932." *Studies in American Political Development,* 2:183–228.

Hansen, Stephen, Thomas Palfrey, and Howard Rosenthal. 1987. "The Downsian Model of Electoral Participation: Formal Theory and Empirical Analysis of the Constituency Size Effect." *Public Choice* 53:277–84.

Hansen, Wendy, L. 1990. "The International Trade Commission and the Politics of Protectionism." *American Political Science Review* 84, no. 1:21–46.

Harwood, John, and Jackie Calmes. 1993. "Politics and Policy: Freshman House Democrats Feel Special Bind as Labor Applies Pressure for Anti-NAFTA Votes." *Wall Street Journal,* October 25, A22.

Hillman, Ayre. 1982. "Declining Industries and Political-Support Protection Motives." *American Economic Review* 72:1180–87.

Hippler Bello, Judith, and Alan F. Holmer. 1990. "The Heart of the 1988 Trade Act: A Legislative History of the Amendment to Section 301." In Jagdish Bhagwati and Hugh T. Patrick, eds., *Aggressive Unilateralism: America's 301 Trade Policy and the World Trading System.* Ann Arbor: University of Michigan Press.

Hudec, Robert. 1990. "Thinking about the New Section 301: Beyond Good and Evil." In Jagdish Bhagwati and Hugh T. Patrick, eds., *Aggressive Unilateralism: America's 301 Trade Policy and the World Trading System.* Ann Arbor: University of Michigan Press.

Ifill, Gwen. 1993. "Clinton is Critical of Labor on Trade." *New York Times,* November 8, A1.

Ingersoll, Bruce, and Asra Q. Nomani. 1993. "Hidden Force: As Perot Bashes NAFTA, a Textile Tycoon Fights It Quietly with Money." *Wall Street Journal,* November 15, A1.

Jones, Joseph M. 1934. *Tariff Retaliation Repercussions of the Hawley-Smoot Bill.* Philadelphia: University of Pennsylvania Press.

Jones, Ronald. 1975. "Income Distribution and Effective Protection in a Multi-Commodity Trade Model." *Journal of Economic Theory* 11:1–15.

Kenen, P. 1988. "The Coordination of Macroeconomic Policies." paper delivered at the

NBER Conference on International Policy Coordination and Exchange Rate Fluctuations, Kiawah Island, October.

Keohane, Robert O. 1984. *After Hegemony: Cooperation and Discord in the World Political Economy.* Princeton: Princeton University Press.

———. 1986. "Reciprocity in International Relations." *International Organization* 40:1–27.

Kilborn, Peter T. 1993. "In Free Trade Accord Little Voices Roar in the Chorus of Trade Pact Foes." *New York Times*, November 13, A10.

Kindleberger, Charles P. 1986. *The World in Depression, 1929–1939.* Berkeley: University of California Press.

King, Gary. 1989. *Unifying Political Methodology.* New York: Cambridge University Press.

Kottman, Richard N. 1968. *Reciprocity and the North Atlantic Triangle 1932–1938.* Ithaca: Cornell University Press.

Krehbiel, Keith. 1991. *Information and Legislative Organization.* Ann Arbor: University of Michigan Press.

Krugman, Paul, ed. 1986. *Strategic Trade Policy and the New International Economics.* Cambridge, Mass: MIT Press.

Kuznets, Simon, Ann Ratner Miller, and Richard A. Easterlin. 1960. *Population Redistribution and Economic Growth: United States, 1870–1950.* vol. 2: *Analyses of Economic Change*, Philadelphia: American Philosophical Society.

Lagerfeld, Steven. 1993. "Nader's Faders." *The New Republic,* March 29, 16–17.

Lake, David A. 1988. *Power, Protection, and Free Trade: International Sources of U.S. Commercial Strategy, 1887–1939.* Ithaca: Cornell University Press.

Lavergne, Real. 1983. *The Political Economy of U.S. Tariffs.* Toronto: Academic.

Ledyard, John. 1984. "The Pure Theory of Two-Candidate Elections." *Public Choice* 44:9–41.

Lefeber, Walter. 1963. *The New Empire: An Interpretation of American Expansion.* Ithaca: Cornell University Press.

Link, Arthur S. 1956. *Wilson: The New Freedom.* Princeton: Princeton University Press.

Lohmann, Susanne, and Sharyn O'Halloran. 1994. "Divided Government and U.S. Trade Policy: Theory and Evidence." *International Organization* 48:595–632.

Lueck, Thomas J. 1993. "Many Companies in Area Disillusioned by Accord." *New York Times*, December 22, B5.

Magee, Stephen P., William A. Brock, and Leslie Young. 1989. *Black Hole Tariffs and Endogenous Policy Theory.* New York: Cambridge University Press.

Martis, Kenneth C. 1989. *The Historical Atlas of Political Parties in the United States Congress, 1789–1989.* New York: Macmillan.

Mayer, Wolfgang. 1984. "Endogenous Tariff Formation." *American Economic Review* 74:970–85.

McArthur, John, and Steven Marks. 1988. "Constituent Interest vs. Legislator Ideology: The Role of Political Opportunity Cost." *Economic Inquiry* 26:461–70.

McCormick, Thomas J. 1967. *China Market: America's Quest for Informal Empire, 1893–1901.* Chicago: Quadrangle.

McCubbins, Matthew, Roger Noll, and Barry Weingast. 1987 "Administrative Procedures as Instruments of Political Control." *Journal of Law Economics and Organization* 3:243–77.

———. 1989. "Structure and Process, Politics and Policy: Administrative Arrangements and the Political Control of Agencies." *Virginia Law Review* 75:431–82.

McCubbins, Matthew, and Thomas Schwartz. 1984. "Congressional Oversight Overlooked: Police Patrols vs. Fire Alarms." *American Journal of Political Science* 28:165–79.

McKelvey, Richard. 1976. "Intransitivities in Multidimensional Voting Models and Some Implications for Agenda Control." *Journal of Economic Theory* 12:472–82.

———. 1986. "Covering, Dominance and Institution-Free Properties of Social Choice." *American Journal of Political Science* 30:283–314.

McMillan, John. 1986. *Game Theory and International Economics.* New York: Harwood Academic.

Miller, Nicholas, Bernard Grofman, and Scott Feld. 1989. "The Geometry of Majority Rule." *Journal of Theoretical Politics* 1:379–406.

Mills, Joshua. 1993. "Business Lobbying for Trade Pact Appears to Sway Few in Congress." *New York Times*, November 12, A1.

Milner, Helen. 1988. *Resisting Protectionism.* Princeton: Princeton University Press.

———. 1990. "The Political Economy of U.S. Trade Policy: A Study of the Super 301 Provision." In Jagdish Bhagwati and Hugh T. Patrick, eds., *Aggressive Unilateralism: America's 301 Trade Policy and the World Trading System.* Ann Arbor: University of Michigan Press.

Nelson, Douglas. 1988. "Endogenous Tariff Theory: A Critical Survey." *American Journal of Political Science* 32: 796–837.

Noll, Roger. 1989. "Economic Perspectives on the Politics of Regulation." in Robert Willig and Richard Schmalensee, eds., *Handbook of Industrial Organization.* Amsterdam: North-Holland.

Nomani, Asra Q. 1993. "Politics and Policy: Corporate America, United on NAFTA Discovers that Coalition Building on GATT is Tougher." *Wall Street Journal*, December 13, A16.

North, Douglass. 1981. *Structure and Change in Economic History.* New York: Norton.

Odell, John. 1990. "Understanding International Trade Politics: An Emerging Synthesis." *World Politics* 43:139–67.

O'Halloran, Sharyn. 1994. *Politics, Process, and American Trade Politics.* Ann Arbor: University of Michigan Press.

Olson, Mancur. 1965. *The Logic of Collective Action.* Cambridge: Harvard University Press.

———. 1982. *The Rise and Decline of Nations: Economic Growth Stagflation and Rigidities,* New Haven: Yale University Press.

Oudiz, Gilles, and Jeffrey Sachs. 1984. "Macroeconomic Policy Coordination among the Industrialized Countries." *Brookings Papers on Economic Activity* 1:1–64.

Oye, Kenneth. 1984. *Cooperation under Anarchy.* Princeton: Princeton University Press.

———. 1992. *Economic Discrimination and Political Exchange: World Political Economy in the 1930s and 1980s.* Princeton: Princeton University Press.

Palfrey, Thomas R., and Howard Rosenthal. 1984. "Participation and the Provision of Discrete Public Goods: A Strategic Analysis." *Journal of Public Economics* 24:171–93.

———. 1985. "Voter Registration and Strategic Uncertainty." *American Political Science Review* 79:62–78.

Pareto, Vilfredo. 1927. *Manual of Political Economy.* New York: A. M. Kelley.

Passell, Peter. 1994. "An End Run on GATT." *The New York Times,* August 6, A33.

Pastor, Robert A. 1980. *Congress and the Politics of U.S. Foreign Economic Policy, 1929–76.* Berkeley: University of California Press.

Pietro, Nivola. 1990. "Trade Policy: Refereeing the Playing Field." In Thomas Mann, ed., *A Question of Balance: The President, The Congress and Foreign Policy.* Washington, D.C.: The Brookings Institution.

Pincus, Jonathan J. 1975. "Pressure Groups and the Pattern of Tariffs." *Journal of Political Economy* 83:757–78.

———. 1977. *Pressure Politics and Antebellum Tariffs.* New York: Columbia University Press.

Poole, Keith and Howard Rosenthal. 1991. "Patterns of Congressional Voting." *American Journal of Political Science* 35:228–78.

Putnam, Robert. 1988. "Diplomacy and Domestic Politics: The Logic of Two-Level Games." *International Organization* 42:427–60.

Rasky, Susan. 1987a. "Trade Amendment Heats Up Debate." *New York Times,* April 9, D1.

———.1987b. "Stock Fall May Affect Trade Bill." *The New York Times,* October 30, D1.

Ray, Edward J. 1981a. "The Determinants of Tariff and Nontariff Trade Restrictions in the United States." *Journal of Political Economy* 89:105–21.

———. 1981b. "Tariff and Nontariff Barriers to Trade in the United States and Abroad." *Review of Economics and Statistics* 63:161–68.

———. 1987. "The Impact of Special Interests on Preferential Tariff Concessions by the United States." *Review of Economics and Statistics* 68:187–93.

———, and Howard P. Marvel. 1984. "The Pattern of Protectionism in the Industrialized World." *Review of Economics and Statistics* 66:452–58.

Reidel, James. 1977. "Tariff Concession in the Kennedy Round and the Structure of Protection in West Germany." *Journal of International Economics* 7:133–43.

Rhodes, Carolyn. 1993. *Reciprocity, U.S. Trade Policy, and the GATT Regime.* Ithaca: Cornell University Press.

Riker, William. 1980. "Implications from the Disequilibrium of Majority Rule for the Study of Institutions." *American Political Science Review* 74:432–47.

Rodrik, Dani. 1994. "Political Economy of Trade Policy." In Gene Grossman and Kenneth Rogoff, eds., *Handbook of International Economics,* vol. 3. Amsterdam: North-Holland.

Rogoff, K. 1985. "Can International Policy Cooperation Be Counterproductive?" *International Economic Review* 18:199–217.

Ruffin, Roy, and Ronald Jones. 1977. "Protection and Real Wages: The Neo-classical Ambiguity." *Journal of Economic Theory* 14:337–48.

Saddler, Jeanne. 1993. "Enterprise—Government Watch: Small Business Boosts Lobbying for NAFTA as Vote Nears." *Wall Street Journal,* November 15, B2.

Sanger, David, E. 1994a. "What's What In the Trade Pact." *New York Times*, November 27, A34.

———. 1994b. "After Years of Talk, Trade Pact Now Awaits Congressional Fate." *New York Times*, November 27, A1.

———. 1994c. "Senate Approves Pact to Ease Trade Curbs. A Victory for Clinton." *New York Times*, December 2, A1.

Sayre, Francis Bowes. 1939. *The Way Forward: The American Trade Agreements Program.* New York: Macmillan.

Schattschneider, E. E. 1935. *Politics, Pressures, and the Tariff.* New York: Prentice-Hall.

Schnietz, Karen E. 1993. "The 1934 Reciprocal Trade Agreements Act: Partisan Institutional Protection of Liberal Trade Policy." Graduate School of Industrial Administration, Carnegie Mellon University. Mimeo.

Stanwood, Edward. 1903. *Tariff Controversies of the Nineteenth Century.* Vol. 2, Boston: Houghton Mifflin.

Steward, Dick. 1975. *Trade and Hemisphere: The Good Neighbor Policy and Reciprocal Trade.* Columbia: University of Missouri Press.

Stigler, George. 1974. "Free Riders and Collective Action." *Bell Journal of Economics and Management Science* 5:359–65.

Stokes, Bruce. 1987. "Everybody's in the Act." *National Journal,* April 18, 927–31.

———. 1988. "The Trade Debate's Winners and Losers." *National Journal,* April 16, 1020–21.

Stone, Peter H. 1994. "GATT-ling Guns." *National Journal,* July 2, 1571–75.

Strauss, Robert. 1987. Forward to Joan E. Twiggs, *The Tokyo Round of Multilateral Trade Negoatiations: A Case Study in Building Domestic Support for Diplomacy.* Washington, D.C.: Institute for the Study of Diplomacy and University Press of America.

Sundquist, James. 1981. *The Decline and Resurgence of Congress.* Washington, D.C.: The Brookings Institution.

Tarbell, Ida. 1911. *The Tariff in Our Times.* New York: Macmillan.

Taussig, Frank. 1966. *The Tariff History of the United States.* New York: G. P. Putnam's Sons.

Terrill, Tom E. 1973. *The Tariff, Politics, and American Foreign Policy, 1874–1901.* Westport, Conn.: Greenwood.

Toner, Robin. 1993. "In Auto-Making Country, Trade Accord is the Enemy." *New York Times*, September 14, A18.

Tosini, Suzanne C., and Edward Tower. 1987. "The Textile Bill of 1985: The Determinants of Congressional Voting Patterns." *Public Choice* 54:19–25.

Twiggs, Joan E. 1987. *The Tokyo Round of Multilateral Trade Negotiations: A Case Study in Building Domestic Support for Diplomacy.* Washington, D.C.: Institute for the Study of Diplomacy and University Press of America.

U.S. Department of Commerce, Bureau of the Census. various years, *Statistical Abstract of the United States,* Washington, D.C.: Government Printing Office.

U.S. Department of Commerce, Bureau of the Census. 1913a. *Thirteenth Census of the*

United States Taken in the Year 1910. Vol. 5: *Agriculture, 1909 and 1910, General Report and Analysis.* Washington, D.C.: Government Printing Office.

U.S. Department of Commerce, Bureau of the Census. 1913b. *Thirteenth Census of the United States Taken in the Year 1910.* Vol. 8: *Manufacturers, 1909, General Report and Analysis.* Washington, D.C.: Government Printing Office.

U.S. Department of Commerce, Bureau of the Census. 1913c. *Thirteenth Census of the United States Taken in the Year 1910.* Vol. 11: *Mines and Quarries, 1909, General Report and Analysis.* Washington, D.C.: Government Printing Office.

U.S. Department of Commerce, Bureau of the Census. 1919. *Census of Manufacturers.* Vol. 2: *Reports on Selected Industries and Detailed Statistics for Industries, by States.* Washington, D.C.: Government Printing Office.

U.S. Department of Commerce, Bureau of the Census. 1926. *Biennial Census of Manufactures, 1922.* Washington, D.C.: Government Printing Office.

U.S. Department of Commerce, Bureau of the Census. 1933a. *Fifteenth Census of the United States, Manufactures, 1929.* Vol. 2: *Reports by Industries.* Washington, D.C.: Government Printing Office.

U.S. Department of Commerce, Bureau of the Census, 1933b, *Fifteenth Census of the United States, Agriculture, 1930.* Vol. 4: *General Report, Statistics by Subject.* Washington, D.C.: Government Printing Office.

U.S. Department of Commerce, Bureau of the Census. 1933c. *Fifteenth Census of the United States, Mines and Quarries, 1929, General Report and Reports for States and Industries.* Washington, D.C.: Government Printing Office.

U.S. Department of Commerce, Bureau of the Census. 1937. *United States Census of Agriculture, 1935, General Report, Statistics by Subject.* Vol. 2: Washington, D.C.: Government Printing Office.

U.S. Department of Commerce, Bureau of the Census. 1938. *Biennnial Census of Manufactures, 1935.* Washington, D.C.: Government Printing Office.

U.S. Department of Commerce, Bureau of the Census. 1939. *Biennnial Census of Manufactures, 1937.* Pt. 1, Washington, D.C.: Government Printing Office.

U.S. Department of Commerce, Bureau of the Census. 1943. *Sixteenth Census of the United States: 1940, Agriculture, 1940, General Report and Statistics by Subjects.* Washington, D.C.: Government Printing Office.

U.S. Department of Commerce, Bureau of the Census. 1944. *Sixteenth Census of the United States: 1940, Mineral Industries 1939.* Vol. 1: *General Summary and Industry Statistics.* Washington, D.C.: Government Printing Office.

U.S. Department of Commerce, Bureau of the Census. 1966. *1963 Census of Manufactures.* Vol. 2, Pts. 1 and 2: *Industry Statistics.* Washington, D.C. Government Printing Office.

U.S. Department of Commerce, Bureau of the Census. 1967a. *U.S. Commodity Exports and Imports as Related to Output 1963 and 1964.* Washington, D.C.: Government Printing Office.

U.S. Department of Commerce, Bureau of the Census, 1967b. *1963 Census of Mineral In-*

dustries Vol. 1: *Summary and Industry Statistics.* Washington, D.C.: Government Printing Office.

U.S. Department of Commerce, Bureau of the Census. 1968. *1964 United States Census of Agriculture* Vol. 2: *General Report.* Washington, D.C.: Government Printing Office.

U.S. Department of Commerce, Bureau of the Census. 1975a. *Historical Statistics of the United States: Colonial Times to 1970.* Washington, D.C.: Government Printing Office.

U.S. Department of Commerce, Bureau of the Census. 1975b. *1972 Census of Manufactures.* Computer file on tape. College Park, Md.: National Archives, Center for Electronic Records.

U.S. Department of Commerce, Bureau of the Census. 1975c. *1972 Census of Mineral Industries.* Computer file on tape. College Park, Md.: National Archives, Center for Electronic Records.

U.S. Department of Commerce, Bureau of the Census. 1977. *1974 Census of Agriculture* Vol. 1, pt. 51: *United States Summary and State Data.* Washington, D.C.: Government Printing Office.

U.S. Department of Commerce, Bureau of the Census. 1979. *U.S. Commodity Exports and Imports as Related to Output 1975 and 1976.* Washington, D.C.: Government Printing Office.

U.S. Department of Commerce, Bureau of the Census. 1989a. *Import Data Bank, 1988.* Computer file on tape. College Park, Md.: National Archives, Center for Electronic Records.

U.S. Department of Commerce, Bureau of the Census. 1989b. *Export Data Bank, 1988.* Computer file on tape. College Park, Md.: National Archives, Center for Electronic Records.

U.S. Department of Commerce, Bureau of the Census. 1990. *1987 Census of Agriculture.* Vol. 1: *Geographic Area Series.* CD-ROM. Washington, D.C.: Department of Commerce, Bureau of the Census, Data User Services Division.

U.S. Department of Commerce, Bureau of the Census. 1993. *1987 Economic Censuses.* Vol. 1: *Report Series* Release 1E. CD-ROM. Washington, D.C.: U.S. Department of Commerce, Bureau of the Census, Data User Services Division.

U.S. Department of Commerce, Bureau of Economic Analysis. 1989. *State Personal Income: 1929–87.* Washington, D.C.: Government Printing Office.

U.S. Department of Commerce, Bureau of Foreign and Domestic Commerce. 1915. *Foreign Commerce and Navigation of the United States for the Year Ending June 30, 1914.* Washington, D.C.: Government Printing Office.

U.S. Department of Commerce, Bureau of Foreign and Domestic Commerce. 1924. *Foreign Commerce and Navigation of the United States for the Calendar Year Ending 1923.* Washington, D.C.: Government Printing Office.

U.S. Department of Commerce, Bureau of Foreign and Domestic Commerce. 1931. *Foreign Commerce and Navigation of the United States for the Calendar Year Ending 1930.* Washington, D.C.: Government Printing Office.

U.S. Department of Commerce, Bureau of Foreign and Domestic Commerce. 1934. *Foreign Commerce and Navigation of the United States for the Calendar Year Ending 1934*. Washington, D.C.: Government Printing Office.

U.S. Department of Commerce, Bureau of Foreign and Domestic Commerce. 1940. *Foreign Commerce and Navigation of the United States for the Calendar Year Ending 1938*. Washington, D.C.: Government Printing Office.

U.S. Department of Commerce and Labor, Bureau of the Census. 1905. *Special Reports: Mines and Quarries, 1902*. Washington, D.C.: Government Printing Office.

U.S. Department of Commerce and Labor, Bureau of Statistics. 1912. The Foreign Commerce and Navigation of the United States for the Year Ending June 30, 1911. Washington, D.C.: Government Printing Office.

U.S. Department of the Interior, Census Office. 1891. *Statistical Abstract of the United States*. Washington, D.C.: Government Printing Office.

U.S. Department of the Interior, Census Office. 1892. *Report on Mineral Industries in the United States at the 11th Census, 1890*. Washington, D.C.: Government Printing Office.

U.S. Department of the Interior, Census Office. 1895a. *Report on Manufacturing Industries in the United States at the 11th Census, 1890*. Washington, D.C.: Government Printing Office.

U.S. Department of the Interior, Census Office. 1895b. *Report on the Statistics of Agriculture in the United States at the 11th Census, 1890*. Washington, D.C.: Government Printing Office.

U.S. Department of the Interior, Census Office. 1902a. *Census Reports*. Vols. 5 and 6: *Agriculture*, Pts. 1 and 2. Washington, D.C.: Government Printing Office.

U.S. Department of the Interior, Census Office. 1902b. *Census Reports*. vol. 7: *Manufactures*, pt. 1. Washington, D.C.: Government Printing Office.

U.S. Department of the Treasury, Bureau of Statistics. 1891. *Foreign Commerce, Navigation, Immigration and Tonnage of the United States for the Year Ending June 30, 1890*. Washington, D.C.: Government Printing Office.

U.S. Department of the Treasury, Bureau of Statistics. 1898. *Foreign Commerce and Navigation of the United States for the Year Ending June 30, 1897*. Washington, D.C.: Government Printing Office.

Verdier, Daniel. 1994. *Democracy and International Trade: Britain, France and the United States, 1860–1990*. Princeton: Princeton University Press.

Weingast, Barry. 1984. "The Congressional Bureaucratic System: A Principal-Agent Perspective (with Applications to the SEC)." *Public Choice* 44:147–91.

Weingast, Barry, and Mark Moran. 1983. "Bureaucratic Discretion and Congressional Control: Regulatory Agency Policy Making and the FTC." *Journal of Political Economy* 91:765–800.

Weinraub, Bernard. 1993. "The World Trade Agreement: The Hollywood Reaction: Clinton Spared Blame by Hollywood Officials." *New York Times*, December 16, A1.

Williams, William Appleman. 1962. *The Tragedy of American Diplomacy*. New York: Dell.

Index